Life-Giving Spring

Life-Giving Spring: The Eternal Fountain

An invitation to reacquaintance
with the Blessed Virgin Mary

ROBERT F. THOMPSON

Cover photograph:

Our Lady as Life-Giving Spring,
18th century painting, Greece (Epirus),
given to the National Museum in Warsaw, Poland,
by Władysław Siemianowski (1849-1938).
Licensing: "This is a faithful photographic reproduction
of a two-dimensional, public domain work of art."
https://commons.wikimedia.org/wiki/File:
Epirus_Our_Lady_as_life-giving_spring.jpg

Blue violet clip art from
Florida Center for Instructional Technology (FCIT)
http://fcit.usf.edu/

On the page of dedication
"Our Lady of the Concourse" refers to
the apparition in 1945 to Joseph Vitolo Jr. in Bronx, New York,
where Our Lady's shrine now is, at 3191 Grand Concourse,
the Bronx's "Boulevard of Dreams"

The quote on the page of dedication
concerning Marjorie Milne appears in Brian Frost,
Glastonbury Journey: Marjorie Milne's Search for Reconciliation
(Oxford, UK: Becket, 1986), pp. 125-126.

Other titles by Robert F. Thompson:

Taliesin's Harp: A Poetics of the Divine-Humanity (2019)
The Anthropocosmic Vision: For a New Dialogic Civilization (2017)
From Glory to Glory: The Sophianic Vision of Fr. Sergius Bulgakov (2016)

A Perennials Study Group publication
Memphis, Tennessee

Printed by Kindle Direct Publishing
https://kdp.amazon.com

Veriditas

To Our Lady of the Concourse
Queen of the Universe

Mother without Borders

And to the memory of
Marjorie Milne of Glastonbury
(1907-1977)
who considered it her task
"to articulate from Glastonbury a vision
of a new world, drawing on the old roots,
but roots where forgiveness had sprinkled
the dust of combats long ago
with a sweet aroma for the future"

and
Fr. Robert Llewelyn of Norwich
(1909-2008)

With thanks for the companionship of
The New Benedictine Community
and other people of Paradise

Succisa virescit
The felled tree flourishes again

Table of Contents

Preface

This is a book of *theotropics*. As the tiny heliotrope "by nature" orients its face to the sun, so each of us orients our face toward the Beloved. The deeper wisdom is not systematic. Spiritual traditions communicate expressions of wisdom that may blend as harmoniously as the many fragrances of a flower garden. This book is about seeing the presentations of our life as occurring under the watchful care of the Blessed Mother. It is, in this sense, a phenomenology of Marian spirituality.

The descending Age to come—premonitions of which are already occurring—can be regarded as an Age of the Blessed Virgin Mary. This book is about the generosity at the heart of the cosmos that is mirrored in the hearts of all beings whatsoever in their original and undefended state. The Blessed Virgin is regarded as both Life-Giving Spring and fire that does not consume. For children of the Mother, she is reality as well as the metaphor that contains many other metaphors. She is also the reality from which arise answers to many questions—a closing of the circle of what is possible in anyone's life.

The book is structured as a mosaic of reflections unfolding from attention to the ancient Greek icon of the "Life-Giving Spring" (*Zoodochos Pighi*), an instance of which is shown on the cover of this book. As a phenomenology, the book makes reference to the imaginal realm as identified principally by the Iranologist, Henry Corbin. This book touches on *hierophanies* of the Virgin Mary as well as on particular locales, such as Glastonbury, Walsingham, and Medjugorje, and on the significance of pilgrimage. There is no attempt at originality in this book. I have tried to identify and give appropriate credit to the many sources from which I have drawn in the writing of it.

The three preceding books, taken as a whole, have a profound kinship of perspective with what is called "ecological civilization," with respect to its methods and its vision. To understand how this is so, consider the question, "Where is 'home' for the (embodied) human being?" In a fundamental sense, can it be anywhere other than this (green) planet Earth? We may be inclined to answer both yes and no. If Earth is our home then there must be recognition of humankind as not simply heliotropic being, but as theotropic being. The ecology goes all the way up, as it were. Is Earth not already in the heart of God—already, even if it is not yet apparent to all? This present book consists of hints and intimations reflecting our actual circumstances. Anything more would put us—the author and the reader alike—at risk of vertigo.

Some of the keynotes of the preceding three volumes are listed succinctly here: The first volume, *From Glory to Glory: The Sophianic Vision of Fr. Sergius Bulgakov*, takes delight in open spaces, Sophia (Holy Wisdom), "perspectival reality," and the nets of language. The second volume, *The Anthropocosmic Vision: For a New Dialogic Civilization*, is concerned with the human person and the possibility of the "human exit." The third volume, *Taliesin's Harp: A Poetics of the Divine-Humanity*, can be said to be a response to the sad fact encapsulated in a line from Tolkien's *The Fellowship of the Ring*: "… and our hands are more often upon the bowstring than upon the harp." As such, the third volume, *Taliesin's Harp*, is concerned with humankind evolving, with the divine melody, with Taliesin/Orpheus, with poetics as that which contributes to this evolution, with Sufism as an expression of the collective imagination, and with a spirituality oriented toward an arriving future that we can believe in and joyfully work toward.

Those three volumes, taken as a whole, are non-systematic. They are constructed as bees construct their hive. They grew out of a desire for "bigger boxes," as it were, to inhabit. They all found their inspiration in these Russian values and experiences: "All-Unity," Freedom, Sophia and sophiology, and the divine-humanity. Listen carefully, because all our works—if they have a beginning in time—are ephemeral and destined to pass away without a trace.

This present volume, although not envisioned as a part of that series, nevertheless of necessity breathes of the same air. This breath is of the divine consciousness that ever flows into myriad manifestations and ever again returns to itself. This flowingness is the deep reality of Blessed Virgin Mary. This is the same flowingness that I honor in the lives of my parents, Audrey & Robert Thompson, as well as in the lives of my maternal grandparents, Lurline & Frank Hurt, and my paternal grandparents, Nettie & Lon Thompson, all of whom made a place for me in their own lives. May you, the reader, find both inspiration and seed-thoughts to sustain you as these unfold, over time, in the course of the journey that is your life.

Robert F. Thompson
February 2, 2020
Purification of the Blessed Virgin (Candlemas)

Life-Giving Spring:
The Eternal Fountain

The angel then showed me the river of life-giving water clear as crystal, which issued from the throne of God and of the lamb, and flowed down the middle of the streets. On either side of the river grew the trees of life which produced fruit twelve times a year, one each month; the leaves served as medicine for the nations.
— Revelation 22:1-2

O Lady graced by God,
you reward me by letting gush forth, beyond reason,
the ever-flowing waters of your grace from your perpetual Spring.
I entreat you, who bore the Logos, in a manner beyond comprehension,
to refresh me in your grace that I may cry out,
"Hail redemptive waters."
— Kontakion (Plagal of Tone 4)

1. *Sanctus - Sanctus - Sanctus*

This present book, having to do with the Blessed Virgin Mary, is largely unfinished because of the nature of the topic itself—a topic so broad and so profound as to surpass the covers of a single book, however well-intentioned or well-researched. In a sense, this does not matter because you, the reader, will unfold, over the time of life given to you, all that is implied within the language of these pages. As Canon Donald Allchin (d. 2010) understood, language of prose constantly moves toward language of poetry and song when we are concerned with the Blessed Virgin Mary.[1]

---

[1] Within Anglican tradition, the dynamic of language tending from prose to poetry and song, when concerned with the Virgin Mary, can be discerned as early as Lancelot Andrewes who, according to Canon Allchin, stands at the root of this tradition. See A. M. Allchin, *The Joy of All Creation: An Anglican Meditation on the Place of Mary* (London: New City, 1993, 1984), pp. xiii-xiv.

In the philosophy of mathematics, there are Godel's incompleteness theorems and Tarski's undefinability theorem that suggest, approximately, in plain English, that there are no "windowless monads" or (entirely self-contained) "wholes" available to perception. What we have, instead, are "holons"—"wholes" that are, at the same time, "parts" of larger wholes. What we call "wholes" are, in fact, "in communication" with something larger and more comprehensive. The reality of the Virgin Mary is of this order. She is the reality, or the bridge, to the larger and more comprehensive (divine) reality. As such, she is and ever has been beyond institutional control—whether ecclesiastical or political.

> *Verbum Dei non est alligatum.*
> The word of God is not chained.
> — 2 Timothy 2:9 (NKJV)

An initial focus of these reflections on the Blessed Virgin Mary concerns one of her many titles—Life-Giving Spring—which also names a particular group of icons of Our Lady, a group of icons whose basic structure is reflected in any number of stylistic variations, one of which appears on the cover of this book. There is a recognized ambiguity in the structure of the Life-Giving Spring icons. This ambiguity can be expressed in these questions: Is the Virgin Mary *in* (or *on*) the font? Or *is* she *herself* the font (the fountain)? Magdalena Lubanska (University of Warsaw) writes:

> When looking at the icons it is not always clear whether the Virgin is sitting in a bowl filled with water, or perhaps it is the bowl that contains water pouring out of the Virgin's body. This ambiguity is presumably intentional, emphasizing the mystery of the healing water's substantiality and its remarkable healing properties. In the Gospel, the water undergoes a process of *metanoia* through its contact with the Lord's angel in the iconographic depictions, the same process occurs through physical contact with the Virgin's body. As a result, the water as it were becomes transformed into a different substance: life-giving water with a whole new set of physical properties. This connection between *ayazma* and holy water is a recurrent element in Orthodox theology and tradition. The pool at Bethesda is mentioned in every *vodosvet* rite, and every *ayazmo* is blessed in

that rite at least once a year. In doing so, the healing properties of the spring become renewed and reinforced.[2]

This is an ambiguity in the structure of the icon that we might highlight and emphasize because it runs through everything we will want to say about the significations of the Blessed Virgin Mary, both as reality and as bridge to reality, as suggested above.[3] The image or notion of "flow" or spring (as of water) associated with this icon is also evocative and central to what we are concerned with in this book. We will have more to say about this aspect of our subject matter further below at "The Great Fountain–Flow and Return."

In the Appendix to this book are sets of triads that can serve as "seed thoughts" for those attuning themselves to the Way of Mary, an expression that will be clarified later in this book. These seed thoughts may help us to see (to understand) the circumstances of our life in terms of the *relationships* between the terms of any particular triad that may be selected as a reflective lens. Contemplation of any of these triads may serve as a *vehicle of ascension*—in the sense that we may begin to discern a (not immediately named) reality, or presence, that effectuates (or constitutes) the three into a particular (interrelated) triad. To state this as an aphorism: "Transcend and include!" While the sets of three terms are proposed as triads, it is up to the reader to discern whether or not they are, in fact, triads. If no (internal) relations can be *discerned*, then they are simply three—not triadic. Or it may be that

---

[2] Magdalena Lubanska, "Life-Giving Springs and The Mother of God / Zhivonosen Istochnik / Zoodochos Pege / Balŭkliyska: Byzantine-Greek-Ottoman Intercultural Influence and Its Aftereffects in Iconography, Religious Writings and Ritual Practices in the Region of Plovdiv," *Slavia Meridionalis* 17, 2017, Article No.: 1252, p. 7. On-line at: <https://www.researchgate.net/publication/320408780_Life-giving_springs_and_The_Mother_of_God_Zhivonosen_Istochnik_Zoodochos_Pege_Balikliyska_Byzantine-Greek-Ottoman_intercultural_influence_and_its_aftereffects_in_iconography_religious_writings_and_rit> (Accessed 1/23/2020)

[3] Places associated with the Virgin Mary also have an ambiguous character. See, for example, Robert Logan Sparks, "Ambiguous Spaces: A Contextualisation of Shared Pilgrimage in Ephesus," Ph.D. dissertation (2011) at Tilburg University (Netherlands). On-line at: <https://research.tilburguniversity.edu/en/publications/ambiguous-spaces-a-contextualisation-of-shared-pilgrimage-in-ephe> (Accessed 8/24/2019)

upon further reflection, at some later time, the internal relations of the three will be *revealed*.

The triads in the Appendix are grouped into sets of seven (heptads). Consider each of the seven triads individually with respect to whether or not one element of the three may be experienced as comprehending the other two. This may or may not be the case. You will experience clarity fairly quickly in some instances, whereas the character of other triadic relations will become clear only after some considerable length of time.

In these exercises, understand yourself to be participating in a tradition—a tradition of coming to know the imaginal realm as the "place" of revelation (unveiling).[4] This is based on the knowledge that all things whatsoever are signs or signatures of the Divine Life. The Swiss visionary and mystic, Joa Bolendas (d. 2005), came to this understanding:

> Revelations have another wavelength. The words, images, sounds (the hymns) come over an extended period of time–with great intervals–which demand a lot of energy from those who receive them. Devotion and concentration are needed. Whenever someone receives revelations, the brain works more quickly and the heart beats more slowly.[5]

From within Jewish spiritual culture, Rabbi Laurence Kushner proposes

> an alternative metaphor by which we may reenter the scriptural text. By reading holy literature as if it were a dream, we gain access to a primary mode of our collective unconscious. The

---

[4] For the range of meanings associated with the "imaginal" realm, see Tom Cheetham, *Imaginal Love: The Meanings of Imagination in Henry Corbin and James Hillman* (Thompson, Connecticut: Spring Publications, 2015). For Corbin, the imaginal realm is not subject to personal (individual) whim or control. The initiative lies with the Angel or the angelic beings. The term, "realm," is the meaningfulness of all things and is not meant to exclude anything.
[5] Joa Bolendas, *So That You May Be One* (Hudson, New York: Lindisfarne Books, 1997), p. 71.

Bible, for us, is an entrance to the cave, perhaps the only entrance. The great dream of Western religion.[6]

He also commends the Hebrew literary form known as Midrash that attempts, by way of creative imagination, to fill in the spaces between the words—to imagine what has not been written in the scriptural text. This, as he explains, is analogous to the psychotherapeutic experience by means of which one seeks to join the fragments of one's life into a greater unity of meaning.

Wisdom school, in Christian context, is similarly exercise in reading the signs. In illustration of this, consider what Catherine Doherty wrote in her book, *Bogoroditza* (Russian for "She who gave birth to God"):

> Just sit down comfortably at Mary's feet and be silent with her. Let your silence have that quality of "listening recollection" that is so necessary for hearing her silence speak.... When you are ... silent—reverently and simply so, with the silence of a great love for Mary the Mother of God—she will arise and, taking you by the hand, lead you into the inner chamber of her Immaculate Heart, where all the words of her Son are still kept, as fresh and alive as when he spoke them. Still silently, she will take each word ... and show it to you. In her hands each word will glow and open as a flower opens in the sun, and will reveal many a hidden or unclear meaning to you. And you will marvel that you did not see before.[7]

This also connects with allusions, at various places further below, about the hiddenness (or the apparent absence) of the Blessed Virgin Mary as well as her presence. As congruent with the above excerpt, the Blessed Virgin Mary can be regarded as the keeper and revealer of all mysteries of the Christian faith.

Understand yourself to be part of the flow that will continue after we have enjoyed our time of embodied human life on this green planet. It is good here, while pondering these triads (in the Appendix), and

---

[6] Laurence Kushner, *The River of Light: Jewish Mystical Awareness*, Special Anniversary Edition (Woodstock, Vermont: Jewish Lights Publishing, 2000), p. xvi.
[7] Catherine Doherty, *Bogoroditza: She Who Gave Birth to God*, Expanded Second Edition (Combermere, Ontario: Madonna House Publications, 2001), p. 55.

always, to remember James Hillman's cautionary advice: "We sin against imagination whenever we ask an image for its meaning, requiring that images be translated into concepts."[8] This also applies to everything we have to say below about the Blessed Virgin Mary.

From within Jewish spiritual culture, Rabbi Laurence Kushner beautifully evokes this notion of "flow" as the pervasive cosmic reality:

> There is a realm of being that comes before us and follows after us. Streaming through and uniting all creation. Knowing who we have been and will be. It contaminates our sleep with visions of higher reality and exalts our waking with stories. It is a river of light. "She is a tree of Life to those who hold on to her" (Proverbs 3:18). Her branches and shoots are the nerves and vessels of this world coursing beneath our surfaces, pulsing through our veins. A blueprint underlying the cosmos. The primary process of being. The inner structure of conscious-ness. The way of the Tao. "And all her paths are peace" (Proverbs 3:17). Just behind and beneath everything. If we could but stand it, everything would have meaning. Everything connected to everything else even as they all share a common Root.[9]

Interestingly, Rabbi Kushner's reference to "river of light" brings to mind Our Lady of Guadalupe. Among the possible meanings that have been suggested for her name, are "hidden river" and "river of light."[10] In 1979, in Mexico, when Cardinal Ernesto Corripio Ahumada and Bishop Torreblanco crowned the image of Our Lady of Guadalupe in Tolpetlac as "Health of the Sick," the Cardinal spoke as follows:

> Mary is like a river always flowing—she is always sending light inspiring love. The endless source of that love and guidance is Jesus Christ. Let's hope that river of light, love and hope reaches every person so that the whole world knows that love.

---

[8] James Hillman, *Re-visioning Psychology* (New York: Harper & Row, 1975), p. 39.

[9] Laurence Kushner, *The River of Light*, previously cited, p. 27.

[10] According to Francis Johnston, *The Wonder of Guadalupe: The Origin and Cult of the Miraculous Image of the Blessed Virgin in Mexico* (Charlotte, North Carolina: TAN Books, 1993), Note 6, p. 46.

She has brought us that light and love not only for us individually but also to unite us and to make us feel that we all belong to the same kingdom and that we must enlarge it and pass it on everywhere, carrying the teaching of Christ to all our brothers and sisters. In that way we will carry Mary with us and people will see Mary through us. Mary's hands extend like a stream of light that makes darkness disappear. Her Love makes the darkness of doubt and fear disappear.[11]

2. Icon of the Life-Giving Spring and the Legends

The full title of the icon type is: Theotokos the Life-Giving Spring or Life-Giving Font of the Mother of God (*Zoodochos Pighi*). There are several layers to the story about the image and icon of the Life-Giving Spring, layers to be found in both history and legend. The first layer has to do with the finding of the spring itself and the sacred constructions associated with it:

> The Sacred Church of the Life-Giving Spring in the City [Constantinople] was first built by Emperor Leo the Thracian, who was virtuous and forgiving, even before he became emperor and was a simple soldier, when he met a blind man outside the Golden Gate of Constantinople. The blind man asked for water to drink, and Leo looked for the source of the spring of water in the area, which was overgrown with trees, and he was unable to find it. He became very sad that he was unable to find water for the blind man. He then heard a voice say to him: "King Leo (he was called a king even though he was just a soldier, which became verified), come deeper into the woods, and after receiving in your hands this turbid water, quinch the thirst of the blind man and wash his eyes, and then you will know who I am who dwells in this place." Leo immediately did what the voice ordered him to do and the blind man received his sight. The voice was that of the Panagia [meaning "All-Holy," one of the titles of the Virgin Mary or Theotokos--RT].

---

[11] As quoted in Robert Feeney, *Mother of the Americas* (Forest Grove, Oregon: Aquinas Press, 1989), p. 55. Lightly edited to implement inclusive language.

Leo, when he became emperor, out of gratitude and honor built on the site of that holy water the sacred church in honor of the Panagia, the Life-Giving Spring. When over a period of time this sacred church collapsed, other emperors—Justinian and Basil the Macedonian—took it upon themselves to have a new church built, even more grand than the previous.

Another tradition says that the first church was built by Justinian, after seeing in a vision while he was hunting there a small church and a priest in front of a spring, saying to him that it is a spring of wonders. There he built a monastery with the materials left over from Hagia Sophia.

This church in the Queen City collapsed in the fifteenth century. According to reports from 1547 the church no longer existed. Only the holy water was there. In 1833 Patriarch Constantios I, with permission from the Sultan, rebuilt the church over the ruins of the old one. Thus on February 2nd in 1835, Patriarch Constantios with twelve other hierarchs dedicated the new Church of the Life-Giving Spring in Baloukli. Baloukli means "the place of the fish," since the Spring contains fish.

In this church many miracles took place, even to noble families of the empire, a typical example being the release from sterility of Empress Zoe, who after the miracle from the Life-Giving Spring gave birth to Constantine Porphyrogenitos, who became emperor in Byzantium. In this church also were healed the emperors Justinian, Leo the Wise, Romanos Lekapenos, Andronikos III, Patriarch Stephen of Constantinople, Patriarch John of Jerusalem, many empresses and many senior officials of the empire, as well as clergy and monks, and many ordinary Christians. In the fourteenth century Nikephoros Kallistos wrote about the holy water of the Spring, and compiled a list of sixty-three miracles.[12]

Concerning the legend of the Spring as it developed, John Sanido-poulos writes:

---

[12] From A.K., "The Panagia, the Life-Giving Spring," as translated by John Sanidopoulos, *Mystagogy Resource Center*, April 25, 2014. On-line at: <https://www.johnsanidopoulos.com/2014/04/the-panagia-life-giving-spring.html> (Accessed 8/9/2019)

Before the second millennium of Christianity, the Spring (*Pege*) of the Theotokos of Baloukli in Constantinople was the source of numerous miracles, but it had not yet received the epithet by which it would become perpetually known—"Life-giving" (*Zoodochos*).

The title *"Zoodochos Pege"* was coined in the ninth century by Saint Joseph the Hymnographer in a hymn he wrote to the Mother of God. It became associated with the icon of the Theotokos at Baloukli and her Spring in the 1000's, when a man from Greece was raised from the dead through the miraculous power of the holy Spring. This miracle cemented its renown with the name "Life-giving Spring" (*Zoodochos Pege*).

According to the story, four pilgrims from Thessaly in Greece were journeying to the holy shrine in Constantinople, but en route one of them died. Before he expired, his dying wish was not to be left behind, but he begged the mariners to take his corpse to the Church of the Spring, and when they arrived they were to pour those holy waters over his dead body. He even specified the amount: three jars of water. His final request was that they afterwards bury him in the surrounding forest. The mariners obliged him, and fulfilled his dying wish. However, after they poured those wonderworking waters over his corpse, the supernatural power of the Theotokos allowed him to rise up and live again.

Therefore, since that time, the Spring has officially become known as *Zoodochos Pege* or Life-giving Spring. In some icons of the Life-giving Spring, this miracle can be seen at the bottom of the Spring.[13]

In the Orthodox Christian world of Greece, the feast day of the Life-Giving Spring is commemorated each year on Bright Friday, which is the Friday following Pascha (Easter), the only feast day which may be celebrated in Orthodoxy during Bright Week. Commemoration of the Life-Giving Spring Icon of the Most Holy Theotokos is observed on

---

[13] John Sanidopoulos, "How Did the 'Life-Giving Spring' Get Its Name?'," *Mystagogy Resource Center*, May 10, 2013. On-line at: <https://www.johnsanidopoulos.com/2013/05/how-did-life-giving-spring-get-its-name.html> (Accessed 8/9/2019)

April 4th.[14] Ephraim the Syrian (d. 373) described Mary as "the fountain of the eternal spirit" and Andrew of Crete (seventh century) was the first to use specifically the Greek phrase *Zoodochos Pighi*—"the life-giving fountain" as a metaphor for the Mother of God.[15] The icon itself is a significant conduit of the Marian (and Sophianic) reality that we are concerned with. It itself is an instance of the transparent and mediating "betweenness" that the Blessed Virgin Mary is and that we ourselves are.[16] This icon, in its various versions, is emblematic of the Christian faith as a therapeutics—first, a therapeutics for ourselves and, second, a therapeutics on behalf of others who are drawn near for healing. This reference to therapeutics may bring to mind the Marian shrine at Lourdes, known for the many dimensions of healing that have been experienced there in the years since the apparitions of 1858. It may be that these therapeutics engage, first of all, the imagination. The poet-priest, Malcolm Guite, has noted the many instances in which the language of Jesus, in the New Testament, engages the imagination.[17]

3. The Great Fountain – Flow and Return

Among the implications of the Fountain as metaphysically and cosmologically apt is the notion that all things are subject to change. All things having their birth in time are subject to passing away. The philosophy of Heraclitus ("All is in flux") comes to mind, as does Oriental teaching concerning the Tao. In Taoist understanding the Fountain is interior as well as all-pervasive. From the *Tao Te Ching*:

---

[14] Other resources for Life-giving Spring can be found on-line at: <https://www.johnsanidopoulos.com/2016/05/zoodochos-pege-life-giving-spring.html> (Accessed 8/9/2019)

[15] According to Jens Fleischer, "The Mother of God—The Life-Giving Fountain," an essay in Søren Kaspersen and Ulla Haastrup, editors, *Images of Cult and Devotion: Function and Reception of Christian Images in Medieval and Post-Medieval Europe* (Copenhagen, Denmark: Museum Tusculanum Press and University of Copenhagen, 2004), p. 257.

[16] For an understanding of the ontological status of icons, see Sergius Bulgakov, *Icons and the Name of God*, translated by Boris Jakim. (Grand Rapids, Michigan: Wm. B. Eerdmans Publishing Co., 2012).

[17] See Malcolm Guite, "As If," video based on his 2019 Laing Lectures at Regent College in Vancouver, British Columbia, on the role of the imagination as a truth-bearing faculty. On-line at: <https://youtu.be/-aQD_W1rSw0> (Accessed 12/5/2019)

Know the glorious,
Keep to the lowly,
And be the Fountain of the World.
To be the Fountain of the World is
To live the abundant life of Virtue,
And to return again to Primal Simplicity.[18]

St. John of the Cross (d. 1591) wrote a poem, as translated into English by Antonio T. de Nicolás, titled "Song of the Soul that Delights in Knowing God by Faith."[19] This poem makes extensive use of the image of the fountain:

Well I know the fountain that runs and flows,
though it is night!

This eternal fountain is hidden deep,
Well I know where it has its spring,
Though it is night!

[In this life's dark night,
Faith has taught where this cold fountain lies,
Thought it is night!]

Its origin I cannot know, it has none,
And I know all origins come from it,
Though it is night!

---

[18] Lao Tzu, *Tao Teh Ching,* John C. H. Wu, translator; Paul K. T. Sih, editor (New York: St. John's University Press, 1961), p. 57. As quoted in John Lindblom, "John C.H.Wu and the Evangelization of China," *Logos: A Journal of Catholic Thought and Culture,* May 2005, pp. 130-164, p. 156. On-line at: <https://www.academia.edu/7509286/John_C._H._Wu_and_the_Evangelization_of_China> (Accessed 11/29/2019)

[19] Antonio T. de Nicolás, translator, *St. John of the Cross (San Juan de la Cruz), Alchemist of the Soul: His Life, His Poetry (Bilingual), His Prose* (York Beach, Maine: Samuel Weiser, Inc., 1989), p. 131-133. Nicolas comments: "This poem is found in the Sanlúcar manuscript. It was composed in prison, December 1577 – August 1578. The verses within brackets are found in another manuscript at Sacro Monte and are considered authentic."

And I know there can be nothing more fair,
The heavens and earth drink there,
Though it is night!

And I know it has no bed,
And I know no one can cross its depths,
Though it is night!

Its clarity is never clouded,
And I know all light shines from it,
Though it is night!

I know her streams swell so abundantly,
They water people, heaven and even hell,
Thought it is night!

The current born of this fountain
I know to be wide and mighty,
Though it is night!

And from these two another stream flows,
And I know neither comes before,
Though it is night!

[I know Three in only one water live,
And each the other feeds,
Though it is night!]

This eternal fountain is hiding from sight
Within this living bread to give us life,
Though it is night!

He calls all creatures to this light,
And of this water they drink, though in the dark,
Though it is night!

This living fountain I desire,
I see it here within this living bread,
Though it is night!

In an essay reflecting on the thought of St. Bonaventure, Fr. Zachary Hayes O.F.M. (Catholic Theological Union, Chicago) (d. 2014) wrote:

> The Trinitarian God of productive, creative love can be compared to a living fountain of water. Flowing from that fountain as something known, loved, and willed into being by the creative love of God is the immense river of creation. The world of nature in its vastness is the expression of a loving, intelligent creator. Like water, the cosmos has many dimensions and diverse qualities. Thinking of water in the form of the oceans, it suggests the overwhelming fullness of creation as it flows from the depths of God. Like an ocean, the cosmos is deep and contains many levels of meaning. Thinking of water in the form of a river, we can see how it reflects the movement and fluidity of the cosmos.[20]

This image of a living and flowing fountain[21] is a profound image that is central to the perspective of this present text. It is central in the sense that it is an image of the imaginal realm wherein the possibilities for each and every being unfold, and also in the sense that it provides an apt image for the dynamism of language as it moves from prose into poetry and song and back into silence. In a profound sense, this is what the Evangel or Gospel is—the liberating possibility of being caught up into the divine double-current or flow of incarnation and ascension, embodiment and return. Also writing from the same Franciscan intellectual tradition as Zachary Hayes, Ilia Delio O.S.F. (Villanova University) has chosen to emphasize the multiplicity that

---

[20] Zachary Hayes O.F.M., "The Cosmos, A Symbol of the Divine," synthesis of a paper originally prepared for the United States Catholic Conference U.S.C.C. meeting in Washington, D.C., June 1997. On-line at: <https://www.franciscantradition.org/images/stories/custodians/09_Cosmos_Symbol_of_the_Divine.pdf> (Accessed 9/1/2019)

[21] For more on the image of the fountain in Saint Bonaventure, see Janet C. Kvamme, "The *Fontalis Plenitudo* in Bonaventure as a Symbol for his Metaphysics," Ph.D. dissertation, Theology Department, Fordham University, 1999. Preview on-line at: <https://fordham.bepress.com/dissertations/AAI9955966/> (Accessed 9/13/2019)

emerges from the evolutionary process as being already divine—as divine as the divine oneness from which it flows.[22]

Bruno Barnhart O.S.B. Cam., Delio, and perhaps others, have used the word "fontality," where it means, in the words of Barnhart:

> God is no longer only the transcendent Other but has become the divine ground of one's identity; even, we might say, the transcendent/immanent Subject, whose light and energies are participated in our own consciousness, our relationships and activities, so that these take on a divine quality. We have given the name "fontality" to this new mode of divine participation, which expresses itself in faith, hope, love, and creativity.[23]

Magdalena Lubanska writes: "The image of the Mother of God of the Life-giving Spring and its veneration goes back to Constantinople, where a small shrine became dedicated to the Mother of God of the Life-giving Spring as early as the fifth century on account of a healing spring located in the vicinity, whose miraculous properties were attributed to an intervention of the Mother of God."[24] In this statement is gathered up key elements of our topic: image (or icon), spring of water, shrine, healing, and the miraculous. Within contemporary Greek culture, these elements are found in what is called the "Romeic" (inside) tradition versus "Hellenic" (public) practice that is deeply secularized, notwithstanding its delimited veneer of Christian Orthodoxy.[25]

---

[22] See Ilia Delio O.S.F., *The Unbearable Wholeness of Being: God, Evolution, and the Power of Love* (Maryknoll, New York: Orbis Books, 2013). Delio has also written extensively on St. Bonaventure, including a paper on "Bonaventure's Metaphysics of the Good," *Theological Studies* 60 (1999) where she notes St. Bonaventure's understanding of God the Father as the "fountain fullness of the good." On-line at: <http://cdn.theologicalstudies.net/60/60.2/60.2.2.pdf> (Accessed 9/5/2019)

[23] Bruno Barnhart, *The Future of Wisdom: Toward a Rebirth of Sapiential Christianity* (New York: Continuum, 2007), p. 132.

[24] Lubanska, pp. 7-8.

[25] As referenced in Evy Johanne Håland, "The Life-giving Spring: Water in Greek Religion, Ancient and Modern, a Comparison," *Proteus: A Journal of Ideas*, Spring 2009, Volume 26, Number 1, pp. 45-54. On-line at: <https://www.ship.edu/globalassets/proteus/volume26-45-haland.pdf> (Accessed 8/10/2019)

The image and physical manifestations in nature of fountains and springs are magical and have always been regarded as holy. These realities are not simply geological, but they are cosmic as well as central to the human person. In his writing, the Irish poet and philosopher, John O'Donohue (d. 2008) used expressions such as "enriching fountain of love" and "wellspring of love within the heart" or "inner fountain" to refer to this "interior" reality.[26] Beatrice Bruteau (d. 2014), a pioneer in the integrated study of science, mathematics, philosophy, and religion, wrote of the cosmic dimensions of this reality.[27] The flow and return is also the *chiasmus* structure that was discussed in my previous book, *Taliesin's Harp*.[28] The appearance of the Blessed Mother is particularly associated with the turning point—or point of crisis—between flow and return, in whatever context, personal or cosmic, we may be considering. "You are this Life that circulates. To acknowledge it with your mass—without words and without desire—that is prayer."[29]

To understand the significance and the dramatic context of the point of crisis it is useful to refer to the work of both René Girard (d. 2015) and Owen Barfield (d. 1997). Girard was a French historian, literary critic, and philosopher of social science in the tradition of philosophical anthropology. He is perhaps best known for his insights into the formation of cultures. It was his discernment that, in general, cultures come into being as a consequence of times of crisis for particular populations—times of crisis that are resolved only by the (murderous) expulsion of a scapegoat following which peace is restored and cultural identity is solidified for that population. As populations move toward periods of crisis they are pervasively *mimetic* and they become maximally *mimetic* at the point of crisis. What do we mean by *mimesis* (adjectival form: *mimetic*)? In Girard's work, *mimetic* theory is

---

[26] See, for example, John O'Donohue, *Anam Cara: A Book of Celtic Wisdom* (New York: HarperCollins, 1998), at pp., 26-27.

[27] See Bearice Bruteau, *God's Ecstasy: The Creation of a Self-Creating World* (New York: The Crossroad Publishing Company, 1997.

[28] Robert F. Thompson, *Taliesin's Harp: A Poetics of the Divine-Humanity*, a Perennials Study Group publication, Memphis, Tennessee (Kindle Direct Publishing, 2019).

[29] Michel Conge, "Presence and Prayer," *Parabola*, October 17, 2018. On-line at: <https://parabola.org/2018/10/17/presence-and-prayer-by-michel-conge/> (Accessed 11/20/2019)

concerned with the pervasiveness of imitative desire—desire that is, for the most part, below the threshold of conscious awareness. In the words of René Girard, "Man is the creature who does not know what to desire, and he turns to others in order to make up his mind. We desire what others desire because we imitate their desires."[30]

The condition of being pervasively *mimetic* is my understanding of what Owen Barfield, philosopher and member of the Inklings, meant by "Original Participation." In this condition there is little self-awareness. In the history of human consciousness there occur what we might call "axial shifts" in human consciousness. According to the psychotherapist and writer, Mark Vernon, fundamental shifts in human consciousness occurred, in the Jewish and Greek worlds, at the time of the Deuteronomists and at the time of the Greek philosophers and in the Western European world at the time of the Reformation.[31] In the Oriental world, a shift can be discerned following the life of the Taoist, Zhuangzi (Zhuang Zhou) (fourth century B.C.E.).

In the Barfield schema, there are what we might call three stages in the evolution of consciousness. This is a movement from Original Participation to a withdrawal from participation to a re-engagement with participation in a more self-conscious way. Barfield terms this third stage "Final Participation." This condition is, as it seems to me, what is also called the divine-humanity—the condition of maximal *theosis* for humankind understood as a reality beyond the individual (in the wake of the European Enlightenment). These shifts, however, are recurrent and not necessarily permanent.

Let's revisit the point of crisis. It is place of decision. The scapegoats (the victimized ones) may appeal to a dimly perceived presence. The victimizers may, also, one by one, wake up and withraw from the sleep of *mimetic* trance, having become aware of a presence manifesting as conscience. These may be said to be under the mantle of the

---

[30] René Girard, "Generative Scapegoating," in Robert G. Hammerton-Kelly, editor, *Violent Origins: Walter Burkert, René Girard, and Jonathan Z. Smith on Ritual Killing and Cultural Formation* (Stanford, California: Stanford University Press, 1987), p. 122. The *Colloquium on Violence & Religion (COV&R)* is a recognized gateway to Girardian scholarship. On-line at: <https://violenceandreligion. com/> (Accessed 9/10/2019)

[31] See Mark Vernon, *A Secret History of Christianity: Jesus, the Last Inkling, and the Evolution of Consciousness* (Alresford, Hampshire, United Kingdom: Christian Alternative, an imprint of John Hunt Publishing, 2019).

Blessed Mother, however her reality is understood. For these, the peace that is experienced is not based on violence. It is experienced as the peace that descends from heaven. What is this reality?

4. The Marian Reality

We gather a certain blurred and feeble and partial image; and our best theologian is not the one who has seen the whole ... but the one who imagines more than the other, and conceives in himself more of an image of the truth, or a shadow, or whatever we may call it.
— Gregory the Theologian, *Oration 30*[32]

Whereas in Girardian understanding, cultures derive from founding murders, the Blessed Virgin Mary, in witness to the contrary, presides over spiritual culture that does *not* depend upon any founding murder. Reflections on the Marian reality can be considered as a region of poetics—the same poetics as presented in my previous book, *Taliesin's Harp: A Poetics of the Divine-Humanity*. The reality of the Blessed Virgin Mary is much more than the "historical" Mary, the mother of Jesus. This "much more" is similar to the meaningful "much more" of our own individual lives that escapes any catalog of (externally witnessed) events that might be included in the history or story of our lives. The same is true of Jesus Christ.

When we confess the faith of Christ, we intend and know a reality beyond the "historical Jesus." In our confession of the faith we affirm that Jesus is the Christ of God—fully human and fully divine. As the Son of God—the Word—he is also the second person of the Holy Trinity. All this is what I have previously called the "Mahayana" vision or version of Christianity—the full-bodied version. I used the term "Mahayana" because it bears some analogy to the widening of vision in the history of Buddhism away from a simple account of the life of the Buddha to the full-bodied Mahayana Buddhism (in contrast to the Hinayana or Theravada Buddhism).

The Roman Catholic Church, in its dogma or doctrine of the Immaculate Conception, has spoken about the Blessed Virgin Mary. What it has said applies to her as a single individual. Beatrice Bruteau,

---

32 As quoted in Thomas Arentzen, *The Virgin in Song: Mary and the Poetry of Romanos the Melodist* (Philadelphia, Pennsylvania: University of Pennsylvania Press, 2017), p. 164.

mentioned in the previous section (The Great Fountain – Flow and Return) above, asks us to consider also the extent to which the Blessed Virgin Mary is an *archetype* whose qualities, as expressed in Church teaching, also manifest in every person. As such—as an archetype—the Immaculate Conception can be understood by reference to the Oriental teaching about our "Original Face"—that is, our face before we or our parents were born. A key text is Bruteau's essay, "The Immaculate Conception, Our Original Face," that appears as Chapter VII in her book, *What We Can Learn From the East*.[33] Bruteau suggests that, if we consider the story of the 1858 apparition of the Blessed Virgin Mary to Bernadette Soubirous in the grotto at Lourdes in southwestern France in all its aspects, we may note the centrality of two things—the Lady and the Spring:

> Is the free-flowing stream of healing and life, springing up from the earth in which it had lain hidden and unsuspected, also an archetype? Why not? Perhaps the Lady and the Spring together reveal the secret meaning of the Immaculate Conception.
>
> The Spring shows that an archetype, though its power comes from its transhistorical significance, need not be unhistorical. There is real water at Lourdes, and real cures take place there. The Blessed Virgin Mary is a historical woman, but as the Immaculate Conception she *means* much more. The Lady and the Spring are a double icon of the purity and unity of the life hidden at the center of things, for us hitherto an unknown life, but one which when liberated and raised to consciousness is healing.[34]

This, of course, blends with the images of our focus icon, Mother of God of the Life-Giving Spring. In both this icon and at Lourdes there is proximity of Our Lady and living (flowing) water. This is richly meaningful in more than a single sense. Bruteau further writes:

---

[33] This essay originally appeared in *Cross Currents*, Vol. XXXIX, #2, Summer, 1989.

[34] Beatrice Bruteau, *What We Can Learn From the East* (New York: The Crossroad Publishing Company, 1995), p. 104.

Our spiritual task is to discover that point in ourselves where *we are the Immaculate Conception*.[35]

Another remark that is perhaps worth making is that the traditional archetypes are available to everyone. You don't have to be a Christian to take the Immaculate Conception to heart as a significant revelation to you personally; nor do you have to be a Buddhist to realize that the emblem of the Original Face was meant for you. Once these highly charged symbols enter the mainstream of human culture, they belong to all of us, and we need not be shy about adopting them as our own.

What I am saying, then, is that this mystery emblem, the Immaculate Conception, is about *us*. It may be also true in the limited and particular sense taught by its official custodians, but my point is that as an archetype it is about *our* true selfhood, *our* consciousness, *our* reality. The view I am proposing regards the whole sacred story, including all its characters, as played out within ourselves by the various aspects of our humanness and our personhood. Taking it this way, we can give a new meaning even to the "exclusive" elements of official dogma.

Our "Mary" aspect is that part of us represented by the icon of the Blessed Virgin Mary. To say that it alone has the privilege of Immaculate Conception is to say that only this central Mary principle in us is free from Original Sin. [...] That there should be at least *one* point in us that *is* free is a great discovery, something to be carefully taught in the sacred mysteries by emphasizing its singularity and uniqueness.[36]

... [T]he Immaculate Conception in us is the presence in us of the "grace of God," the sharing of divine life, something that quite transcends the principles on which the natural universe operates. It is the presence of *personhood* in us, something that cannot be reduced to the motions of molecules.[37]

Bruteau goes on to connect her remarks about this Original Face (or Immaculate Conception) in us with what Thomas Merton referred to

---

35 Bruteau, *What We Can Learn From the East*, p. 105.
36 Bruteau, *What We Can Learn From the East*, pp. 111-112.
37 Bruteau, *What We Can Learn From the East*, p. 112.

as "the virgin point" (*Le Point Vierge*), that central point in us that never loses its connection with the divine. This is that certain emptiness within us that is also *paradisal.*

The Immaculate Conception as archetype can also be understood, it seems to me, as an image of the present moment in the sense that the present moment is that "place" where we have the maximum freedom to welcome and to shape the arriving future and to re-conceive the receding past in ways that reveal the divine generosity that is the ever-flowing fountain of grace. In regard to the receding but ever-present past, we begin to forgive and to understand—as a mother would, her errant children.

The greatest obstacle to our awareness of and responsiveness to the Marian reality, it seems to me, is the realm of our own thoughts. It is within the domain of our thoughts that words of the Accuser (Satan) form themselves. Proliferation of the Accuser's language, if and as we follow its traces, involves us in blockages and obsessions that impede our participation in the free-flowing nature of the divine goodness. Wisdom school teaches us to maintain equanimity in the face of the Accuser's language. Transcending this realm of slander, we find ourselves in the Marian realm of of spaciousness, freedom, and beauty. When this happens, we then have the grace to enact this divine generosity in our worlds of manifestation.

A high view of the Marian reality is expressed in the *Enzira Sebhat*, a medieval Ethiopian poem dedicated to the Virgin Mary:

> Justly are you the beginning of the creation of this world,
> For you are at once the foundation and the gateway of the
>   whole endeavor.
> O Dawn which knows no eventide,
> It was on your account that God created the heaven and the
>   earth,
> The sea and its depths, the sun, the moon and stars,
> The times and seasons, the winter and summer,
> Days and Sabbaths, festivals and jubilations,
> All the worlds, whether visible or hidden.
> It was on your account that God instituted the passage of the
>   days of the week.

Fr. John McGuckin, translator of the work, writes in his Introduction, "A rabbinical tradition stated that it was on account of the beauty of the Torah, pre-existently conceived by God, that the Creator made the world." Similarly, according to Fr. McGuckin, the Ethiopian author of the poem "sees God finding in the beauty of the Theotokos a motive not only for his own entrance into creation, but for the whole conception of the world order. There is also a sense intended that the week, as it is liturgically conceived as a way of dividing up the praises of Mary in the churches, finds its true fulfillment."[38]

To consider the Marian reality is to enter, in the words of the Perennialist philosopher, Frithjof Schuon (d. 1998), "an extremely subtle domain, in which definitions are always hazardous."[39] We shall avoid definitions in this present text but we shall have recourse to selected titles of the Blessed Virgin Mary and to certain of the traditions about her. Following is a succinct summary of the approach to the Marian reality that is commended:

> The Virgin Mother Mary has always been venerated … far beyond her scriptural role. […] [W]e propose a symbolic framework of deep culture … [for] understanding the prominence of Mary and the manner in which she plays a role in people's lives …. The framework begins with a mystical/ esoteric perspective to appreciate Mary as a symbol that is multivalent, irreplaceable, archetypal, interior, and manifest yet hidden. […] Mary's significance … is best understood in her role as symbolic doorway to mystical religiosity. This role is highly agentic, although not in the sense in which agency is typically—exoterically—understood as analytical and external,

[38] John Anthony McGuckin, translator, *The Harp of Glory: Enzira Sebhat: An Alphabetical Hymn of Praise for the Ever-Blessed Virgin Mary from the Ethiopian Orthodox Church*, Popular Patristics Series (Yonkers, New York: St. Vladimir's Seminary Press, 2010), pp. 83, 117.
[39] As quoted by James S. Cutsinger in his paper, "Colorless Light and Pure Air: The Virgin in the Thought of Frithjof Schuon," 2007, previously published in *Sophia: The Journal of Traditional Studies*, 6:2 (Winter 2000); reprinted in *Maria: A Journal of Marian Studies*, 3:1 (August 2002) and in *Ye Shall Know the Truth: Christianity and the Perennial Philosophy*, ed. Mateus Soares de Azevedo (Bloomington, Indiana: World Wisdom, 2005). On-line at: <https://www.cutsinger.net/pdf/colorless_light_and_pure_air.pdf> (Accessed 8/30/2019)

but rather as esoterically affective and internally transforma-tive.[40]

This approach recognizes and honors the "poetic basis of the mind"[41] in attending to the appearance of the Blessed Virgin Mary in the imaginal realms. This approach also commends a Marian *metaxology*, a term that recalls the work of the Irish philosopher of religion, William Desmond (Leuven and Villanova), on the hermeneutic and heuristic uses of all that is "between." In other words, there is recognition of the Blessed Virgin Mary as mediating between the concerns of philo-sophy and theology. The Marian reality is, in the words of Patrick Ryan Cooper (Saint Martin's University), the integral site of an "open porosity" between philosophy and theology. The concerns of this approach exceed the bounds of a Mariology proper.[42]

The Marian reality is deeply associated with the natural world. As such, this reality resists all that is merely mechanical, including the mechanics (logic) of human thought. Consider the forest, for example. Animals run into the forest when they are injured and are about to die. The forest is a place where it is ok to cry. The forest accepts all the suffering. The Virgin Mary is like that. The Virgin Mary is the Mother who (as Nature) accepts everything. The Virgin is the hope of all those who have lost hope. Most of all, the Virgin Mary associates with the

---

[40] Ali Qadir and Tatiana Tiaynen-Qadir, "Deep Culture and the Mystical Agency of Mary in Eastern Christianity," *Religions* 2018, 9, 383; doi:10.3390/rel9120383. On-line at: <https://www.researchgate.net/publication/329155659_Deep_Culture_and_the_Mystical_Agency_of_Mary_in_Eastern_Christianity> (Accessed 9/2/2019). The authors of this paper are in the Faculty of Social Sciences in the University of Tampere, Finland.

[41] This expression comes from James Hillman, *Re-visioning Psychology*, previously cited, at p. xi.

[42] See Patrick Ryan Cooper, "The Virginal Middle: Towards a Marian Metaxology," in *Medieval Mystical Theology*, Volume 25, 2016, Issue 1. Abstract on-line at: <https://www.tandfonline.com/doi/full/10.1080/20465726.2016.1163972>. In this article Cooper elaborates his Marian *metaxology*, recog-nizing that "Mary's irreducible significance is to be found in maintaining this excessive, 'virginal middle' from which 'one infers the lesser from the greater' (i.e. God becomes man) and 'also the greater from the lesser (i.e. man becomes divine)', themes of which direct us to the very core of the use of analogy and the metaphysical, the economy of salvation overall and mystical theology in particular."

flower and herb gardens of the planet—especially those with springs or fountains.[43] There is a flowingness associated with the eternal feminine—an eternal feminine that the philosopher and Jesuit priest, Teilhard de Chardin (d. 1955), referred to as the "envelope of God."[44] Through this flowingness that we may refer to as the eternal feminine (Sophia), the world is created and the Incarnation has manifested in time. The Marian reality is also about us. A saying attributed to Meister Eckhart is: "What good is it to me if Mary gave birth to the son of God and I do not also give birth to the son of God in my own time and my own culture? We are all meant to be Mothers of God for God is always needing to be born."[45]

Christian sage, Owen St. Victor, wrote of the Marian reality as it has been perceived in the West beyond Roman Catholic and Eastern Orthodox spiritual contexts. He mentions, for example, well-known figures from within Protestant tradition—Jacob Boehme, Emmanuel Swedenborg, and William Blake. Interestingly and insightfully, he also mentions and gives attention to the American historian and journalist, Henry Adams (d. 1918):

---

[43] Accounts of the Marian apparitions at Litmanova and Turzovka in Slovakia, for example, include references to both the forest environment and to associated springs of water. Other examples could be cited. An on-line account of Litmanova: <http://www.divinemysteries.info/litmanova-slovakia-1990-1995/> (Accessed 10/24/2019). An on-line account of Turzovka: <http://www.free-rosary.net/?p=945> (Accessed 10/24/2019)

[44] See Henri de Lubac S.J., *The Eternal Feminine: A Study on the Text of Teilhard de Chardin* (London: Collins, 1971).

[45] As quoted in William J. Byron S.J., *The Word Proclaimed: A Homily for Every Sunday of the Year; Year A* (Mahwah, New Jersey: Paulist Press, 2013), at Sermon 5 for Christmas Vigil. In a paper titled, "Giving Birth to God: Meister Eckhart and Symeon the New Theologian on Spiritual Maternity," Archimandrite Maximos Lavriotes (Orthodox) has compared the teaching on the giving of birth to the Divine Word in the believer as found in a sermon of Eckhart and in a sermon of St. Symeon the New Theologian, the 10th-century Byzantine mystical writer. He thinks Eckhart comes close to the Eastern Orthodox teaching on deification, but believes Eckhart's God "is concerned only with perfect souls." (*Eckhart Review*, Volume 4, Issue 1, 1995, pp. 36-56. Limied access on-line at: <https://www.tandfonline.com/doi/abs/10.1179/eck_1995_4_1_005> (Accessed 12/2/2019)

In 1895, Adams began a study of Gothic architecture and its religious and social context that resulted in the 1904 publication of his celebrated and still read classic, *Mont St. Michel and Chartres*. However his road to the Virgin at Chartres began earlier. This we can see in his autobiographical, *The Education of Henry Adams* published in 1905. Unconsciously, Adams was already attracted to the figure of the Virgin during his stay in Rome (1859-1860). In one place he wrote how he sat "more than once, at sunset, on the steps of the Church of Santa Maria di Ara Coeli" musing. On another visit, in 1865, on hearing of the assassination of President Lincoln, "he went to meditate on the steps of the Santa Maria in Ara Coeli." Returning again, in 1900, he wrote: "The church of Ara Coeli seemed more and more to draw all the treads of thought to a centre."

To understand what follows in a description of Adams' apprehension of the Virgin it is necessary to know one thing: that the humanist, already in his sixties at the turn of the century, was dumfounded at the discoveries in science that were unfolding. His studies in philosophy directed his attention particularly to the new physics of radiant energy (magnetism, electricity, X-rays) and to their practical utilization as power (through the appropriate engineering). Thus chapter XXV in *The Education* discusses "two kingdoms of force," described by the chapter heading: "The Virgin and the Dynamo."

Adams wrote of the newly discovered forms of physical radiant energy: "The rays ... were occult, supersensual, irrational; they were a revelation of mysterious energy like that of the Cross ...." Philosophically, he felt that forces in human history and forces of energy in the natural world must have some relationship. He wrote that he wished "to reduce all these forces to a common value." However, he went on to observe, while his compatriots flocked to scientific and technological exhibitions and were quite aware of physical forces, no matter how invisible, they were completely ignorant of something else. As he put it: "The force of the Virgin was still felt at Lourdes and seemed as potent as X-rays; but in America ... the Virgin never had value as force...." (Her emanation) "was the highest energy ever known to man, the creator of four-fifths of his noblest art, exercising vastly more attraction over the human mind than all the steam-engines and dynamos ever dreamed of; and yet this energy was unknown to the American mind.[46]

Fascination with the mechanical sciences, in the interests of power and material wealth accumulation, served to obscure an awareness of the life-giving and life-sustaining generosity of the tended garden. This trend had begun long before. Carolyn Merchant, American ecofeminist philosopher and historian of science, wrote:

> During the seventeenth century, the Christian narrative of dominion over nature was combined with science, technology, and capitalist development to reinforce the possibility of remaking the earth as a controlled, managed Garden of Eden. Social values of order and control paved the way toward acceptance of a new narrative of dominion over nature. The mechanical worldview created by the "fathers of modern science" drew on philosophical assumptions consistent with the power of machine technologies to control the natural world. Early capitalist development was based on watermills, windmills, furnaces, forges, cranes, and pumps that transformed and multiplied the energy of sun, wind, wood, and coal to produce ships, guns, cannons, ammunition, cloth, paper, planks, flour, glass, and a myriad of iron implements and utensils. The large pumping, milling, and lifting machines found everywhere in daily life made plausible a model of nature as a machine. The cosmos was likened to a clock that regulated time in equal units. God was depicted as a clockmaker, mathematician, and engineer who constructed and directed the world from outside.[47]

The notion of a tended garden is the image of a right-relation with nature understood as *theophanic* nature. Contemporary philosopher,

---

[46] Owen St. Victor, *The Masked Madonna: Studies in the Mystical Symbolism of The Secret Sovereign: The Queen of Heaven* (Leuven, Belgium: Sancta Sophia, 1988), pp. 9-10.
[47] Carolyn Merchant, *Reinventing Eden: The Fate of Nature in Western Culture* (New York: Routledge, 2003), p. 72.

cultural historian and gardener, Jeremy Naydler (Oxford, England), advocates for the recovery of a theophanic view of nature. He writes:

All of nature cries out for this turn of our attention towards the kind of knowing that is not based on manipulation and control in order to fulfil our utilitarian needs and desires, but issues from a genuine desire to relate to the creatures with which we share the world as they are in themselves and for their own sake. The affirmation of the wholeness and inherent integrity of creatures is, then, a first step towards restoring a more harmonious relationship to nature. We do not have to be scientists to know the inner nature of other creatures: it is a question rather of how open or closed we are as human beings to the forms and qualitative attributes of the multiple natural phenomena that surround us.

But there is a further step that can be taken. By intensifying our focus on something's innate qualities, we may deepen the experience of "the idea within the thing" to the point at which the numinous ground of its existence becomes present to our consciousness. Then the spiritual source of the idea, or organising principle, begins to speak to us. This source is not in the sense-perceptible world but in the creative energies out of which the sense-perceptible world unfolds into manifestation. What is sense-perceptible is thus revealed to be the exteriorisation of a deeper, spiritual level of existence. For the creative energies that pour into the world belong to a sphere of reality that is intrinsically numinous, and it is within this numinous sphere of reality that the organizing principles are rooted. Encountered as creative powers, they are traditionally referred to as spiritual archetypes, or "ideas *prior* to things" (*universalia ante res*).

This is of course a quite different kind of knowledge to that pursued by contemporary science. It is sacred knowledge. In the Western philosophical tradition, the spiritual archetypes are conceived as being "in the mind of God," a phrase which signifies that their provenance is beyond space and time, and that they have a purely spiritual mode of existence before they manifest in any material form. This spiritual mode of existence is as thoughts or ideas within the greater cosmic intelligence, or cosmic *Logos*, which endows them with generative power. As thoughts in the greater cosmic intelligence, they possess a creative potency that human thoughts do not have.[48]

To the extent that we are able to see the natural world as permeated with Divine light and life, we may also discern the Blessed Virgin Mary standing at the pinnacle of the angelic world that enlivens and maintains the natural world. We are invited to cooperate in that world maintenance.

The Garden

In both literature and art there is a long-standing and rich tradition of the Virgin Mary in association with gardens, the closed garden (*hortus conclusus*) in particular.[49] The garden contains flowering plants and medicinal herbs. In an essay on the art of the garden, Jemima Montagu writes:

> The symbol of the garden recurs throughout the cultures of the globe—from the various incarnations of the Garden of Eden in paintings, tapestries and literature across the Judaeo-Christian world, to formal Islamic gardens and their philosophical counterparts in the Far East, whether they be classical Chinese park-

---

[48] Jeremy Naydler, "The Perennial Philosophy and the Recovery of a Theophanic View of Nature," p. 6. Published on-line at *The Harmony Project*, March 14, 2019, and re-published at *The Matheson Trust* website. PDF version accessible on-line at: <https://www.themathesontrust.org/library/naydler-perennial-philosophy-recovery> (Accessed 12/15/2019)

[49] The image of the "closed garden" presents a great paradox because sometimes one is present within this garden and sometimes one is not. Like the Klein bottle (or Moebius strip) of topographic theory, the inside manifests as outside and vice versa. This is particularly characteristic of the imaginal realms and their phenomena. An image similar to the closed garden, but not exactly the same, is the image of the tended garden with porous borders. The tended garden is not meant to be radically discontinuous from regions beyond it. Somewhat like a Benedictine monastery, the world and the monastery (or tended garden) are not impervious to each other. The suggestion is that the presence of the Virgin Mary signifies a mandalic center (tended garden) from which there is an expanding (and indefinite) number of outer perimeters (walls) having doorways. The Tibetan mandala is a schematic image of these plural and dynamic relations.

lands or Zen landscape design. Gardens have also played a talismanic role in British culture, offering fertile imagery for art and literature across the centuries, and acting as a barometer for the country's changing social and cultural landscape.

In Western iconography the image of the garden has been shaped and defined by the Biblical story of Adam and Eve, the original sinners thrown out of their paradise for tasting the forbidden fruit, and cast into the wilderness. It is surprising, however, how little description the Book of Genesis gives of the original garden:

> The Lord God planted a garden in Eden, away
> to the East, and there he put the man whom he had
> formed. The Lord God made trees spring from
> the ground, all trees pleasant to look at and good
> for food; and in the middle of the garden he set
> the tree of life and the tree of the knowledge of good and
> > evil.
> There was a river flowing from Eden to water the garden.

This rudimentary outline has given rise to many interpretations of the mythical garden, often depicted in early religious paintings as a rich, verdant orchard, full of flowers and trees. The imagery was enriched by the florid verses of the Song of Solomon, where the dialogue between bride and bridegroom is a contest of compliments using the metaphor of the garden. The bridegroom calls his love "an orchard full of rare fruits," and uses the now well-known metaphor of his virginal bride as a secret garden: "My sister, my bride, is a garden close-locked, a fountain sealed."

The "close-locked" garden, or *hortus conclusus*, as it became known in the Renaissance, was one of the most influential early garden images. As a metaphor for virginity, as well as a reference to the prelapsarian paradise, it appears in many early religious paintings and tapestries. In works such as *The Garden of Paradise* (c.1415) by the Master of Oberrheinische Kunst, the Virgin Mary sits safely with her companions in a garden with castellated walls; they read, pick fruit and play musical instruments, surrounded by blossoming flowers. The painting is not just a leisure scene, but also an image for religious meditation, dense with Christian symbolism such as the slayed dragon of evil and the fountain, source of spiritual life and salvation. The physical arrangement of the Renaissance garden bore a close resemblance to a stage set, a similarly enclosed and contained area for playing out fantasies and dramas, a source of transformation, dream and fantasy. However, while the early garden emphasised small-scale, enclosed spaces, later ones took inspiration from the open expanse of the Biblical wilderness. The opposition between garden and wilderness reflected man's complex relationship to nature, where an impulse to shape, tame and control the natural world lived alongside a desire to yield to its wildness and danger—a duality that has shaped and influenced the way gardens have been visualised, both in life and art.[50]

Of all the flowers in the garden, the rose and its fragrance have always and especially been associated with and emblematic of the Blessed Virgin Mary. The rose was also said to have been the Prophet Muhammad's favorite flower. In my previous book, *Taliesin's Harp: A Poetics of the Divine Humanity*, primacy was given to the divine melody. Here, in this present text, primacy is given to the divine fragrance. Melody—like a poem—requires time. It unfolds in time. Fragrance, however, is timeless, instantaneous. Rose petals and their fragrance also figure in the American story, not recounted here, of Our Lady of Guadaloupe. Listen to her words to Juan Diego (in 1531) below. Are not her very words permeated with the fragrance of roses?

Hear and let it penetrate into your heart, my dear little son: let nothing discourage you, nothing depress you. Let nothing alter your heart or your countenance. Also do not fear any illness and vexation, anxiety or pain. Am I not here who am your mother? Are you not under my shadow and protection? Am I not your fountain of life? Are you not in the folds of my

---

[50] From Jemima Montagu, "Earthly Delights: The Art of the Garden," *Tate Etc.*, magazine of the Tate galleries, Issue 1, May 1, 2004. On-line at: <https://www.tate.org.uk/tate-etc/issue-1-summer-2004/earthly-delights> (Accessed 9/10/2019)

mantle, in the crossing of my arms? Is there anything else that you need?[51]

As in the garden, fragrances from many flowers blend, so the fragrances of wisdom traditions—non-systematic wisdom from varying traditions—easily blend. This is a deeper meaning of Our Lady's garden. The deepest wisdom is manifested in the tiny garden heliotropes. For us, this is simple recognition of ourselves as *theotropic* being. Our prayer blends with the ceaseless prayer of the tiny heliotropes. A prayer,[52] in the garden, to Our Lady:

I greet you, White Lily of the Glorious and always Peaceful Trinity.
I greet you, Beautiful Rose from the courts of Heavenly Joy.
O You Precious Queen who the Heavenly King
Allowed to carry and give birth to Him.
Fill our souls with Godly Grace.
Amen.

The above prayer makes reference to the "courts of Heavenly Joy." Canon Allchin recognized this joy as a keynote of the Blessed Virgin Mary:

Here in the classical Christian faith there is a very great affirmation of the goodness of the human, despite all its empirical disorder and decay. The human is capable of the divine. Through the gift of God, the divine life is rooted in the human, the human in the divine. And here precisely is the cause of great joy and amazement. For precisely in "man's animal exigencies" the ultimate glory is revealed, just where we had least expected it. Hence everywhere in the Christian world where she is known, Mary's name is associated with joy. She is the joy of joys, the cause of our joy, the joy of all creation. Latin, Greek, Russian, Syriac all proclaim the same thing. In her there is a meeting of opposites, of God and humankind, of

---

[51] As quoted in the front pages of Janice T. Connell, *Queen of Angels: Mary's Answers to Universal Questions* (Brewster, Massachusetts: Paraclete Press, 2008).
[52] Prayer associated with particular devotion to Our Lady of San Damiano (Italy). On-line source: <https://www.marypages.com/san-damiano-(italy)-en.html> (Accessed 10/18/2019)

flesh and spirit, of time and eternity, which causes an explosion of joy, a kind of ecstasy.[53]

The symbolic depths and range of the garden as image and emblem can be seen in considering all that we know and feel not only about the (primal) Garden of Eden but also about the Garden of Gethsemane. Both gardens, together, associate with the dimensions of Paradise in its fullness.

Transcend and Include

Recalling the image of a fountain, there is a forceful upward movement, within time, as well as a falling back. The forcefulness, however, is not "brute force," but is rather the gentle force of the radiant heart[54] that involves if not our direct "choice" or decision, then at least our conscious consent ("Be it unto me according to thy word," as Mary said to Gabriel at the Annunciation). Within eternity, or timeless perspective, the "upward" movement and the "falling back" are seen as one and the same; the forcefulness of the upward movement and the acceptance in the falling back as one and the same. Our consent to participation is key:

> For there to be a return, I have to wake up to my situation and consent to participate in this returning, upward movement of energies, or influences. We may come to understand that there really are currents of energies that pass from one cosmic level to another. In certain passages the flow is only possible if organisms are placed there. In the downward direction, the movement happens by itself. In the upward direction it will not happen unless there are men and women who become aware of their condition as seeds and acknowledge that they are placed there to enable the energies to return and thereby receive a new possibility. If I enable this return of energies, I am transformed. But I must understand that the higher levels have just

---

53 A. M. Allchin, *The Joy of All Creation*, previously cited, p. 18.
54 See discussion of the unicorn further below where it is suggested that the piercing strength of the unicorn's horn is the sword of St. Michael.

as great a need of that as the lower levels do. In a single whole, everything has need of everything.[55]

What if nature and culture (or history and myth[56]) are "not two" (distinctly different) entities? It may be that these are best regarded as two sides of a Moebius strip.[57] In his preface to the 2005 revised translation of *The Fountain of Life* (*Fons Vitae*) by the Andalusian poet and Jewish philosopher, Solomon ibn Gabirol (d. 1070), Leonard Levin writes:

> Soul and body, form and matter are not stark dichotomies ..., but the two sides of a Moebius strip, or two strands whose complex interweave depict a subtle tapestry of being in which everything is the flip-side of its counterpart and inextricably bound up with it. What is form in one instance can become matter in another connection, and vice versa.[58]

Levin also points out that, in the tradition, the same can be said of other similar dichotomies such as physical/spiritual. The work of Ibn Gabirol does bear a relationship with the Neo-Platonic intellectual tradition wherein imagery of the living fountain or of the ever-flowing fountain is, in the West, particularly at home. Levin's reference to the Moebius strip is significant in that it is the "place" (*topos*) where transformation is experienced with respect to elements of any given binary.

---

[55] Michel Conge, *Inner Octaves* (Toronto: Dolmen Meadows Editions, 2013), pp. 71-72.

[56] C.S. Lewis and J.R.R. Tolkien may be said to have regarded Christianity as "true myth." This is similar to what Rudolf Steiner argued in his 1901-1902 lectures, later published in book form as *Christianity as Mystical Fact and the Mysteries of Antiquity*. A fourth edition of this book, with an Introduction by Christopher Bamford, was published by SteinerBooks/Anthroposophic Press in 1997.

[57] The Moebius strip has been described as a surface with only one side and only one boundary component. (In topological mathematics, the Klein bottle is similar to the Moebius strip, except that the Klein bottle has no boundary.)

[58] Solomon Ben Judah ibn Gabirol, *The Fountain of Life* (*Fons Vitae*), originally translated by Alfred B. Jacob, revised by Leonard Levin (New York: The Jewish Theological Seminary, 2005), Levin's Preface, p. ii.

The binary (as a set of polar "oppositions") is transcended.[59] This is also, exactly, the "place" or the character of the Blessed Virgin Mary as she comes into manifestation—and as Spirit becomes incarnate within and from her. The movement—as Word comes from out of Silence—is one of unfoldment—as the rose petals unfold. The fragrance of the rose does not take one into the Kingdom—with the fragrance one discovers that one is already there! In the Litany of Loreto, the Blessed Virgin is the *Rosa Mystica*, the Mystic Rose.

If image and word are taken as polarity, there is a dynamism and yearning love in their relation. This is suggested and embodied in the human brain consisting of right and left lobes associated respectively and typically with responsiveness to images and with logic and language.[60] Consider meditatively the image of the Virgin and Holy Child—from the Great Silence come both the Image and the Word. The image (her authentic icon) leads or points one to the Word (that clothes itself in words). Gaze upon the Mother and listen! Listen for the Word who is the Son! Marian spirituality is predominantly imagistic, but it is these images that prepare one to hear the Word.[61] Otherwise, as in the Parable of the Sower, the ground may be hard and dry.

Characteristically, the Blessed Virgin Mary may be taken as sign and signature of the possibility of the miraculous—a function of the pervasive flowingness of meaning (the Moebius strip of nature/supernature). Scholars have used the term "miracular sensitivity" to indicate a characteristic of Marian spirituality. According to one statement of it, this expression can be taken to mean "anticipation of the extraordinary

---

[59] "Overstanding" (as opposed to "understanding") is a term within the Rastafarian *Iyaric* (dialect) that intends the most comprehensive view (that transcends and includes binaries).

[60] See Chapter 1, "A World of Polarities," in Istvan Cselenyi, *The Maternal Face of God?: Explorations in Catholic Sophiology* (Kettering, Ohio: Angelico Press, 2017), for a window into the pervasiveness of polarities and the purposes they serve.

[61] Wim Bonis (scholar of the goddess tradition and contributor to Leiden Law Blog, University of Leiden, Netherlands) writes: "Generally we can say that in Marian worship the power of imagery came to the foreground and the power of the written word was diminished." From Wim Bonis article, "The Hidden Wealth of the Virgin Mary," 2018, p. 9. On-line at: <http://eng.wimbonis.nl/wp-content/uploads/2018/09/The-Hidden-Wealth-of-The-Virgin-Mary-Wim-Bonis.pdf> (Accessed 11/19/2019)

... which stresses the importance of the authentic state of grace," and which is characterized by "the need for divine apparitions and divine interventions in worldly matters but also the need for extraordinary events which are, nevertheless, in accord with a traditional and enduring system of values."[62]

Marian spirituality is also the "art of real presence," to use an expression from John O'Donohue.[63] Also, because the internal relations of binaries or polarities in nature and in language come to be seen not as warring oppositions, but as paired lovers, we may suspect there is something like a Marian hermeneutic—a sensitive way of reading and a sensitive way of exposition that invites the interior light in all things to reveal itself. This seems similar if not identical to the *agapeic* criticism that has been commended by Michael Martin (Center for Sophiological Studies, Michigan) with respect to literary studies. This is a criticism grounded in contemplation.[64] Along similar lines, the late Stratford Caldecott wrote the following,[65] citing the Catholic theologian and cultural historian, Hans Urs von Balthasar:

> Christian gnosis, or Balthasar's "seeing the form" (the title of the first volume of *The Glory of the Lord*), is the place where we might integrate (with appropriate adjustments!) much of what the Persian tradition tells us about the Interworld or *mundus*

---

[62] From Andrzej Hemka and Jacek Olędzki as quoted in Konrad Siekierski (King's College, London), "Charismatic Renewal and Miracular Sensitivity at a Catholic Marian Apparition Site in Poland," *Journal of Global Catholicism*, Volume 2, Issue 2, 2018, Article 6. On-line at: <https://crossworks. holycross.edu/jgc/vol2/iss2/6> (Accessed 11/15/2019)

[63] John O'Donohue, "Spirituality as the Art of Real Presence," *The Way* Supplement (London: Burns & Oates, 1998), p. 85. On-line at: <https:// www.theway.org.uk/back/s092ODonohue.pdf> (Accessed 11/25/2019)

[64] See Michael Martin, *The Incarnation of the Poetic Word: Theological Essays on Poetry & Philosophy • Philosophical Essays on Poetry & Theology* (Kettering, Ohio: Angelico Press, 2017). Reference to this and other books and articles by Michael Martin can be found at the Center for Sophiological Studies website at: <https://www.thecenterforsophiologicalstudies.com/> (Accessed 11/22/2019)

[65] From Stratford Caldecott, "The Deep Horizon," an essay reproduced at The Matheson Trust website by permission of Second Spring (secondspring.co.uk). On-line at: <https://www.themathesontrust.org/ library/the-deep-horizon> (Accessed 12/27/2019)

imaginalis. Despite widespread suspicion of the imagination among the Desert Fathers and other Christian authorities, Balthasar concentrates less on the imagination as a capacity for deception and as a source of distraction and temptation than on its role in prophecy and in the revelation of spiritual truths, as the locus for visionary experience, and as the home of symbolism, of poetry and of creativity. It is, Balthasar seems to suggest, the world of the "heart" where the Virgin Mary ponders the words and deeds of God, and where she first conceives the Word in humble obedience to the great Angel. Thus from the gnosis of faith, hope and love, infused into the human soul by the Holy Spirit, we have moved easily to the "feminine": the Church or Bride of Christ, with Mary his Mother as the unblemished, esoteric heart mediating all his graces, radiating him into the world. Balthasar notes:

> The terrible havoc which the 'historical-critical method' is today wreaking in the world of faith is possible only in a spiritual sphere from which the Church's Marian dimension has been banished and which has, therefore, forsaken all spiritual senses and their ecclesial communication. This devastation is spreading not only over the whole theological realm [he wrote this in 1961]; it is penetrating even the area of philosophy. Here the world is becoming imageless and valueless; it is a heap of 'facts' which no longer say anything and in which an equally imageless and formless naked existence is freezing and anguishing unto death. The philosophy and the theology of the image stand and fall together, and when the *image* of woman has vanished from the theological realm, and exclusively masculine, imageless conceptuality and thought-technique takes over, and then faith finds itself banished from the world and confined to the realm of the paradoxical and the absurd.

In the Darkest Nights

French Orthodox lay theologian, Annick de Souzenelle, writes about the silences associated with the darkest nights and with the Virgin Mary:

Nothing is said about Christ during the three days and three nights in the darkness of the tomb, the matrix of light. Tradition however offers for our meditation the image of Christ in hell.

About it Karlfried Graf von Durckheim, speaking at an international interreligious conference organized by Pir Vilayat Inayat Khan in March 1969, had this to say:

> A long time ago, near Paris, I encountered an extraordinary man, Father Gregory, a hermit who painted icons. Among these icons, one represented Christ full of love leaning towards Adam in hell. I asked Father Gregory: "Father, tell me what this represents for you." He answered: "If man encounters himself in his deepest and most wicked depths and finds himself face to face with the dragon that he is deep within himself, if then he is capable of embracing that dragon, of uniting with him, the divine breaks out, and it is the resurrection!"

Nor is anything said about Mary, the mother of Christ, carrying these same three days and nights in her inner tomb:

> Shall I go with you or wait for you?
> Say something, O Word,
> Do not pass by in silence!

are Mary's words in a liturgical hymn for the morning of the Passion.

Every mother resonates intimately with the hell of her child and with its journey toward the marriage with its inner dragons. Receiving a human seed in one's womb, bringing a child into the world, means agreeing in advance to accompanay him or her, without expectations, on their inner path. It means dying with them in silence and unknowing.

"Say something, O Word!"

But the Word is silent for Mary, as the Father is silent for Christ. Accepting that nothing can be known anymore, nothing wanted ...

Then the unbridgeable chasm is bridged. With her son, Mary crosses the abyss; she shows us that the impossible is possible. Mary is suffering humanity, accomplishing itself through deaths and maternities conjoined. She is the silence that becomes Word.[66]

Here is a "thought question" for us. Which is the preferred condition—to experience temptation together with its successful resistance or to experience no temptation at all? On reflection, it may become clear that the first condition is a divided state whereas the second is not. The first condition (the experience of temptation together with its resistance) is a signification or deeper meaning of "hell" (as purgatorial) whereas the (unitive) second condition is what is signified by "paradise." The feeling tone of the first condition is one of suffering. What is especially important to know is that the Blessed Virgin Mary is present (if not always obvious) to us in both of these conditions. Our prayer is should always be "Lead us not into temptation" (and suffering) and yet, if He does, ….

And what is the value of the first condition (of temptation and suffering)? There is a wisdom tradition that *all* experience is redeemed or taken up into the divine melody and the divine work of art. Consider, for example, the existence of William Blake's "Songs of Experience" that he paired together with his "Songs of Innocence." He celebrates (sings) the value of both. The Prodigal Son, when he has returned to his father's house, has something of value that his brother does not. Consider the language in the *Exsultet* chanted in connection with the lighting of the Paschal candle at Easter, *O Felix Culpa*: "O happy fault, O necessary sin of Adam, which gained for us so great a Redeemer." Look also for deeper layers of meaning in the Christian expression, "joyful sorrow." In the seventeenth century, the Anglican theologian, Jeremy Taylor (Bishop of Down and Dromore in Northern Ireland), made reference to the "joyful solemnities" of the Church.[67] In our own time, Fr. George Metallinos (Greek Orthodox) wrote:

---

[66] From Annick de Souzenelle, *The Body and Its Symbolism: A Kabbalistic Approach* (Wheaton, Illinois: Quest Books / Theosophical Publishing House, 2015), pp. 273-274.
[67] See "A Collision of Joys: Jeremy Taylor," Chapter Three in Allchin, *The Joy of All Creation*, previously cited.

Paradise and hell are not two different places. Such an idea is an idolatrous concept. Rather they signify two different conditions [ways or states of being], which originate from the same uncreated source, and are perceived by man as two, differing experiences. More precisely, they are the same experience, except that they are perceived differently by man, depending on his internal state.[68]

If we understand that paradise and hell are not different "places," it may be less surprising to discern the presence of the Blessed Virgin Mary in both conditions.

Three sovereign roles of the Blessed Virgin Mary are Queen of Heaven, *Mediatrix*, and Empress of Hell. Let's consider further her role as Empress of Hell.[69] There is no hell in which the Virgin Mary does not appear. There is no one beyond the possibility of redemption. Perhaps, as we suggested above in regard to nature and culture, God's Justice and God's Mercy are also "not two." In the same way, the occasions of God's Justice and God's Mercy are blended within each of us and among all of us. The Lebanese-American poet, Khalil Gibran (d. 1931) wrote:

Often times have I heard you speak of one who commits a wrong as though he were not one of you, but a stranger unto you and an intruder upon your world. But I say that even as the holy and the righteous cannot rise beyond the highest which is in each one of you, so the wicked and the weak cannot fall lower than the lowest which is in you also. As a single leaf turns not yellow but with the silent knowledge of the whole tree, so the wrong doer cannot do wrong without the hidden will of you all ... You cannot separate the just from the unjust and the good from the wicked ... you can not lay remorse upon the

---

[68] From Fr. George Metallinos, "Paradise and Hell According to Orthodox Tradition," *OrthodoxyToday.org*, 2009. On-line at: <http://www. orthodoxytoday.org/articles-2009/Mettalinos-Paradise-And-Hell-According-To-Orthodox-Tradition.php> (Accessed 9/14/2019)
[69] See Effie Karpodini-Dimitriadi, "The Descent of the Virgin Mary into Hell: A short presentation and free translation of a handwritten text from the island of Kythira." On-line at: <http://ekarpodini.com/en/files/2013/03/The-descent-of-Virgin-Mary-into-the-Hell1.pdf> (Accessed 8/24/2019)

innocent nor lift it from the heart of the guilty .... you who would understand justice, how shall you unless you look upon all deeds in the fullness of light? Only then shall you know that the erect and the fallen are but one man standing in twilight between the night of his pigmy-self and the day of his God-self, and that the corner stone of the temple is not higher than the lowest stone in its foundation.[70]

These words, written by a poet, may be helpful in commending to us a perspective from which the Blessed Virgin Mary can be seen as both the Queen of Heaven and also the Empress of Hell.

Although the Virgin Mary, in her messages, is capable of "chastisements," that is not the dominant note or chord associated with her presence, especially as she appears in the Life-Giving Spring icon. In Kabbalah, the glyph referred to as the Tree of Life has left and right columns that are sometimes used to imagine the left and right arms of God—the divine "arms" of justice (or rigor/severity) and mercy. In Kabbalistic tradition, the divine mercy prevails over the divine severity. So it is with the Blessed Virgin Mary whose foot, in some Marian imagery, restrains the serpent. Similarly, in a relief on the Royal Gate at Chartres Cathedral, she holds a tamed dragon like a lap dog.[71] Imaginative attention to the reality of the Black Virgin brings to awareness the full range of these aspects of the Blessed Virgin Mary.[72]

Oftentimes, the hells we may find ourselves in are pervaded with illusion. It is the Blessed Virgin's gift to lead us through and beyond all

---

[70] From Khalil Gibran, *The Prophet*, as quoted in Bahar Davary, "Forgiveness in Islam: Is it an Ultimate Reality?," *Ultimate Reality and Meaning*, Volume 27 Issue 2, June 2004, pp. 127-141, p. 127. On-line at: <https://www.utpjournals.press/doi/pdf/10.3138/uram.27.2.127> (Accessed 12/30/2019). Reflect on these words from Gibran together with Jesus's parable of the wheat and the tares (Matthew 13:24-30).

[71] See image at Ella Rozett, "The Mysterious Black Faces of the Madonna," at Interfaith Mary Page. On-line at: <http://interfaithmary.net/black-madonna-introduction> (Accessed 12/10/2019)

[72] Especially commended is the video presentation by Bishop Paul Dupuis (Celtic Orthodox) on the topic of "Black Virgin: The French Mother Kali," given at the Vedanta Society of Providence (Rhode Island), October 8, 2017. On-line at: <https://youtu.be/vRahjadv9Kw> (Accessed 12/11/2019)

that is illusory. The Estonian-Russian Christian mystic and hermeticist, Valentin Tomberg (d. 1973) wrote:

> ... [E]very Hermeticist who truly seeks authentic spiritual reality will sooner or later meet the Blessed Virgin. This meeting signifies, apart from the illumination and consolation that it comprises, protection against a very serious spiritual danger. For he who advances in the sense of depth and height in the "domain of the invisible" one day arrives at the sphere known by esotericists as the "sphere of mirages" or the "zone of illusion." This zone surrounds the earth as a belt of illusory mirages. It is this zone which the prophets and the Apocalypse designate "Babylon." The soul and the queen of this zone is in fact Babylon, the great prostitute, who is the adversary of the Virgin.
>
> Now, one cannot pass by this zone without being enveloped by perfect purity. One cannot traverse it without the protection of the "mantle of the Blessed Virgin"—the mantle which was an object of worship and of a special cult in Russia (*Pokrov Presvyatyya Bogoroditsy*—"Mantle of the Very Holy Mother of God"). It is therefore the protection of this "mantle" which is absolutely necessary in order to be able to traverse the "sphere of mirages" without falling prey to the influence of its illusions.[73]

Seen from a different perspective, however, the Blessed Virgin Mary herself *is* Paradise—so that wherever the Blessed Mother is discerned, that "place" *is* Paradise. Abbot Joseph Homick (Superior of Holy Transfiguration Monastery, a Byzantine-Catholic community in Redwood Valley, California) writes:

> The titles "deliverance of Eve" and "mystical Paradise" are related by their reference to the Garden of Eden at the beginning of creation. Mary is called "mystical Paradise" because within her grew the new "Tree of Life" which is Christ Himself. Through communion with Him in the Holy Eucharist, we

---

[73] Anonymous, *Meditations on the Tarot: A Journey into Christian Hermeticism* (New York: Jeremy P. Tarcher / Putnam, 1985, 2002), p. 281. The excerpted language appears in Letter XI, "Force."

eat the fruit of this Tree and live forever. Mary herself is a kind of Paradise in the sense that in her there is no sin, just like the first terrestrial paradise which was pristine in its beauty and purity prior to the sin of Adam and Eve.[74]

One of the more intriguing titles of the Blessed Virgin Mary—together with her previously mentioned role as Empress of Hell—is Queen of the Dead. This title or appellation is particularly associated with Our Lady of San Damiano (Italy). As we reflect on this title—Queen of the Dead—we may be led to recall the mystery of Holy Saturday in which Christ decends into Hell (or Hades) to rescue Adam and Eve and, implicitly with them, all their children who were held captive in Hell. This is sometimes referred to as the Harrowing of Hell. The incarnation of spirit into flesh is a constriction. To be subject to persecution and illness is a further constriction. The falling asleep that is death can be said to be the maximum of constriction. Our Lady does not fail to appear in each and every place of perceived constriction. The life of (Mama) Rosa Quattrini-Buzzini (d. 1981), for example, illustrates and manifests a range of constriction and it was to her that Our Lady chose to appear in San Damiano.[75]

Salve, Regina, Mater misericordiæ,
vita, dulcedo, et spes nostra, salve.
Ad te clamamus exsules filii Hevæ,
Ad te suspiramus, gementes et flentes
in hac lacrimarum valle.

Eia, ergo, advocata nostra, illos tuos
misericordes oculos ad nos converte;
Et Jesum, benedictum fructum ventris tui,
nobis post hoc exsilium ostende.
O clemens, O pia, O dulcis Virgo Maria.

---

[74] Abbot Joseph Homick, *A Place Prepared by God: Through the Virgin Mary, the New Eve, Paradise Will Not Fail Twice* (Sunnyvale, California: Patsons Press, 2010), pp. 42-43.
[75] See Chapter Two in Sandra L. Zimdars-Swartz, *Encountering Mary: Visions of Mary from La Salette to Medjugorje* (New York: Avon Books, 1991) for an account of Mama Rosa and the events in San Damiano.

Hail, holy Queen, mother of mercy,
Hail our life, our sweetness, and our hope.
To you we cry, poor banished children of Eve;
to you we send up our sighs,
mourning and weeping in this valley of tears.

Turn, then, most gracious advocate,
your eyes of mercy toward us;
and after this, our exile,
show unto us the blessed fruit of your womb, Jesus.
O clement, O loving, O sweet Virgin Mary.

The Unicorn

The unicorn is an ambiguous creature—both real and imaginary. The unicorn's single horn associates with what is called the Third Eye.[76] The Rev. Dr. John Dupuche (Archdiocese of Melbourne, Australia) writes about the Third Eye as follows:

> ... [T]he first center to be blessed is between the eyebrows, the "Third Eye," the symbol of insight.
> The meditator understands the eyebrow center as a radiance or vortex of energies. Actually touching this place can help sensitize it. Then with full confidence, indeed with the power of the Spirit and in union with the Word made flesh, the mantra and the breath are imparted.
> The place has been marked by the Spirit and takes on the character of the Spirit, a freedom beyond words, real but intangible, beyond time, spacious, open, and wide as the sea. The Spirit who hovers over the deep at the very origin (Genesis 1:1) and who, in the end, calls out with the Bride, "Come Lord Jesus" (Revelation 22:17), the same Spirit is located at the place of the "Third Eye," the eye of perception which sees beyond

---

[76] Annick de Souzenelle, prefers the term "threefold vision." About the unicorn, she writes: "The unicorn symbolizes the highest degree of fertility and power. It is light, linked with threefold vision." By "threefold vision" is meant vision beyond duality. From de Souzenelle, *The Body and Its Symbolism*, previously cited, p. 254, and illustration at p. 366.

the visible to what no one has seen or imagined, "things beyond the human mind" (1 Corinthians 2:9).

Indeed, surprisingly, the breath of the Spirit seems to be felt at this point, moving freely in and out as though through an opening, not forced, full of peace, pleasurable, enjoyable. There may also be a slight contraction, which occurs naturally, as though wishing to feel the friction of the breath more intently.

From this center, like spokes from a wheel, the energies move in and out, as so many gifts: wisdom counsel, right judgment, reverence, awe and wonder. The practitioner allows the energy to radiate from that point into the very center of the head where the pituitary gland is located, the gland which governs all the others. In time the energy of the Spirit flows into the whole person, bringing tranquility and balance, strength and energy to every part of the body.

A great calm and sense of stability develops, a sense of authority and strength—indeed all the gifts of the Spirit start to manifest themselves. There is an increase in wisdom and a growing reverence for all things. The conflicting passions are put to rest and an equanimity results, which copes with both good and bad knowing that the transcending Spirit overcomes all obstacles. The strength of a good conscience gives vigour and assurance. Sight becomes clear and the eyes acquire a lustre and a penetration because they see beyond the perceptible. The eye of faith opens further and things unseen become evident. In fact, so wonderful is the sight that glamour holds little attraction and the inner quality of things becomes apparent.

It is recommended that a definite level of experience be attained at the eyebrow center. This place of insight and wisdom, of authority and reverence, provides a suitable guide for the power, which will become apparent in the other centers.[77]

The image of the unicorn may be contrasted with the image of the centaur in the Integral philosophy of Ken Wilber. In a sense, they are

---

[77] John Dupuche, *Jesus: The Mantra of God: An Exploration of Mantra Meditation* (Melbourne, Australia: David Lovell Publishing, 2005), pp. 39-40. Spelling and capitalization have been standardized in this excerpt. --RT

both hybrid creatures. If the centaur is both human and animal, we might say of the unicorn that it is both animal and something angelic. The unicorn's horn pierces beyond the realm of thought to the clear awareness—the clear awareness that is the Uncreated Light. This piercing strength of the unicorn's horn is also the sword of St. Michael. The unicorn associates with the conviction that the arriving Kingdom *will* manifest. As the enclosed garden frequently associates with the Blessed Virgin Mary, there is a similar association in visual art and literature of the Virgin and unicorns. Further reflection may bring to mind the image, in sacred literature, of the mystical marriage.

Mary as Proclaimed in the Early Church and Later

To more fully appreciate the Marian reality it is important to know something of how the Virgin Mary was understood in the early years of the Church. In her book on the symbolic theology of the Virgin Mary, Madonna Sophia Compton writes that "… from very early in the Church's history, the Theotokos emerges with a clear mission: she appears as the revealer of divine mysteries."[78] This is, I believe, the fundamental interpretive key to the Marian reality. Beyond this insight, Compton helpfully summarizes the development of Marian oral tradition as associated chronologically with the seven Ecumenical Councils of the Church:

> 1) The First Council of Nicaea in 325 … developed the Nicene Creed. By this time, Mary had already received the titles "New Eve" and "Advocate" (Irenaeus, d. 193). Also, Gregory of Nyssa records that Gregory the Wonderworker has received

---

[78] Madonna Sophia Compton, *The Mother of God: Symbolic Theology of the Virgin Mary* (Berkeley, California, and Kansas City: The Raphael Group, 2010, 2018), p. 9. It can also be noted here that in Sufism, according to Henry Corbin (*Creative Imagination in the Sufism of Ibn Arabi*, Princeton University Press, 1969, p. 221), it is the heart that attains knowledge (*gnosis*) of God and perceives the divine mysteries. Contemporary Christian mystic, John Butler, has also pointed out that true knowledge is revealed, not learned (by empirical inquiry). Butler's comment appears in his talk, "Be Still and Know that I Am God" (video), at 5:30 minutes in. On-line at: <https://youtu.be/MYMWliD11rw> (Accessed 10/16/2019)

the first apparition of Mary (207).[79]   In addition, the early Alexandrian Fathers such as Origen (d. 253) and Clement (d. 215) had affirmed her perpetual virginity.

2) The Council of Constantinople in 381 ... defined the Trinity and clarified that the Holy Spirit's role was fully divine. ... By this time the Syrian Fathers had written so eloquently about Mary and the Holy Spirit; and the apocryphal tradition of the *Protoevangelium of James* had been in circulation for nearly two hundred years.

3) The Council of Ephesus in 431 ... proclaimed Mary as the Theotokos, or Mother of God, not simply the Mother of Christ. Mary had now received titles like the "Burning Bush," the "Ark," [and] numerous other associations with Old Testament types were appearing in homilies. Mary's role as Mediatrix had been affirmed by Cyril of Alexandria (d. 444); and Proclus (d. 446) had proclaimed the salvific character of Mary's motherhood.

4) The Council of Chalcedon in 451 ... affirmed that Christ has two natures in one person ... and reaffirmed Mary the Virgin as Theotokos. Liturgical poetry and prayers to Mary had developed and the tradition of the Dormition was already in circulation, based on the legend of Empress Pulcheria, who went to the Council to procure Mary's coffin and funeral garments.

5) The Second Council of Constantinople in 553 ... refuted monophysite writings and confirmed the dual natures of Christ. By this time, the first known Akathist had been written and the great Byzantine hymnographer Romanos the Melodist (d. 560), for whom Mary was the "powerful mediatrix, the rampart, the defense, and the haven of whoever trusts in her," had composed some of the most beautiful liturgical poems and prayers to Mary known to the Church. Byzantine iconography reaches a pinnacle under Justinian (d. 565), who was an enthusiastic promoter of the cult of the Theotokos and who may also be

---

[79] Michael O'Neill, who is quoted further below, has suggested that the earliest known apparition is that of St. James the Greater who saw the Virgin Mary while he was in preaching on the banks of the Ebro River in Saragossa, Spain, in 40 A.D.

responsible for "a universal acceptance ... of her final glorification."

6) The Third Council of Constantinople in 680 ... refuted monothelitism (and affirmed the two wills of Christ). By the advent of the 6th Ecumenical Council, Mary's role as advocate, intercessor, mediatrix, and queen was well established in the liturgical tradition and in the lives of the faithful.

7) The last Council of Nicaea II in 787 declared that icons are acceptable aids in worship.[80]

At this point in our narrative we might insert a personal story from the life of St. Gregory Palamas (d. 1359), a noted defender of hesychast spirituality. The following account of the personal relationship of St. Gregory Palamas with the Theotokos is from a book by Metropolitan Hierotheos (Vlachos) of Nafpaktos, *Saint Gregory Palamas as a Hagiorite*. Metropolitan Hierotheos is drawing upon the *Vita* of St. Gregory Palamas by Patriarch Philotheos of Constantinople (d. 1379):

Every Saint loves the Panagia. Sainthood is not understood without this Theotokophilia. It occurs because the Saints, after tasting the Love of God, communing of the Body and Blood of Christ, and experiencing the gifts of the incarnation of Christ, feel the need to give thanks also to that person who was the cause of this great joy. It is well known that the Saints are very sensitive and are therefore grateful for even the smallest gifts which they receive, and much more for the great gift of the deification of human nature, which came about in the Tomb of the Theotokos. She gave her flesh to the Son and Word of God for His incarnation.

This is also the case with St. Gregory Palamas. However, the Saint felt love for the Panagia also for other reasons. He was granted to see her in his life; he was her protege. We shall give more details to demonstrate this truth, as his biographer Philotheos Kokkinos, Patriarch of Constantinople, describes them.

The first indication is the fact that from an early age he was given into the protection of the Theotokos by his father.

---

[80] Compton, pp. 186-187.

Before his father died, St. Gregory's mother asked him to ask the emperor to protect his children. That Saintly man not only did not accept her words, but rebuked her in a way and said to her: "I do not leave my children to some earthly rulers, but I leave my children to the Mistress of all, the mother of the King of heaven." And indeed at the time when he said these things he was looking at the icon of the Theotokos which was in front of him. St. Philotheos says in the biography of St. Gregory that the words of his holy father came true, because the Theotokos herself persuaded the emperor to take care of the orphan children, and also later "she was seen to be their protectress and guide, and in every way the savior of both their souls and their bodies."

The second circumstance which shows that his father's prophetic words were actually fulfilled and the Theotokos was a wonderful sponsor, governess and guide, came from the period of his studies. At the beginning of his studies the Saint had difficulty in memorizing. Then he placed a restriction on himself not to come near the books and not to begin reading without first having knelt three times before the icon of the Theotokos, saying a prayer at the same time. When he did this every day he succeeded very easily in memorizing and reciting the lessons. But if he sometimes forgot to follow this rule even the recitation failed right away. At the same time, as Philotheos says, the Panagia persuaded the emperor to be the guardian of the children and to assume all their personal expenses. Furthermore the emperor showed particular sympathy, for he invited them to come to see him and talked with them in a kind and loving way.

The third sign is from the period of his asceticism on Mount Athos. Immediately after he came to the Holy Mountain he gave himself over with great zeal to ascesis, fasting, vigil and unceasing prayer. It is significant, according to the information of St. Philotheos Kokkinos, that he prayed unceasingly to the Theotokos. He prayed day and night to God, projecting the Mother of God "as guide, protector and mediator, all the time bringing before his eyes her aid and her countenance, with words and prayers and noetic movements, and pondering the way of obedience with her guidance." So in the first two years the Saint was praying constantly to God, with the Panagia as his guide and mediator. The prayer which he was saying at that time was "enlighten my darkness."

During a great stillness, while his *nous* had turned inward and to God, John the Evangelist appeared to him, not in a dream, but in a vision, and assured him that he had been sent "as a messenger from the Queen beyond," to find out why he was constantly praying: "Enlighten my darkness, enlighten my darkness." St. Gregory replied that, since he is a passionate man, he was praying to be enlightened by God to be conformed to His saving will. Then John the Evangelist said: "Do not be afraid, do not doubt... the Queen of all is giving the order through us: 'I myself will be your help'." And when again St. Gregory asked when the Theotokos would be his help and ally, in the present or future life, then the Evangelist replied: "Both before and now, and in both the present and the future."

This appearance of St. John the Evangelist, sent by the Most Holy Theotokos, was revealed by St. Gregory himself years later to his fellow-monk Dorotheos, later Metropolitan of Thessaloniki. It is characteristic that the Theotokos heard the prayer and assured him that, just as long ago, so also now and in the future, she would be his helper and defender, and moreover, that she was filling him with divine gifts.

The fourth sign is the revelation which the Theotokos herself made to St. Gregory. It was at the time when he had returned to the Lavra, but he was staying at St. Savas frontisterion outside the Monastery of the Great Lavra. He once prayed for himself and his fellow monk to the Panagia, "the usual governor and deliverer," that both their guidance and their journey toward God might be unimpeded, but also that they might have what they needed for their nourishment, in order not to be very much occupied with collecting supplies and neglect prayer. Then the Panagia, the Queen of all, appeared in a vision, "dressed modestly and purely," just as the holy icons present her. Many saints had appeared and were following her. Then the Theotokos turned and gave them the order to serve St. Gregory and his companion: "From now on you are to be stewards and distributors of the necessities for Gregory and his companion." And St. Gregory was assured that from then on "all that was necessary for our bodily needs was offered us without effort wherever we happened to be."

From what we have said it is clear that St. Gregory Palamas had a close relationship and communion with the Theotokos. All the things that he writes about her, which we shall see further on, are obviously not dry, intellectual thoughts and reasoning conjectures, but experiences of the Panagia. This explains his great love for her. We can also see the progressive manifestation and revelation of the Theotokos. At first, through his father's prayer, she took up his protection. Then she showed him clearly that he must trust in her, for she would protect him throughout his studies. Then, through John the Evangelist, she assured him that she would be his helper and protector, and finally she herself was revealed personally. Throughout his life the Saint was convinced that he had the protection and help of the Theotokos, and therefore he struggled with strength and courage, expounded the theology of the Church in an Orthodox way and defeated the heresies of his time.[81]

A more extensive and thorough survey of the Marian reality would also attend to relations and resonances with the Shekinah in ancient Judaism as well as with Sophia and the Holy Spirit in Christian understanding. In the Roman Catholic and Anglican churches, joint studies have been done since 1970 by the Anglican/Roman Catholic International Commission (ARCIC). These resulted in an Agreed Statement on the Blessed Virgin Mary that identifies the following commonalities that Anglicanism and Roman Catholicism share today:

> We together agree that in understanding Mary as the fullest human example of the life of grace, we are called to reflect on the lessons of her life recorded in Scripture and to join with her as one indeed not dead, but truly alive in Christ. In doing so we walk together as pilgrims in communion with Mary, Christ's foremost disciple.

---

[81] From Metropolitan Hierotheos (Vlachos) of Nafpaktos, *Saint Gregory Palamas as a Hagiorite* (Levadia, Greece: Birth of Theotokos Monastery, 2000), as reproduced at Mystagogy Resource Center (John Sanidopoulos) blog, August 17, 2009. On-line at: <https://www.johnsanidopoulos.com/2009/08/relationship-between-saint-gregory.html> (Accessed 11/23/2019)

Including Mary in praise and prayer belongs to our common [Anglican and Roman Catholic] heritage, as does our acknowledgement of her unique status as Theotokos [Mother of God], which gives her a distinctive place within the communion of Saints.

The practice of believers asking Mary to intercede for them with her son grew rapidly following her being declared Theotokos at the Council of Ephesus [A.D. 431]. The most common form today of such intercession is the "Hail Mary." This form conflates the greetings of Gabriel and Elizabeth to her (Luke 1:28, 42). With this background in mind, we [Anglicans and Roman Catholics] seek a theologically grounded way to draw more closely together in the life of prayer in communion with Christ and his Saints.

The Scriptures invite Christians to ask their brothers and sisters to pray for them, in and through Christ (James 5:13-15). Those who are now "with Christ," untrammelled by sin, share the unceasing prayer and praise which characterizes the life of heaven (Revelation 5:9-14; 7:9-12; 8:3-4). In the light of these testimonies, many Christians have rightly found that requests for assistance in prayer can rightly and effectively be made to those members of the communion of Saints distinguished by their holy living (James 5:16-18). It is in this sense that we affirm that asking the Saints to pray for us is not to be excluded as unscriptural, though it is not directly taught by the Scriptures to be a required element of life in Christ.

Among all the Saints, Mary takes her place as Theotokos [Mother of God]: alive in Christ, she abides with the one she bore, still "highly favored" in the communion of grace and hope, the exemplar of redeemed humanity, an icon of the Church. Consequently she is believed to exercise a distinctive ministry of assisting others through her active prayer.

Many Christians find that giving devotional expression to their appreciation of this ministry of Mary enriches their worship of God. Authentic popular devotion to Mary, which by its nature displays a wide individual, regional, and cultural diversity, is to be respected. The crowds gathering at some places where Mary is believed to have appeared suggest that such apparitions are an important part of this devotion and provide spiritual comfort. There is need for careful discernment in assessing the spiritual value of any alleged apparition. This has been emphasized in recent Roman Catholic teaching. We are agreed that, within the constraints set down in this teaching to ensure that the honor paid to Christ remains pre-eminent, such private devotion is acceptable, though never required of believers.[82]

5. For the Healing of Nations

In the context of theater, there is the concept of foregrounding and backgrounding—moving theatrical elements to the fore or to some less conspicuous place on the stage or into the wings. Similarly, we may speak of a foregrounding, a moving into greater prominence, of the Blessed Virgin Mary in our time. This foregrounding manifests as advocacy on behalf of some future promulgation by the Roman Catholic Church of what is called a Fifth Marian Dogma, of Mary as Co-Redemptrix. As explained by a Catholic media source:

Up to the present time in the history of the church, four Marian doctrines have been defined as central Catholic truths by the Church: the Motherhood of God, the Immaculate Conception, the Perpetual Virginity of Mary, and her Glorious Assumption into heaven. It is now time for the church, at the summit of this Marian era, to proclaim and define the fifth and final Marian doctrine, that is, Mary's universal mediation as Core-demptrix, Mediatrix of all grace, and advocate for the people of God.[83]

---

[82] From Q&A document on the Agreed Statement on the Blessed Virgin Mary between Anglicans and Roman Catholics on-line at: <http://stpaulsparish. org/education/documents/mary_ARCIC.pdf> (Accessed 8/13/2017). The authoritative statement can be found on-line at: <https://www. anglicancommunion.org/media/105263/mary-grace-and-hope-in-christ_english.pdf> (Accessed 11/13/2019).

[83] Vox Populi, "The Fifth Marian Dogma," an undated petition to Pope John Paul II, from the Library of documents at Eternal Word Television Network (EWTN). On-line at: <https://www.ewtn.com/catholicism/library/fifth-marian-dogma-5671> (Accessed 10/26/2019)

Whether such a dogma will be proclaimed in the near future or not, advocacy for it underscores recognition of Our Lady's active role in our world on behalf of created beings.

As Queen of Angels, the Blessed Virgin Mary's presence in Planet Earth serves a healing function. This is what Divine Wisdom does. Hieromonk Silouan (Wisdom Hermitage, St. Davids, Wales) writes of the healing fire:

> Wisdom is vision of glory envisioned in some icons of the Virgin of the Unburned Bush as the Virgin of the Flame, whose vermilion glory consumes confusion and division but not the union in difference that characterises paradise restored. She is the burning wisdom of the Spirit's Pentecostal flame that does not consume wholesome creation but extinguishes the confusion that divides creation from God. Her wisdom function is to transmit God the consuming fire in such a way that creation is not consumed but healed.
>
> The vermilion Virgin is the wisdom of the unburned bush who cures fire by fire. Destructive demonic fires are overcome by the uncreated fire of glory, the fire of the Holy of Holies present in our midst. The vermilion and gold of Holy Wisdom transmit theosis, deification, whose wisdom injunctions are to turn and see. Turning awakens the heart to the grace of seeing, theoria, where seer and seen are one. Seeing is God's union of seer and seen in Holy Trinity. It is the fruit of wisdom experienced as the tree of life, whose gift is timeless awareness of the eternal presence. It is the way, truth and life of the Holy Name, whose glory births timeless wisdom.[84]

If the crisis of climate change is front and center in the English-language media in our time, it should be said that this is also a symptom of a more deeply rooted illness within our societies and within us as individuals. Our treatment of the tribes of the animal kingdom as having value only to the extent that they serve humankind is another symptom of this illness. As such, we are, in many respects, blind to it (even as in our grocery stores we have kept the slaughter houses of this

---

[84] Excerpt from Hieromonk Silouan, "Virgin of the Flame," blog entry at *Wisdom Hermitage*, April 13, 2018. On-line at: <http://www.wisdomhermitage.org.uk/2018/04/13/virgin-of-the-flame/> (Accessed 9/13/2019)

world out of sight). But do not lose heart! With God, all things are possible.

If we may return for a moment to the icon (or icon-like painting) on the front cover of this book and reflect on its detail, here is the description of this object from Epirus in northwestern Greece (bordering Albania and the Ionian Sea), now in the National Museum of Warsaw, Poland:

> In the center of the icon is the image of the Mother of God with Christ at her chest. The Virgin and Child, who are frontally depicted, emerge from a richly decorated fountain, from which gargoyles pour streams of water into a pool. Above these figures, the Greek letters of the Marian and Christological monograms are visible. The fountain and water pool are surrounded by people who draw water, including a lame man waiting for healing and a man in a loincloth who drinks water from a pitcher. In the upper corners of the icon are shown angels kneeling in the clouds, turned to Mary in prayer gestures. Beside the fountain there is a Greek inscription that means "Source of Life." The faces of the persons are rounded, modeled with chiaroscuro. In the way the human body is depicted, especially the robes, there is apparent schematization, which also applies to the landscape outlined in the background with a row of trees (cypresses), with an attempt to use the aerial perspective. The color scheme of the whole—saturated and strongly contrasting, in which red, pink, green, ocher and gold predominate—is typical for the iconic painting of Macedonia as well as Mount Athos in the 18th-19th centuries. Eighteenth-century icons from Epirus are similar to this icon with respect to both the design of the faces and the ornamentation used.[85]

I would add to this description that, when reflecting further on structural details of this icon, we may note that the fountain or font is round or circular and that the pool beneath is square or four-sided. It is as if the unitive Glory of the Holy Trinity—the Glory (Sophia/Holy

---

[85] This description is my lightly edited version of a machine-translation, from the Polish into English, of the National Museum of Warsaw's description written by Aleksandra Sulikowska. On-line source: <http://cyfrowe.mnw.art.pl/dmuseion/docmetadata?id=18146> (Accessed 10/6/2019)

Wisdom) that is both Light (*Phos*) and Life (*Zoe*)—images forth as the Holy Mother who, together with her Son, is the healing Water of Life that all people, wandering within more obscure realms of manifestation and aware of their own need and that of others, seek. With regard to the pool in this icon, we might be reminded of the Gospel stories of the healing pools at Bethesda and Siloam.

There is also the notion or association of vision with pools of water. When the waters become still we see more, we become aware of more, in the reflecting and transparent waters. It has also been noted[86] that the Blessed Virgin, in her appearing, inspires devotion rather than desire. It has been argued that her virginity is the source of her power.[87]

We have noted above the resonance between the Blessed Virgin Mary and Holy Sophia. We might also take note of the resonance, in connection with holy wells and springs, particularly in Britain and Ireland, between the Virgin Mary and the pre-Christian feminine presence, Brigid. Gary R. Varner, in his book, *Sacred Wells: A Study in the History, Meaning, and Mythology of Holy Wells & Waters*, writes:

> The Brennemans' research of holy wells in Ireland concluded that the ancient wells previously dedicated to Bridgid are in a decline. This is due, in the most part, because these wells "are taken out of the sphere of the sacred and placed into that of the secular. It is a matter of removing the well from the mytho-logical realm to the realm of history." This would appear to address the various traditions of holy or healing wells losing their powers due to such mundane practices as the bathing of animals and children or washing clothing in the wells. The invasive nature of everyday labor nullifies the sacred. However, as the Brennemans also note, those wells dedicated to the Virgin Mary are prospering. In fact, new holy wells are being

---

[86] By Angela Voss (Canterbury Christ Church University), for example, in her paper, "The Secret Life of Statues," p. 6. On-line at: <https://www.academia.edu/472457/The_Secret_Life_of_Statues> (Accessed 10/17/2019)

[87] See Martin Clive Warner, "Virginity Matters: Power and Ambiguity in the Attraction of the Virgin Mary," Ph.D. dissertation, 2003, University of Durham. Warner thesis seeks to account for virginity as the source of Mary's power to attract. On-line at: <http://etheses.dur.ac.uk/3140/> (Accessed 11/19/2019)

"born" in Ireland because of the growth in the power of wells dedicated to Mary. However, this is not due to the Christian nature of Mary, but to the combination of the powers intrinsic to Brigid/Mary. "What appears to be emerging," according to the Brennemans, "is a form of syncretism in which the loric, in the figure of Brigid, presents itself in a quiet or tacit manner, while the sacred, in the figure of Mary, plays a predominant role in terms of the overt symbols that are present at the well. Thus, it is not simply a matter of Mary taking over Brigid wells but rather a change in the relationship of Brigid and Mary...a change in the symbolic meaning of the holy well."

I believe that we can safely say that Brigid is Mary as Mary is Brigid. The age old influence and perceived powers of the feminine spirit continue to be felt regardless of what terms are applied to it. This power simply is as it always has been but the effects ebb and flow in accordance to the amount of attention paid to it by the faithful at certain locations—Christian or pagan faithful. As the Brennemans summed up their study of Irish holy wells:

> We began to think that perhaps there was a connection between the appearances of the Virgin Mary in Ireland and the ancient lady at the well. Could the lady be appearing now in modern Christian form with a message not for the kings of ancient Ireland but for the entire world, a message that is grounded in the power of place, the well? Could these modern postindustrial apparitions be a survival of earlier myth and ritual modes appearing at a different point in history and thus presenting a universalized message?[88]

---

[88] Gary R. Varner, *Sacred Wells: A Study in the History, Meaning, and Mythology of Holy Wells & Waters*, 2nd Edition (New York: Algora Publishing, 2009), pp. 146-147. The complete Brennemans reference is: Walter L. Brenneman and Mary G. Brenneman, *Crossing the Circle at the Holy Wells of Ireland* (Charlottesville, Virginia: University Press of Virginia, 1995).

The Healing Water of Life: From *Zoe* into *Bios*

In the Epirus icon, then, there is reproduced that flow that is cosmic in scope and in scale. This is the flow that was discussed above in Section 3 (*The Great Fountain – Flow and Return*). This is the flow from *zoe* (deathless life) into *bios* (temporal life). Among contemporary theologians attentive to relations between *zoe* and *bios* in Christian understanding has been Joseph Ratzinger, Pope Bendict XVI. The spiritual Christology of Joseph Ratzinger has been characterized as follows in a dissertation by Peter John McGregor (Catholic Institute of Sydney)[89]:

> Ratzinger holds that, from another point of view, love is stronger than death only when someone values love more highly than life. However, the only way that this can be so is if love can be superior to and encompass mere *bios*. In a way that acknowledges an insight of Teilhard de Chardin, Ratziner states that such a "mutation" or "evolution" would take *bios* up into *zoe*—a definitive life which is not subject to death. This last development would not be achieved "within the realm of biology but by the spirit, by freedom, by love." (p. 70)

> He [Jesus] is the one who possesses *zoe*, a life beyond the realm of *bios* and history, a reality borne out by the Resurrection narratives. However, his new life has been begotten in history. (p. 71)

> According to Ratziner, this hermeneutic enables us to see that the Resurrection of Jesus is no mere resuscitation. His new life is no longer governed by the laws that govern *bios*. Hence, encounters with Jesus are termed "appearance." In these [Resurrection narratives], the recognition of Jesus is his initiative. He must open hearts and minds to recognize his *zoe* in the midst of *bios*. (p. 71)

---

[89] Peter John McGregor, "Heart to Heart: The Spiritual Christology of Joseph Ratziner," Ph.D. dissertation (2013), School of Theology, Australian Catholic University. Subsequently published in book form (2016) by Wipf and Stock and its imprint, Pickwick Publications, Eugene, Oregon. Dissertation on-line at: <https://researchbank.acu.edu.au/theses/477/> (Accessed 10/9/2019)

Thus, for Ratzinger, heaven is not physically "above" the world. Nor is it an eternal metaphysical region independent of the world. Rather, Heaven and the Ascension of Jesus are indivisible. The Ascension brings Heaven into existence. Ratzinger puts it thus:

> Heaven is to be devined as the contact of the being "man" with the being "God"; this confluence of God and man took place once and for all in Christ when he went beyond *bios* through death to new life. Heaven is accordingly that future of man and of mankind which the latter cannot give to itself, which is therefore closed to it so long as it waits for itself, and which was first and fundamentally opened up in the man whose field of existence was God and through whom God entered into the creature "man." (p. 74)

Where Ratzinger does seem to be dependent upon Teilhard de Chardin is in the taking up of *bios* into *zoe*. Ratzinger thinks that Teilhard de Chardin has overcome an anthropological/cosmic dualism, has enabled the reconciliation of anthropology and cosmology within Christology, by demonstrating that full "hominization" includes not only the union of God and man, and the creation of the "corporate man," but the unification of the cosmos with the personal, of the ultimate union of all matter with spirit in the person of Jesus Christ. (p. 84)

However, in his treatment of the High Priestly Prayer of Jesus, Ratzinger identifies four major themes in this prayer which outline how the Church participates in this prayer of Jesus. First, Jesus prays that his disciples may have *zoe*—"life." This "life" is eternal. It is not life after death, but it is a real "life" which can be lived in this life. This life is obtained through "recognition," one which creaetes communion. The "key to this life is not any kind of recognition, but to 'know you the only true God, and Jesus Christ whom you have sent.' In the encounter with Jesus 'we experience the recognition of God that leads to communion and this to 'life'." (p. 160)

How can love be stronger than death? According to Ratzinger, it is only when someone is ready to put life second to love. In the Resurrection of Jesus, the power of love has risen to be superior to the power of mere biological life. In him, *bios* has been encompassed by and incorporated in the power of love. This love of Jesus for us has become the love that actually keeps us alive. In this "evolutionary leap," *bios* has become *zoe*, definitive life. This "leap" is achieved "by the spirit, by freedom, by love. It would no longer be evolution but decision and gift in one." (p. 283)

In the Cross and Resurrection of Jesus, *bios* has been transformed into *zoe* through the transformation of human eros into divine agape, human freedom into the freedom of God. This new state of affairs Ratziner attributes also to "the spirit." (p. 284)

Since the communion of God and man in the Resurrection and Ascension of Christ has broken down the frontier of *bios* and transformed it into *zoe*, the eschaton has already begun. Ratziner identifies the Resurrection as the eschatological event. In Christ the temporal has been taken up into the eternal. The barrier between "being" and "becoming" has been breached. Time has been drawn into God. (p. 285)

For Ratzinger, anthropology and cosmology coincide in Christology. That is to say, in Christ, man and the cosmos have been reconciled. In the assumption of eros into agape, *bios* has been taken up into *zoe*. The cosmos was not created as a mere "container" for human history. Rather "the cosmos is movement … it is not just a case of history existing in it … cosmos itself is history." This history is moving towards its "omega" point, the second coming of Jesus Christ. (pp. 285-286)

In my first book, the book on Bulgakov,[90] I called attention to the perspective of *panzoism*, one strand (or tradition) among the many

---

[90] Robert F. Thompson, *From Glory to Glory: The Sophianic Vision of Fr. Sergius Bulgakov*. A Perennials Study Group publication, Memphis, Tennessee. (CreateSpace, 2016).

strands that constitue the beautiful fabric of Slavic Christian spiritual culture. A powerful sense of *panzoism* in reflected, for example, in the work of Nikolai Fedorov (d. 1903) who wrote in his *Philosophy of the Common Task* that

> The Divine Being, which is itself the perfect model for society, a unity of independent, immortal persons, in full possession of feeling and knowledge, whose unbreakable unity excludes death –such is the Christian idea of God. In other words, in the Divine Being is revealed what humanity needs to become immortal. The Trinity is the Church of the Immortals and its human image can only be a church of the resurrected. Within the Trinity *there are no causes for death, and all the conditions for immortality.* An understanding of the Divine Trinity can be attained only by achieving universal human multi-unity. So long as in actual life the independence of individuals is expressed in their disunity, and their unity in enslavement, universal human multi-unity modeled on the Trinity will only be a mental image, an ideal. If, however, we reject the separation of thought from action, then the Three-in-One will be not merely an ideal but a project, not merely a hope but a commandment.[91]

In times of forgetfulness, it is the healers and those who are being healed and especially those who, as we may say, are being raised from the dead, who most clearly recognize the Water of Life as it flows without end (but invisibly to the inattentive or, we may say, to those who have severed their connection with the Source of Life) through the realms of manifestation as the Blessed Virgin together with her Son.

There is the necessity of *bricolage*. As the bees construct their hive, so is the bringing together or the convergence of the contrasting primal images. The *zoe* (deathless Life) associates with "Living Water," which also associates with the divine and transforming Fire. Andrew Simsky (Research Center for Eastern Christian Culture, Moscow) writes about the range of significations of fire and the hierotopy of fire in Dionysian tradition:

---

[91] Nikolai Fedorovich Fedorov, *What Was Man Created For: The Philosophy of the Common Task: Selected Works* (Lausanne, Switzerland: Honeyglen Publishing/ L'Age d'Homme, 1999), p. 71. Emphasis added.

The Biblical themes of fire were interpreted by Dionisius Pseudo-Areopagite in the spirit of his teaching about "dissimilar, figurative symbols, which are employed to represent the ineffable qualities of the Divine. Fire is one of those symbols. His understanding of the *Fire of God* was essentially based on the ideas of ancient physicists about fire being the all-pervasive omnipresent element which imparts matter with dynamics and the ability to change and even be alive. The real fire, being a visible manifestation of this invisible internal fire, was understood by the ancients as the symbol of Life. In the Christian context, it became the symbol of the eternal life of God and his immanence and also of the deification of man. Since we now know that fire is a chemical process which is limited in space and duration and is external to substances, it is not surprising that our contemporary perception of the sacral fire has lost most of its rational foundation and has a predominantly intuitive, almost instinctive character.

The ideas of Dionisius were put into spiritual practice by medieval mystics. Characteristic examples can be found in the works of John of Ruysbroeck, a Flemish monk of the fourteenth century. He wrote that the soul of a God-seeing man is craving to burn its "otherness" in "the eternal fire of love" and to become one with "the simple Unity of God." In this transcendent state the soul "finds neither beginning nor end and feels itself one with this fire of love." Richard Rolle, a British hermit, wrote that the "fire of love" entered his heart with its "honey-sweet flame."

... The Bible describes the creation of sacred spaces around altars and sacrificial fires. In the Christian tradition the sacral fire is also lit upon the altar, thus making obvious its direct link to the fire sacrifices of the Old Testament. Of course, liturgical fire also has other aspects: it symbolizes the Judgment and is also emblematic of the love of God and His eternal life. These multiple meanings have the common basis, which we find in the paradigmatic image of the *Fire of God* which is experienced by the faithful as a foretaste of the future meeting with God, entailing an inseparable mix of yearning and fear. In brief, liturgical fire is the symbol of the *Fire of God.*[92]

The Virgin Mary herself is said to be "Similar to Fire."[93] There is an Ethiopian/Rastafarian old saying that the rainbow is the Virgin Mary's belt and that the red, gold, and green colors of the Ethiopian flag are symbolic of this.

Angelic and Imaginal Realms

In a book titled, *Rose of the World*, by Daniil Andreev (d. 1959), there is the verbal image of each deeply rooted people having, in some upper or transcendent realm—beyond the ordinariness of our day-to-day life—a council of great souls who once lived among the particular people and who now, after their deaths, continue to inspire and to guide the aspirations of their people. These great souls, we may say, help to shape the long-term destinies of their particular peoples. In a still more elevated or comprehensive realm (and I don't recall that Andreev suggests this) the Blessed Virgin Mary presides over all of these councils. When it is said that the Virgin Mary is Queen of Angels and the angelic realms, something important about the ontological location of the Virgin Mary is being indicated to us. The angelic realms are mediating or intermediating realms, which are (or are the domain of) Sophia, the Holy Wisdom of God.[94] Ioana Cosma (Centre for Comparative Literature, University of Toronto) wrote:

[92] Andrew Simsky, "The Image-Paradigm of the Fire of God in the Bible and in the Christian Tradition," in Alexei Lidov, editor, *Hierotopy of Light and Fire in the Culture of the Byzantine World* (Moscow: Theoria, 2013), pp. 73-81, pp. 75-76.
[93] As in the title of the book by William Hart McNichols and Mirabai Starr, *Mother of God Similar to Fire* (Orbis Books, 2016).
[94] For a classic Orthodox Christian study see Sergius Bulgakov's *Jacob's Ladder: On Angels*, translated by Thomas Allan Smith (Grand Rapids, Michigan: Wm. B. Eerdmans Publishing Co., 2010). According to Tikhon Vasilyev (St. Theosevia Centre for Christian Spirituality, Oxford), the angelic realm figures in, or is an aspect of, Bulgakov's metalanguage (as distinguished from traditional philosophical and theological language) of sophiology. See Vasilyev, "Christian Angelology in Pseudo-Dionysius and Sergius Bulgakov," D.Phil. thesis, Wolfson College, Oxford University, 2019. On-line at: <https://ora.ox.ac.uk/objects/uuid:667ef5e8-a005-4bb4-8e2d-cc7b0424d4a7> (Accessed 10/22/2019)

In considering the aspect of "excessive presence" in relation to angelophanies, we direct our attention to one of the three fundamental theological modes of addressing the problematics of theophany: the kataphatic way ..., the apophatic way ... and the perspective of the *coincidentia oppositorum* (both presence and absence) such as we find it in the works of Sohravardî, Ibn Arabî, Nicholas of Cusa and Sergei Bulgakov, to give just a few examples.[95]

The above comment has to do with the *metaphysics* of the angelic realms, with our experience of angelic phenomena. With respect to the *imaginal* realm we may allude to the work of Henry Corbin:

... Corbin revolutionizes our philosophy by reintroducing in their proper places the metaphysical categories and figures that we no longer have the courage or strength to think about—categories that the evolution of European thought had obliterated in its movement of laicization. Corbin tells us that there is no space for the soul, there is no vision and participation in the [O]ne, there is no *ascension* through the various degrees of being *except under the direction of the angel.* Or should we say *angels*, each one of whom is specific to each one of us? It is because *a "subtle" space for the angel exists* that the soul, in effect, is able to develop and be led once again to its true place of existence, which is that of *a placeless place,* that of the imaginal world dear to Corbin and which, in the first place, gave birth to the soul that animates us.

The figure of the *angel,* from then on, becomes the central figure, and ... there is *a profound and urgent "necessity for angelology"* for anyone trying to understand our connections with the Divine—*the angel being the relationship that unites us to God* and allows us to pass from the stage of individual to the status of person.

---

[95] Ioana Cosma, "Angels In-Between: The Poetics of Excess and the Crisis of Representation," Ph.D. dissertation, Centre for Comparative Literature, University of Toronto, 2009, p. 89. On-line at: <https://tspace.library. utoronto.ca/bitstream/1807/26454/7/Cosma_Ioana_I_200911_PhD_thesis. pdf.pdf> (Accessed 11/3/2019)

... Henry Corbin is a hundred times richer than what we are able to suggest here. What I have tried to bring out here is the originality of a study that is at the same time a quest. It is the updating of a certain number of structures of being that will allow us tomorrow to think beyond the breach that today affects "Western" thinking. It is the opening of life to the being beyond being that will allow us to go beyond the ambient nihilism of an impoverished culture. This vision of the *angel* upon whom we have closed our metaphysical eyes, bringing instead a purely terrestrial look, will allow us to rethink the Divine when it rises up in our soul where it assumes a form and a face.[96]

A traditional understanding of the angelic orders names nine orders within three hierarchies. In descending order, the first hierarchy consists of Seraphim, Cherubim, and Thrones. The second (or middle) hierarchy consists of Dominions, Virtues, and Powers. The third hierarchy consists of Principalities, Archangels, and Angels. In Dante's *Convivio*, each of these orders associated with a particular discipline of learning, which together came to form the *Trivium* and *Quadrivium* of the Liberal Arts along with the Physics, Metaphysics, and Moral Science that constituted Philosophy. Theology was a separate division of Philosophy not associated with any one of the nine orders, but was associated with God Himself.[97] Chartres Cathedral was a center of this learning. Composer and writer, Andrew Baker, describes how the wisdom at Chartres associates with the Blessed Virgin Mary:

Chartres is also a sign of the growth of "The Cult of the Virgin." Mary had long been patroness of Chartres, which had long been a pilgrimage site focussed on a relic of the Virgin's shirt, or chemise. There was also an image in wood, a "Black Virgin." The new cathedral raised her image in new and dra-

---

[96] From the chapter titled, "Angel Logic," by Michel Cazenave in Henry Corbin, *Jung, Buddhism, and the Incarnation of Sophia: Unpublished Writings from the Philosopher of the Soul* , edited by Michel Cazenave (Rochester, Vermont: Inner Traditions, 2019), pp. 184-185. Emphases added.

[97] As found, for example, in the entry for "University" in *Johnson's Universal Cyclopedia: A New Edition*, Volume 8 (New York: D. Appleton and Company, 1895), p. 389. Other sources could be cited.

matic ways, with the spectacular representation of Mary in glass, and the first representation of Mary in stone, above a doorway, surrounded by the Seven Liberal Arts.

The concept of the Seven Liberal Arts originated with Boethius, who was so influential in the philosophy of Music. This idea of seven areas of learning had previously been described in a pagan context by Martianus Capella but Boethius ensured the idea would become the framework for education for centuries. All the Arts stem from the view that number, or harmony, was at the heart of all things and the understanding of this would lead to the knowledge of Unity in God. The number seven reflects the number of planets, which in turn derives from the seven notes of the diatonic musical scale. All worldly wisdom stems from this Inherent Law of Harmony.

Mary, at Chartres, is not only Mother of God, but also patroness of wisdom and the divine truth that we can discover in Nature through Knowledge and Art—and Music is the key to all the Arts and Sciences—and has an intimate association with the ancient Hebrew idea of Wisdom, as the Inherent Law.

To the right of Mary, in this doorway at Chartres, Pythagoras is shown with his monochord, a single stringed instrument with which he could measure the Harmony of Creation.

This was how Mary was seen in the middle ages—the image of Wisdom and the teacher of worldly wisdom to her son— sometimes represented as "*sedes sapientiae*," Seat of Wisdom, seated with her son on her knee.[98]

Contained "within" the *imaginal* realm, so to speak, is a *cosmological* realm.[99] With regard to specific angelic beings, using the language of

---

[98] Andrew Baker, *Dancing Before God: A Franciscan Composer's Theology of Creation* (September 12, 2018). On-line at: <https://andrewbakercomposer.files. wordpress.com/2018/10/dancing-revised-september-20th-with-new-ending-2018-complete.pdf> (Accessed 12/27/2019)

[99] Domestic piety and religiosity are also realms within the imaginal. Christian dogmas function as *koans* to move awareness beyond the constrictions of logic into the profundity of myth and image. This also happens in the imaginal. The Christian faith is, in other words, non-systematic. It is about the Presence of God and all the splendid ramifications of the Presence. See, along these

cosmology and culture formation, there is some variation in accounts of the identities of, for example, the archangels. In a substantial study of the involvement of the angelic realms in nature and in human history, the contemporary Bratislavan mathematician and sophiologist, Emil Páleš, names the archangels as follows:[100] Gabriel, Raphael, Anael, Michael, Samael, Zachariel, Oriphiel. The account given by Páleš is not a Christian account *per se*, but purports to have discerned commonalities in Christian and Arabic accounts that are also congruous with ancient Babylonian temple wisdom. The archangels are differentiated by their gifts.

Here is my summary of the archangelic traits as identified by Páleš. *Gabriel*, as archangel of the Moon and the most picturesque of the angels, is enlivener of nature and and inspirer of childhood and the Baroque. *Raphael*, as archangel of Mercury, is patron of physicians, botanists and linguists. He presides over the geological age of Mercury and the birth of the Gothic. He is inspirer of rationalism and the Enlightenment. He is joker and protector of youth. *Anael*, as archetype of love and beauty is the spirit of puberty and the muse of fine arts. He is also the inspirer of compassionate saints, romantics, mystics, and revolutionaries. He is patron of alchemists. *Michael*, as sun of truth is the spirit of the Paleozoic era, Michaelic art, and sun cults. He is the inspirer of philosophy. He is involved in the history of democracy and the task of the present day. *Samael* presides over the gods of war and the geological age of dragons. He is at the heart of universal conflagration, when it comes. He is implicated in the rhythm of the goddess Eris. He associates with the twentieth century and with the new knighthood. *Zachariel*, as god of the celestial dome presides over the geological age of Sagittrius. He is the patron of Indo-Europeans. He associates with the arising of the great kings and with Renaissance aesthetics and thinking. He is the inspirer of geometry and geography. He is intimate with the blue souls of those in their fifties. *Oriphiel* calls attention to the function of the metal, lead, in the human soul. He presides over the geological age of Capricorn. He is patron of hermits

---

same lines, the essay by Michael Martin titled, "Catholicism isn't a Religion, it's a Field," Angelico Press, blog, undated. On-line at: <https://angelicopress.org/catholicism-isnt-a-religion-its-a-field/> (Accessed 1/6/2020)

[100] Emil Páleš, *Seven Archangels: Rhythms of Inspiration in the History of Culture and Nature* (Bratislava, Slovakia: Sophia, 2009).

and emperors. He is the inspirer of geometries having to do with the circle and of Saturnian sciences. He presides over times when people understand themselves as architects of their own fortunes.

It should be emphasized here that, on this understanding, each of the angelic gifts is subject to diversion that unwittingly serves evil ends, in the sense that the *telos* or greatest possibility of the angelic gift fails to be realized. It is clear from the above that the angelic realm, on this account, is intimately involved in human history and in individual human lives. This involvement, according to Páleš, displays a periodicity (of 72-year and 354-year cycles and, for individuals, intervals of seven years). One does not have to accept this overall picture of the angelic world in detail to have a sense of what is involved in the angelic world. One might, for example, make some connection with the language of "implicate order," "morphic fields" (or "morphic resonance"), and "formative causation" used in the sciences associated with David Bohm, Rupert Sheldrake and others, especially as these concepts are deployed in philosophical reflections on biological life.

It can also be said, parenthetically, that as we enlarge our perspective of the processes and features that constitute for us "the world," the means by which we engage the world is *alchemical.* Alchemy, in this sense and usage of the word, is more like art than science. It is also something done (or worked) by the Divine realms— rather than something we (unilaterally) do at our own initiative.

The important aspect of all this is the understanding that the angelic realm is not simply "immaterial," it is intimately involved in the evolution or the unfolding of the "material" that includes both nature and culture, terms that are also highly ambiguous and not discrete entities. The angelic world interpenetrates our "common" world. Angelic beings can and do manifest in human form. Peter Mogila (d. 1647), Metropolitan of Kiev, is said to have written: "If you wish to see God's servants in human likeness, go to the Carpathians, where two hundred angels in human flesh dedicated their lives to God by their service."[101] The Assumption of the Virgin Mary is not simply a Roman

---

[101] As quoted in the Wikipedia entry on Theodosius of Manyava. On-line at: <https://en.m.wikipedia.org/wiki/Theodosius_of_Manyava> (Accessed 11/9/2019)

Catholic understanding.[102]   It is acknowledged also in the Eastern Christian world in, for example, the Armenian Church. The Assumption is about the possibility of being taken up into the angelic world. This is an invitation to a level of consciousness beyond names and forms.

According to Renaud Fabbri, director of the Perennialist website *Religio Perennis*, "Schuon defines the level where religious divergences are reconciled as the domain of the Virgin Mary, Sayyidatna Maryam in Islam."[103] Along similar lines, Otto F. A. Meinardus (Ellerau, Germany) wrote about traditional sites of Marian piety—grottoes, springs, and trees—that have appealed both Christians and Muslims:

> For many centuries, grottoes, springs and isolated trees have served as pilgrimage sites where both Christians and Muslims have venerated the Virgin Mary. Grottoes and caves, as sites of divine revelation, have played important roles in the Abrahamitic religions. Moses experienced the hand of the Lord in a cleft of the rock (Exodus 33:22), and, nearby, Elijah lodged in a cave where the Lord spoke to him (I Kings 19:9). Jesus was born in a cave which served as a stable, and Muhammad received his call in the night of power, the *laylet at-qadi*, in the cave at the foot of Mount Hira (S.97:1-5).
>
> In view of these traditions, it is not surprising that the Virgin repaired to grottoes and caves. For example, there is the Saiyideh al-Mantara, or Notre Dame de la Garde, south of Saida (Sidon). Originally, this cave served a Phoenician deity; later, Astarte was worshipped there. Christian traditions identify this cave as the place were Mary rested while waiting for her son who was at Sidon (Matthew 15:21). In spite of the Islamic prohibition of the veneration of icons, I have repeatedly

---

[102] See Stephen J. Shoemaker, *The Ancient Traditions of the Virgin Mary's Dormition and Assumption*, Oxford Early Christian Studies (Oxford, UK: Oxford University Press, 2003).

[103] Renaud Fabbri, "The Milk of the Virgin: The Prophet, the Saint and the Sage," in M. Ali Lakhani, Editor, *Sacred Web* 20, 2007, p. 11. On-line at: <http://www.worldwisdom.com/public/viewpdf/default.aspx?article-title=The_Milk_of_the_Virgin_the_Prophet_the_Saint_and_the_Sage.pdf> (Accessed 7/24/2019)

observed Muslims venerating there the miraculous icon of the Holy Virgin. Christians and Muslims see in her the mother of all mothers, especially in view of the biblical confession: "Blessed is the womb that bore thee and the paps that thou has sucked" (Luke 11:27). Irrespective of their religious identity, women in travail repair to the different Marian grottoes and caves in which they expect blessings for lactation, be it in Saiyidah ad Darr near Bsarre in northern Lebanon or in the Magharat as-Saiyidah, the well-known Franciscan "Milk Grotto" in Bethlehem.

The significance of water, be it a spring or a well, is generally related to life and fertility. Moses smote the rock in Sinai and water came out of it (Exodus 17:6). Jesus spoke about the rivers of living water (John 7:38), and, in the Qur'an, Mary is being comforted with the words: "Grieve not! Thy Lord hath placed a rivulet beneath thee (S. 19:24). Since the thirteenth century, Christian pilgrims have gone to St. Mary's Well at Matariyah near Cairo, which used to be under the custody of the Mameluke sultans. The visit of the Holy Family to this site is attested by the apocryphal Gospel of St. Matthew and the Coptic and Ethiopic *Synaxaria*. Here, so it is said, the child Jesus dug with his hands a well and there flowed from it water which had an exceedingly sweet odor. And Jesus took some of the water and watered therewith the pieces of Joseph's staff which he had planted. And they took root and put forth leaves, and an exceedingly sweet perfume was emitted by them ... and they called them "Balsam." Muslims used to identify this well with the above-mentioned Qur'anic rivulet.

In the Kidron Valley, outside the city-walls of Jerusalem, Muslims and Christians visit St. Mary's spring. According to medieval Christian tradition, Mary is said to have bathed and to have washed the swaddling clothes of her son here. On the other hand, Muslims of the nearby village of Silwan named the spring after Sitt al-Badriya, a descendant of 'Ali, another cult-transfer.

Taqi ad-Din Ahmad al Maqrizi (1304-1442), a noted Islamic historian, refers to a Coptic tradition about the sojourn of the Holy Family at al-Bahnasa. In this upper Egyptian town, the waters of the spring were known to heal pilgrims from their infirmities. An Islamic tradition identifies this spring with that mentioned in the Qur'an: "And we made the son of Mary and his mother a portent, and we gave them refuge on a height, a place of flocks and water-springs" (S. 23:50). However, the Arab traveller Ibn Batuta (1304-1377) located this Qur'anic spring on the slopes of Gebel Qasiyfin, just outside of Damascus.

As springs and wells are sites of divine-human encounters, so also isolated trees have been regarded as places of special revelations. The Qur'anic verses of Surah 19 have served as a foundation: "And the pangs of childbirth drove her [Mary] unto the trunk of the palm tree (23)." Samuel E. Zwemer reports that at the Shi'ite Mashad Husain in Kerbela, southwest of Baghdad, there are two palm trees under which Mary is said to have delivered her son. Numerous communities in the Islamic world claim to possess such palm trees. In Matariyah, just outside of Cairo, the Emir Yashbek built, around a special tree and the above-mentioned spring, a resort to entertain Qait Bey (1467-1496) and other wealthy Mamelukes. The waters were believed to be "holy and medicinal."[104]

For the benefit of those who have some familiarity with the term, "imaginal" and its uses by James Hillman and, before him, Henry Corbin, there is a valuable critique by Matthew Del Nevo (Catholic Institute of Sydney) that brings this into connection with Christian tradition. The connection is made with attention to St. John of Damascus (d. 749), the Council of Nicaea, and the Iconoclast Controversy.

> In his discussion of imagism and iconoclasm in *Healing Fiction*, Hillman is making a point which he thinks is in defense of the image and the imaginal, and to some extent that is certainly the case, but to some extent also, it is certainly not the case, and from this point of view Hillman's perspective cuts short the lengths of imagining that are archetypally possible. This other point of view reflects a Christian (as opposed to a theophanic)

---

[104] Otto E A. Meinardus, "The Virgin Mary as Mediatrix Between Christians and Muslims in the Middle East," *Marian Studies*, Vol. 47, Article 10, 1996, pp. 88-101, pp. 93-94. On-line at: <https://ecommons.udayton.edu/marian_studies/vol47/iss1/10> (Accessed 11/3/2019)

metaphysic, and one which profoundly, and archetypally extends the imaginal conception. This discussion in *Healing Fiction* is particularly symbolic for Hillman's view of the imagination as expounded elsewhere in his essays and books, and in the works of imaginal psychologists who have followed him.

Hillman discusses the ecumenical Council of Nicea in 787 C.E., and his account of it goes as follows: although history says the imagists won and the iconoclasts lost, a closer look leads one to the conclusion that, in a crucial way, the imagists lost and the iconoclasts won. In other words, Christianism once again failed the anima. The crux of this closer look is that although the imagists held that the image was itself full of power "containing in itself the person who is imaged," according to John of Damascus, when it came to the crunch they said that the image merely represented the power and/or person and did not contain it.

For instance, the image of Christ was not Christ but only his representation. This, Hillman thinks, is a move away from the previous idea held by the imagists, that the image contains in itself the person who is imaged. It is a move away which locates the power of the image elsewhere than the image, thus denigrating it.

Hillman's explanation for this compromise on the part of the imagists is that a literalistic theology of spirit was battling with an imaginational psychology of image; it then moved away from the position cited by John of Damascus. It was, at a level the imagists were not conscious of, an encroachment upon and victory over soul by spirit. Furthermore, symbolically, the two camps, imagists and iconoclasts, were drawn up along gender lines, with the Empress Irene heading the imagists.

Before we go on, let us recall what a theophanic view of the image is. It says that the divine manifests by the image in the image. The image does not merely correspond, as in allegory or analogy with its divine archetype, rather, it leads back to it (Corbin's *ta'wil*). This leading-back is also a process of soul-making, in Hillman's sense. The connection between image and archetype is qualitative, and the nearer, as it were, the image stands to its Origin, the greater the (qualitative) likeness is to be found, and the more archetypal it is.

The distance between image and Origin is not simple or logical, it is rather an abyss in which birds fly. When John of Damascus says the image contains in itself the person who is imaged, as Hillman quotes him saying, this is precisely the theophanic view—or so Hillman thinks—for, qualitatively speaking, it does. To say, as the Council then went on to say, that the image is a representation, is to move away from theophanic thinking in which the image is a symbol, to another literalist way of thinking where it is merely an allegory. For the theophanic view of the image sees that a symbol symbolises with that which it symbolises, whereas an allegory merely attempts to picture something external to itself. The theophanic view of the image is symbolic and never allegorical. In this metaphysic of the image Hillman is deeply indebted to Corbin, as is all imaginal psychology.

But—and here is the disabling move that is typical of imaginal psychology—when Hillman brings this theophanic view of the image to Nicea in 787, he measures against it what he reads there. Hillman quotes with approval John of Damascus that the image contains in itself the person who is imaged, because he reads it as a theophanic statement. As such, he sees it in distinction, even in opposition to the Council's final decision, which called the image representational. Hillman's theophanic metaphysic leads him into imaginative oversight, exposing the disability of imaginal psychology. For John of Damascus, as an Orthodox Christian, did not think theophanically in the same sense.

Under a Christian metaphysic, theophany is slightly and somewhat different. In this type of thinking the image may both contain in itself the person who is imaged (as John says) *and* confess to represent the person (as the Council decided). Far from there being an unconscious conspiracy here by spirit against soul, as Hillman suggests, there is a certain homology. Thus John's imagism comprehends both an equivalent to a *ta'wil*, and what Hillman would criticize as literalistic "substantive" thinking. How can this be so?

The answer involves distinguishing Hillman's imaginative oversight, which is just this: the icon is an *historic* picture. As an historic picture, the icon is both representative *and* actual. In this sense it represents things seen and testified (Christ as a man in Galilee and Jerusalem), but the icon is actual as well, in the sense that the community of faith whose expression this is and who have stabilised this expression over time, see the person imaged actually (theophanically) present. Christ, for instance, is seen in His actuality and in the faithful believers'.

John of Damascus is not speaking theophanically in Hillman's sense. In fact, he would regard Hillman as an image-destroyer, an iconoclast, rather than as the imagist Hillman believes himself to be. The reason for this is that under John's metaphysic a theophany is not something merely embodied in the image in the imaginal realm (*mundus imaginalis*), but it is something down-to-earth embodied *in the flesh*.[105]

A reason for calling attention to this extended excerpt is to avoid a possible misconception on the part of some readers who may understand the word, "imaginal," to mean "immaterial" (and therefore non-historical). Our use of the term, "imaginal," in connection with Blessed Virgin Mary and her appearances (apparitions) is not meant to entail exclusively "interior" phenomena. The imaginal transcends the distinction between "inner" and "outer." The angelic beings serve to reveal and to enable (to imagine) our individual or particular possibilities. We are being imagined—not the other way around. It is our responsibility, our task, to cooperate with the possibilities that are shown to us by these emissaries (angels) of the divine realm—possibilities specific to our particular situations in embodied life.

6.   Glastonbury as Heart Chakra of the Earth

The environs of Glastonbury, England, are a vortex of timeless and interpenetrating layers of dream—a dreamscape of all the yearnings of humans and other created beings interacting with each other across the

---

[105] Matthew Del Nevo, "Imaginal Psychology's Disability," *Spring: A Journal of Archetype and Culture*, Issue 53, 1992, pp. 113-120. Article available on-line at: <https://www.pantheatre.com/archives/pages/forum_2006_ metaphysics.pdf> (Accessed 12/2/2019)

great stretches of time.[106]   Elements of these layers of dream are also generated by the understandings and expectations of Glastonbury's many pilgrims who are drawn to the place. Glastonbury scholar, James Carley, writes:

> "There are only about a dozen reservoirs of world magic on the whole surface of the globe," says the hero of John Cowper Powys' *A Glastonbury Romance*, "Jerusalem … Rome … Mecca … Lhasa—and of these Glastonbury has the largest residue of unused power. Generations of mankind, aeons of past races, have—by their concentrated will—made Glastonbury miraculous." In spite of its lack of surface appeal, then, Glastonbury emanates to a remarkable degree a sense of mystery and power; there is an overwhelming *genius loci*, so much greater than mere physical circumstances would warrant. And because there is no longer any real, or at least tangible physical correlative on which to pin the transcendent atmosphere which Glastonbury generates, mysteries tend to be invented, the numinous demystified and made specific by an appeal to hidden structures anciently imposed on the landscape. The formless, in other words, is made formal. … Every pilgrim worthy of his scrip … returns from Glastonbury with his own small miracle, his own private myth of the place.[107]

Consider for a moment all that may be implied by the stories of King Arthur who, in some tellings, is associated with Glastonbury. Here is a contemporary account of the association of Arthur with Glastonbury:

> One of the most intriguing of associations with Glastonbury is that of the hero King Arthur. Giraldus Cambrensis, Gerald of Wales, wrote a history in the twelfth century based on older records. Gerald asserts that Arthur had a great devotion to Our Lady of Glastonbury and had her image painted on his shield.

---

[106] For the pre-history of these environs, discussed in the most comprehensive way, see the writings of Gordan Strachan (d. 2010), especially his *Jesus the Master Builder: Druid Mysteries and the Dawn of Christianity* (Edinburgh, Scotland: Floris Books, 2010).

[107] James P. Carley, *Glastonbury Abbey: The Holy House at the head of the Moors Adventurous* (Glastonbury, England: Gothic Image Publications, 1996), p. viii.

This story is corroborated by another account which says that in the eighth of his twelve great battles to establish the freedom and peace of ancient Britain, Arthur carried an image of Our Lady on his shoulder into battle. So it is not surprising that when Arthur was mortally wounded by his illegitimate son Mordred at the battle of Camlan, the King was carried off to the Isle of Avalon—an ancient name for Glastonbury—and at his death was buried near the old church. In 1190, his supposed grave was opened and in it was found the bones of a giant of a man, with the clear marks of a death wound to his head. With him was a smaller skeleton, a woman with golden hair. What is particularly notable about this burial is that the coffin was not a marble sarcophagus, as one might expect if a fraud was intended by some medieval entrepreneur. Rather, the bones lay in the hollowed out trunk of a tree, which, unknown to the monks, was the usual method of burial by the Celts. In 1278, King Edward I and his Queen kept Easter at Glastonbury, and assisted in the transferral of the ancient bones to a splendid new tomb near the high altar. The tomb is gone, but the place is still marked in the ruins.[108]

There is a saying in some Sufi circles that if the heart chakra becomes healthy and radiant, the other chakras will, in due course, become similarly healthy and balanced as well. Glastonbury can be considered as a "heart chakra" of the earth.[109]

---

[108] From an essay on "Our Lady of Glastonbury and Saint Joseph of Arimathaea" at the Full Homely Divinity website. The text of the essay is copyright of the Consortium of Country Churches, 2005. On-line at: <http://fullhomelydivinity.org/Glastonburytraditionsfullpage.htm> (Accessed 10/10/2019)

[109] For a good discussion of the tensions in Glastonbury, in this century and the last, arising from competing or contrasting imaginaries, see Adrian Iwachiw (Ivakhiv), "Places of Power: Sacred Sites, Gaia's Pilgrims, and the Politics of Landscape (An interpretive study of the geographics of New Age and contemporary earth spirituality, with reference to Glastonbury, England, and Sedona, Arizona)," Ph.D. dissertation, York University, Ontario, Canada, June 1997. On-line at: <https://oatd.org/oatd/record?record=oai%5C%3Acollectionscanada.gc.ca%5C%3AOOAMICUS.18222596> (Accessed 8/15/2019). Attention to "heartfulness" in contemporary spiritual psychology is particularly characteristic of the work of Robert Sardello.

A chronicle of the tensions in Glastonbury from the mid-1980s up through the late 1990s can be found in the fourteen annual newsletters written in those years by the Rev. James Turnbull (d. 1998). These newsletters were subsequently collected and published in book form. In his 1984 newsletter, Turnbull wrote:

> So far this letter has stated an outline of the problem we face both nationally and locally at a time when thousands upon thousands of people pour into Glastonbury each year, some seeking spiritual answers and finding little if any spiritual food in our churches. They include Roman Catholics, Anglicans, Orthodox, Free Church, charismatic fellowships, Israelites, Druids, Essenes, natural occultist and spiritist healers, astrologers, CND [Campaign for Nuclear Disarmament] supporters, Hare Krishna devotees, some part-Christian, unemployed people or drifters, pilgrims from many lands, each bringing his own idea of spirituality including some "leaders" who build up separatist groups, often of young people. As TV programmes bear witness, the initiative lies mainly with those on the fringes or outside of Church life.
>
> In reflection, it is not surprising that the Church is wallowing in Glastonbury as it is elsewhere in the country; no doubt it was doing so in medieval times when Glastonbury was a great centre of pilgrimage after the Crusades when "Christians" had been thrown out of the Holy Land following Arab and Turkish "Holy Wars" against western European imperialism. Inevitably this gave rise to power struggles. Then as now other faiths were brought into this country, and butchering of "infidels" gave way to persecution of "heretics." Western Europe now has to grow up.[110]

Given the magnitude and diversity of the influences at work in contemporary Glastonbury, as indicated above, the ruins of the Abbey and its present-day environs have provided and continue to provide a test case of the ability of the Christian vision, as manifested in local communities, to foster cultural reconciliation. As it seemed to Canon Allchin in the 1980s:

---

[110] James Turnbull, *The Prophetic Role of Glastonbury: To be a blessing for the world* (Glastonbury, England: Abbey Press, 2001), p. 14.

We live at a time when there is a steadily increasing interest in prayer and spirituality and a growing sense that in the life of Christian faith we need to understand more of our poetic and intuitive capacities as well as our strictly rational ones. Everywhere too there is a concern to find ways of rediscovering the sacredness of the earth, for in many different situations people have suddenly realized how fragile and vulnerable our planet is.[111]

It is widely recognized that we are entering a new age, the Age of Aquarius, the water pourer. We may understand the water pourer to be Jesus Christ as the bearer of the Water of Life. The Age of Aquarius is understood to be a Sophianic age wherein the dry parched lands may be revived by the rain of Holy Wisdom. What is called the "New Age" is not to be feared, but is rather to be regarded as a cauldron of many possibilities, similar to Ceredwin's cauldron of changes in medieval Welsh legend. The Order of Saint Michael (Michaelines),[112] founded by the American fantasy writer, Katherine Kurtz,[113] and others, is an example of a contemporary Christian religious community that happily engages with New Age events and thought without feeling any need to diminish their Trinitarian Christian faith in so doing. In the mid to late twentieth century, in British counterculture, it was not unusal to hear— or to see on a bumper sticker—the happy expression, "*Jah Glastafari!*" Such a blended expression was expressive of the atmosphere at Glastonbury as it then was and, to some extent, is today, especially in connection with the now annual Glastonbury Festival since the

---

[111] A. M. Allchin, *The Joy of All Creation*, previously cited, p. xiv.

[112] "The Order of Saint Michael is an esoteric, ecumenical Christian community oriented toward self-knowledge (gnosis in its original meaning) and spiritual growth. The Order provides a community for those seeking to enrich their traditional faith experiences and for those searching for a personal path to the Divine. Members seek contemporary meaning in traditional forms of worship and prayer, combining the rich traditions of the past with an exploration of contemporary mysticism and ritual." On-line at: <https://www.michaelines.org/> (Accessed 11/24/2019)

[113] Katherine Kurtz (b. 1944) is author of sixteen historical fantasy novels in the *Deryni* series, as well as occult and urban fantasy. Resident in Ireland for over twenty years, she now lives in Virginia.

1970s.[114] In Glastonbury there have been and are cultures associated with the various "layers" of Glastonbury history and myth or legend—Glastafarians, connected in some way with the Festival, and Glastonians—the townspeople who have preferred to keep their distance from the Festival, but have not been hesitant to make money from it when there is opportunity.

What is at issue with the New Age for Christianity is, using other terminology, the relationship between what can be called "folk religion" and the institutions and practices of the prevailing or established religion.[115] In the West, there has been this cleavage between the cultures of popular (pastoral, vernacular or folk) religion and of official religion since the realist/nominalist debates of the Middle Ages.[116] Historically, when the Church—in its rationalizing of itself—fails to take up into itself the common world (of carnival, pagan, and fairy traditions) the populace begins to become detached in various ways from that established religion.

---

[114] See Marion Bowman, "More of the Same?: Christianity, Vernacular Religion and Alternative Spirituality in Glastonbury," in Marion Bowman and Susan Sutcliffe, editors, *Beyond New Age: Exploring Alternative Spirituality* (Edinburgh: Edinburgh University Press, 2000), pp. 83-104.

[115] With regard to methodology, folklore/ethnology scholar, Marion Bowman (The Open University, England), writes: "The particular aspects of folklore studies which complement the study both of traditional forms of religion and contemporary spirituality include a refusal to grant privilege to written forms of expression over oral ones, the recognition that belief spills over into every aspect of life and behaviour, an appreciation of the dynamic nature of tradition, and the directing of attention to narrative forms such as legend and *memorate*." For this and other methodological considerations, see Marion Bowman, "Vernacular religion and nature: The 'Bible of the Folk' tradition in Newfoundland," *Folklore*, Volume 114, Issue 3, 2003, pp. 285-295. On-line at: <https://www.tandfonline.com/doi/abs/10.1080/0015587032000145333> (Accessed 11/30/2019)

[116] See the chapter titled, "Robert Herrick, Little Gidding, and Spectres of an Old Religion," in Michael Martin, *The Incarnation of the Poetic Word*, previously cited.

Prayer to the Mother of God
Our Lady Saint Mary of Glastonbury

Holy Theotokos, most gracious Queen, Our Lady Saint Mary of Glastonbury: We implore you by your powerful intercession, together with that of Blessed Michael the Archangel, Blessed Joseph of Arimathaea, and all of the martyrs and saints of Glastonbury, that true unity of Faith may be restored among all Christians and that, by your help and protection, we your children may ever rejoice in health of mind and body to render fitting service to our great God and Saviour, the Holy and Undivided Trinity, whom we ever adore, the Father, the Son, and the Holy Spirit, now, and forever, and unto ages of ages. Amen.[117]

As the historian, Jaroslav Pelikan (d. 2006), observed, "One of the most profound and most persistent roles of the Virgin Mary in history has been her function as a bridge builder to other traditions, other cultures, and other religions."[118] It is this recognition that we would hope for Glastonbury and for the world. For the latter part of her life the Anglican mystic, Marjorie Milne (d. 1977), manifested the spirit of Marian bridge-building in Glastonbury. As Natalia Ermolaev (Center for Digital Humanities, Princeton University) has written about Mother Maria Skobtsova (d. 1945, Orthodox), Marian spirituality entails God-motherhood as a social principle. For Skobtsova, Mary is "the great symbol of any genuine relationship among people."[119] More recently, Milne, who has been referred to as a "holy fool," was an embodiment of this quality in Glastonbury in the late 1960s and 1970s. The epithet

---

[117] Contemporary language style applied to prayer from the Full Homely Divinity webpage, previously cited, at: <http://fullhomelydivinity.org/Glastonburytraditionsfullpage.htm> (Accessed 10/10/2019).
[118] Jaroslav Pelikan, *Mary Through the Centuries: Her Place in the History of Culture* (New Haven: Yale University Press, 1998, 1996), p. 67.
[119] As quoted by Ermolaev in "The Marian Dimension of Mother Maria's Orthodox Social Christianity," *Philanthropy and Social Compassion in Eastern Orthodox Tradition: Papers of the Sophia Institute Academic Conference* (New York: Theotokos Press, Dec. 2009). On-line at: <https://academiccommons.columbia.edu/doi/10.7916/D8XS64SK> (Accessed 10/26/2019)

"holy fool" recalls the tradition of being a "fool for Christ," a tradition most clearly discerned in Byzantine and Russian Orthodox Christianity:

> As Sergey Ivanov argues, holy foolery in Russia emerged simultaneously with the formation of czarism. Holy fools kept the gap between secular authority, however despotic, and divine authority from closing. The genealogy of the figure of the "holy fool" can be traced from the Paul of 1 Corinthians 1-4 to Dostoyevsky's "idiot." While the criteria of "holy foolery" vary historically, one constant feature that Ivanov observes is that holy fools functioned as "cultural antennae" and rehearsed the hypocrisies, idolatries, and abuses of a religious community fallen into sin and decline.[120]

As noted elsewhere in this present text, it is the Grail that all beings seek and that the Blessed Virgin Mary together with her Son *are* the icon of that Life (*zoe*). That Life—the Glory of the Holy Trinity—is the Holy Sophia of God.[121] If the icon of the Life-Giving Spring is especially associated with healing, Rublev's icon of the Hospitality of Abraham (also known as the icon of the Holy Trinity) is particularly associated with the Sophia of God as reconciling Love. In the context of Glastonbury, this icon of reconciling Love (the Holy Grail in its

---

[120] From Larisa Reznik (then a Ph.D. student in Theology at the University of Chicago Divinity School), "'We Are All Pussy Riot' But Who Are 'We?',"
September 20, 2012, an article in the *Sightings* series at the University of Chicago Divinity School website. On-line at: <https://divinity.uchicago.edu/sightings/articles/we-are-all-pussy-riot-who-are-we> (Accessed 10/28/2019). The reference to Sergey Ivanov is a reference to the book, *Holy Fools in Byzantium and Beyond*, by Ivanov and translated by Simon Franklin (New York: Oxford University Press, 2006).

[121] "J. Daniélou wrote, "The real metaphysical questions are those which reveal the limits of metaphysics." Life does, in fact, seem to be one of these very questions that poses a challenge for human thought." These are opening lines from a paper by Giulio Maspero (Pontifical University of the Holy Cross, Rome), "Life as Relation: Classical Metaphysics and Trinitarian Ontology," *Theological Research*, Volume 2 (2014), Number 1, pp. 31-52. On-line at: <http://dx.doi.org/10.15633/thr.677> (Accessed 12/7/2019). This paper is an important resource for considerations arising from the movement of *zoe* into *bios*. Maspero was also one of the presenters at the Cambridge conference on New Trintarian Ontologies in September 2019.

deep reality) comes to the fore. This is the icon that Fr. Pavel Florensky (d. 1937) referred to as proof of the existence of God: "There exists the icon of the Trinity by St. Andrei Rublev; therefore, God exists."[122]

Christ-Consciousness as Paradise-Consciousness

The Blessed Virgin Mary always points, in some way, to Jesus, her son, the Christ. The self-consciousness of Christ is the consciousness of Paradise. It is "Paradise-consciousness"—the spiritual fragrance of Ethiopia, Persia, and Glastonbury. Shame and fear are unknown to Paradise-consciousness. Paradise-consciousness does not arrive by any force that sets up resistances. Sufism as spiritual culture is permeated with Paradise-consciousness. Sufism expresses itself in the language of Islam and it dances to the divine melody manifesting in the play of "ordinary" circumstances and occurrences. Thomas Merton:

> All really valid poetry (poetry that is fully alive, and asserts its reality by its power to generate imaginative life) is a kind of recovery of paradise. Not that the poet comes up with a report that he, an unusual man, has found his own way back into Eden; but the living line and the generative association, the new sound, the music, the structure, are somehow grounded in a renewal of vision and hearing so that he who reads and understands recognizes that here is a new start, a new creation.[123]

Aidan Hart, iconographer, wood carver, and Fellow of the Temenos Academy, commented as follows on Paradise as the first temple:

> We can say that the first temple was in fact Paradise, for it was a place where God and the human race were to meet and commune, and for man to enter union with God. Eden was a temple "not made with human hands." We have seen that a temple is a source and starting point for the whole world to be

---

[122] Gabriel Bunge, *The Rublev Trinity: The Icon of the Trinity by the Monk-Painter Andrei Rublev*, translated by Andrew Louth (Crestwood, New York: St. Vladimir's Seminary Press, 2007), p. 107.

[123] As quoted in George Kilcourse, "'The Paradise Ear': Thomas Merton, Poet," *The Kentucky Review*, Summer 1987, Volume 7, Number 2, p. 119.

sanctified. And so when God tells Adam and Eve to "fill the earth and subdue it" He is telling them to make the whole world a paradise, to extend the borders of the garden-temple so that the whole world might become garden-temple.

Seen in this context, we shall see later how Mary's encounter with the unfallen angel Gabriel can be related to Eve's encounter with Satan. By her life on earth and obedience to God, Mary, like a second Eve, begins to undo the work of the first Eve and so becomes a means of establishing the new and eternal temple-garden of the Church.[124]

We are invited to become troubadours of the Blessed Virgin Mary. When I try to imagine the music of Paradise, I think of certain contemporary musicians whose musical repertoire, at least in parts and on some occasions, brings Paradise to mind—the music of self-described "modern day troubadour," Estas Tonne (Ukraine), and Nóirín Ní Riain (Ireland),[125] for example.

> *Tell me the landscape in which you live And I will tell you who you are.*
> — Ortega y Gasset

In the season of Advent, especially, the Church calls to mind these passages of scripture from the prophet, Isaiah:

> A shoot shall come out from the stump of Jesse, and a branch shall grow out of his roots. The spirit of the LORD shall rest on him, the spirit of wisdom and understanding, the spirit of counsel and might, the spirit of knowledge and the fear of the LORD. His delight shall be in the fear of the LORD. He shall not judge by what his eyes see, or decide by what his ears hear; but with righteousness he shall judge the poor, and decide with

---

[124] From Aidan Hart, "Mary and the Temple in Icons," a talk given at the Temple Studies Group at the Temple Church, London, June 15th, 2013. On-line at: <http://www.templestudiesgroup.com/Papers/Hart_Maryandthetemple.pdf> (Accessed 9/16/2019)

[125] See Nóirín Ní Riain, "The Specificity of Christian Theosony: Towards a Theology of Listening," Ph.D. dissertation (2003), Mary Immaculate College, University of Limerick (Ireland). On-line at: <https://dspace.mic.ul.ie/handle/10395/2039> (Accessed 8/26/2019)

equity for the meek of the earth; he shall strike the earth with the rod of his mouth, and with the breath of his lips he shall kill the wicked. Righteousness shall be the belt around his waist, and faithfulness the belt around his loins. The wolf shall live with the lamb, the leopard shall lie down with the kid, the calf and the lion and the fatling together, and a little child shall lead them. The cow and the bear shall graze, their young shall lie down together; and the lion shall eat straw like the ox. The nursing child shall play over the hole of the asp, and the weaned child shall put its hand on the adder's den. They will not hurt or destroy on all my holy mountain; for the earth will be full of the knowledge of the LORD as the waters cover the sea.[126]

And further from Isaiah:

The wilderness and the dry land shall be glad, the desert shall rejoice and blossom; like the crocus it shall blossom abundantly, and rejoice with joy and singing. The glory of Lebanon shall be given to it, the majesty of Carmel and Sharon. They shall see the glory of the LORD, the majesty of our God. Strengthen the weak hands, and make firm the feeble knees. Say to those who are of a fearful heart, "Be strong, do not fear! Here is your God. He will come with vengeance, with terrible recompense. He will come and save you." Then the eyes of the blind shall be opened, and the ears of the deaf unstopped; then the lame shall leap like a dear, and the tongue of the speechless sing for joy. For waters shall break forth in the wilderness, and streams in the desert; the burning sand shall become a pool, and the thirsty ground springs of water; the haunt of jackals shall become a swamp, the grass shall become reeds and rushes. A highway shall be there, and it shall be called the Holy Way; the unclean shall not travel on it, but it shall be for God's people; no traveler, not even fools, shall go astray. No lion shall be there, nor shall any ravenous beast come up on it; they shall not be found there, but the redeemed shall walk there. And the ransomed of the LORD shall return, and come to Zion with

---

[126] Isaiah 11:1-9 (NRSV)

singing; everlasting joy shall be upon their heads; they shall obtain joy and gladness, and sorrow and sighing shall flee away.[127]

The language in these texts anticipate the arrival of a state of being (or state of consciousness) that we may name Paradise-consciousness. It is characterized by a harmonizing of elements that are, in our fallen state, seen as warring against one another. How does one, therefore, act in the world? A contemporary English mystic has stated that it seems to him that whereas saints in the West are most often people of action, saints in Russia and elsewhere in the East are especially noted for being people of prayer. He also identifies with the view that the world is, in some fundamental sense, perfect as it is, because it reflects the will of God.[128]

To live in Paradise-consciousness is to see the perfection of the world in conformity with Divine melody. Elsewhere in this present text the image of the Moebius strip is used to illustrate certain relationships. The image of the Moebius strip is applicable in this instance as well because Marian spirituality entails both the consciousness of Paradise and fearless cooperative action toward the restoration of all things. If the fundamental perfection of the world and the necessity for action seem contradictory, two things can be noted. First, the perfection of the world includes the work of its healers who in their work contribute to the restoration of all things. The restoration of all things in harmony

---

[127] Isaiah 35:1-10 (NRSV)

[128] See John Butler in conversation on the topic of prayer in his video on-line at: <https://youtu.be/p-bnP4g9nuU> (Accessed 12/2/2019). Bruce Charlton has criticized Butler as being "not Christian," but Matthew Del Nevo's remarks about Meister Eckhart could apply to Butler as well. Del Nevo wrote: "Eckhart gives us an anthropology that shows us inhabiting a world of personality, and also a world we call spiritual that is apprehended *in experience*, by the soul (inner sensibilities) and the ego (little self). Now this anthropology is not contingent on religious belief …. Only Eckhart's *idiom* is Christian, the *ideas* belong to the ancient wisdom of East and West." (From the Introduction to Del Nevo, *The Metaphysics of Night: Recovering Soul, Renewing Humanism*. New York: Routledge, 2014). A contemporary Orthodox monastic of the island of Mull, Hieromonk Seraphim Aldea, like John Butler, takes a quietist position with respect to action in the larger world but, unlike Butler, this is not because he sees the perfection of the world but because, to the contrary, the world (and therefore political action) lacks interest for him.

with the Divine melody is a *cooperative* task of the divine-humanity. Second, in the process of *theosis* (transformative life in God), the agent of all action comes to be seen as God rather than oneself.

> The purpose of economic activity is to defend and to spread the seeds of life, to resurrect nature. This is the action of Sophia on the universe in an effort to restore it to being in Truth. Sophia acts through the medium of historical humanity, and it is Sophia that determines the teleology of the historical process. The world as Sophia, though it has fallen into a false and hence mortal condition, must regain being in Truth through labor, or through the economic process. If selfness in man could only be vanquished through self-improvement or religious dedication, selfness in nature is vanquished through labor and in the historical process. Economic activity overcomes the divisions in nature, and its ultimate goal—outside of economics proper—is to return the world to life in Sophia.[129]

The Blessed Virgin Mary can be seen as the bridge across these and other kinds of logical divides that present themselves to the rational mind. Imagine, if you will, the *Stella Maris* (Our Lady of the Sea) to whom sailors appeal from the stormy and treacherous sea. Though their life is in peril, the sailors are at peace so long as they are in the awareness of Our Lady. This is the consciousness of Paradise. Jesus said to the penitent thief, "This day you will be with me in Paradise." This is a consequence of the divine alchemy, to see differently. In this prayer/poem, St. Mariam Baouardy (d. 1878), a Melkite Greek Catholic Carmelite mystic, wrote of the Virgin Mary as her paradise—where life returns:

> Lord, send your dew upon this sterile earth,
> and it will return to life.
>
> At the feet of my mother, Mary,
> I come back to life.
> All you that suffer,

---

[129] Sergei Bulgakov, *Philosophy of Economy: The World as Household*, Catherine Evtuhov, translator (New Haven, Connecticut: Yale University Press, 2000), p. 153.

Come to her.
All you that work in this house of God,
Mary knows your labors and counts your steps.
Tell yourselves:
At the feet of Mary, I come back to life.
You that dwell in this monastery,
let go of material things.
Your life and your salvation are at Mary's feet.
I dwell in my mother's heart,
there I find the One I love.
In the heart of Mary
I have found life.
Do not say I am an orphan.
I have Mary for my mother, my father is God.
The serpent, the dragon, wished to take my life;
But at the feet of Mary, I recovered my life.
She called me to this monastery, and here
will I forever remain.
At the feet of Mary, I came to life again.[130]

Beyond the familiar titles of Christ—Son of God, Son of the Father, Son of Man, etc.—we may also understand His reality as Son of the Mother. As such, He shares with her all the qualities that make for Paradise-Consciousness—qualities commended in the Sermon on the Mount.

Grail Tradition

What is called the Holy Grail has been long associated with the Virgin Mary. According to one recent account (Joseph Goering, University of Toronto), the Grail tradition in Western Europe derives from the presence in Spanish religious art of images of the Virgin Mary holding a bowl. Some fifty years before Chrétien de Troyes wrote about the

---

[130] From Mary Ford-Grabowsky, Editor, *Spiritual Writings on Mary* (Woodstock, Vermont: Skylight Paths Publishing, 2005). A slightly different translation can be found in Penny Hickey, Editor, *Drink of the Stream: Prayers of the Carmelites* (San Francisco, California: Ignatius Press, 2002). The reference to "material things" can be read in the sense of attachment to things of the world-system that resists the arrival of the Kingdom.

Grail, images of the Virgin Mary with a simple but radiant bowl (called a "grail" in local dialect) appeared in churches in the Spanish Pyrenees. Part of the allure of the Grail was that neither Chrétien nor his audience knew exactly what it represented or why it was so important. It was out of the attempts to answer those questions the literature of the Holy Grail was born.[131]   According to a different and earlier account (Julius Evola, d. 1974), the Grail is of Hyperborean origin and its legend deals with an initiatory mystery according to which the Grail is a symbolic expression of hope and of the will of specific ruling classes in the Middle Ages (namely, the Ghibellines) who wanted to reorganize and reunite the entire Western world as it was at that time into a Holy Empire having a transcendental and spiritual basis.[132] These two accounts do not exhaust the variety of attempts to comprehend the Grail and the appearance of its legends.

Psychologist, Robert Sardello, has understood that humans are, timelessly, pulled from the future rather than primarily being pushed, within the time stream, from the past.[133]   As such, it is important that we give attention to imagining—attempting to envision—the kind of future we hope to grow into. The Grail tradition is a multivalent and general image of that future—a future under the mantle or protection of the Blessed Virgin Mary. To inhabit the Grail tradition is to live in a condition of sufficiency—having enough—as opposed to a condition

---

[131] See Joseph Goering, *The Virgin and the Grail: Origins of a Legend* (New Haven: Yale University Press, 2005).

[132] See Julius Evola, *The Mystery of the Grail: Initiation and Magic in the Quest of the Spirit* (Rochester, Vermont: Inner Traditions International, 1997, 1994). On-line at: <http://www.cakravartin.com/wordpress/wp-content/uploads/2006/08/Julius-Evola-The-Mystery-of-the-Grail.pdf> (Accessed 10/19/2019)

[133] Robert Sardello, Ph.D., is co-founder of the School of Spiritual Psychology. At the University of Dallas, he served as chair of the Department of Psychology, head of the Institute of Philosophic Studies, and graduate dean. He is also co-founder of the Dallas Institute of Humanities and Culture and is a former faculty member of the Chalice of Repose Project in Missoula, Montana. Dr. Sardello is now an independent teacher and scholar. He is author of several books, including *Facing the World with Soul; Love and the World; Freeing the Soul from Fear; The Power of Soul: Living the Twelve Virtues,* and *Silence.*

of the fear of insufficiency. The Blessed Virgin provides more than enough.[134]

At some deep level Grail tradition is emblematic of the divine-humanity as characterized by *sobornost*, a togetherness that implies both sharing and the willingness to share. To inhabit the Grail tradition is to experience paradise now. In paradise there is no separation of action and contemplation. In paradise, humankind are good stewards of planet Earth; they do not aspire to mastery of the planet or of the animal kingdom. The animal kingdom is a congregation of innumerable tribes of wonder belonging to God alone—not to humankind. Animals were created, according to the Genesis story, because it was not good for the human to be alone. The animals were created to keep us company and, I believe, to teach us empathy and compassion.[135]

The Blessed Virgin Mary is an image of the ladder spanning the realms. She is the image of those ascending/descending energies that connect *Zoe* (deathless life) and *Bios* (life incarnate).[136] As such, she

---

[134] See, for example, Sonja Petrović (University of Belgrade), "Legends of the Virgin Mary: Miracles of Abundance out of Scarcity," in *Belief Narrative Genres*, International Society for Folk Narrative Research, 2012, pp. 139-146. On-line at: <https://www.academia.edu/5978905/Legends_of_the_Virgin_Mary_Miracles_of_abundance_out_of_scarcity> (Accessed 9/9/2019)

[135] The most spiritually authentic images (icons) of St. George and of the Virgin Mary, in terms of their symbolics, have them subduing the dragon and the serpent—not killing them. Images of the Virgin Mary sometimes show her bare foot resting lightly on serpent's back, not on its head—the serpent seeming relaxed and in submission to Mary. The phenomenon of the "Holy Snakes of the Virgin Mary" occurs regularly in the month of August during the Theotokos festivities in the village of Markopoulo on the Greek island of Kefalonia. The story that is told about these snakes is that when the local monastery was attacked by pirates in 1705, the nuns prayed fervently to the Virgin Mary for protection. The nuns were then transformed into the snakes and thus avoided being taken prisoner. In regard to this phenomenon, see Wikipedia entry at: <https://orthodoxwiki.org/Holy_Snakes> (Accessed 1/6/2020)

[136] A significant essay that ought especially to be included in the bibliography of Grail literature is John Carey's essay, "Henry Corbin and the Secret of the Grail," *Temenos Academy Review* 14 (2011), pp. 159-178. This essay was based on the text of a lecture presented to the Temenos Academy on September 2, 2010. On-line at: <https://www.temenosacademy.org/JOHN%20CAREY%20Henry%20Corbin%20and%20the%20Secre%20of%20the%20Grail.pdf>

manifests the reality of the Sophia, the Holy Wisdom of God.[137] We may further suggest here (based on a reading of Fr. Sergius Bulgakov together with Henry Corbin) that Sophia, as the Life and the Glory of the Holy Trinity, *is herself* the Holy Grail that all created beings seek, whether they are clearly conscious of this or not.[138] It can be noted, however, that whereas Grail tradition was associated in the West with the literature and customs of courtly love, this was not the case in Russia:

> Medieval Russia had known neither the practice nor the poetry of courtly love. Up to the modern epoch, no Russian Dante has ever dared to glorify his Beatrice and to transform the idealized image of the Beloved in an allegory of some sacred thing. Not adoring love, but *compassionate care*, is typical for the emotional background of medieval Russian literature, including its secular sector.[139]

Independent scholar, Peter Critchley, has observed: "As Dante's instructor, guide, and lure, Beatrice is an amalgam of Christ, Mary and

---

(Accessed 10/16/2019)

[137] In the Litany of Loreto one of the titles of Blessed Virgin Mary is "Seat of Wisdom." In her paper, "The Images of Mary in the Litany of Loreto," Old Testament scholar, Margaret Barker, wrote: "The titles for Mary in the Litany of Loreto derived from the titles for the Great Lady in Solomon's temple. Known as the Queen of Heaven and Wisdom, she was the Mother of the Lord, but denigrated by the title Asherah. She was purged from the temple by King Josiah in 623 BCE. Traces of her survive in the Bible and other ancient texts, and in icons of the Mother of God, but most remarkably in the Akathist Hymn of the Orthodox Church, and in the Litany of Loreto." On-line at: < http://www.margaretbarker.com/Papers/USU_Barker.pdf> (Accessed 11/2/2019). We eagerly await the companion volume to Barker's book, *The Mother of the Lord: Volume 1: The Lady in the Temple* (New York: Bloomsbury/T & T Clark, 2012).

[138] See Hadi Fakhoury, "Henry Corbin and Russian Religious Thought," Master of Arts thesis, 2013, Institute of Islamic Studies, McGill University, Montreal, Quebec, Canada, together with the previously cited essay, "Henry Corbin and the Secret of the Grail," by John Carey.

[139] Sergey S. Averintsev, "The Image of the Virgin Mary in Russian Piety," *Gregorianum* 75, 4 (1994), pp. 611-622, p. 611. On-line at: <https://www.jstor.org/stable/pdf/23579744.pdf> (Accessed 11/20/2019). Emphasis added.

the Church. Her beauty establishes a powerful link between love and knowledge."[140] This linkage between love and knowledge, mediated by the Blessed Virgin Mary, is the common heritage of Christian culture, in whatever language it may be embedded or, we may say, incarnated. The Sophianic beauty that links love and knowledge is, as suggested above, the Holy Grail that all created beings seek. It is this Sophianc beauty that is manifested in the Blessed Virgin Mary. Witnesses to her appearance have attested to her radiant, even blinding, beauty.[141] It is the function of this beauty embodied in Blessed Virgin Mary to lead us more fully and more deeply into the life of the Holy Trinity. It is a central purpose of this present book to elaborate this truth.

Service to the Grail does not seek power but may cooperatively join in efforts to retrieve or resurrect all that is life-giving and life-sustaining in our layered environments on this planet. As if to provide an over-view of the necessary characteristics of such cooperative effort, Irena Ateljevic (Wageningen University, Netherlands) has used the term, "transmodernity," as "an umbrella term that connotes the emerging socio-cultural, economic, political and philosophical shift." She writes:

> Transmodernity can generally be characterized by optimism to provide hope for human race. [Marc Luyckx] Ghisi describes transmodernity as a *planetary vision* in which humans are beginning to realize that we are all (including plants and animals) connected into one system, which makes us all interdependent, vulnerable and responsible for the Earth as an

---

140 Peter Critchley, "Dante's Enamoured Mind: Knowing and Being in the Life and Thought of Dante Alighieri" (2013), p. 422. On-line at: <https://www.academia.edu/4771579/Dantes_Enamoured_Mind> (Accessed 11/29/2019)

141 In the affective tradition of reading Dionysius, from Thomas Gallus (d. 1246) of the School of St. Victor and others, acquired knowledge falls away or is transcended. What remains is Love and beauty as its emblem. The elaboration in language of the beauty which is seen (revealed) is the true knowledge. The Blessed Virgin Mary stands at the head of this mystical stream. An important study of Thomas Gallus and the affective theological tradition is Boyd Taylor Coolman's *Knowledge, Love, and Ecstasy in the Theology of Thomas Gallus* (Oxford, U.K.: Oxford University Press, 2017). St. Bona-venture (d. 1274) also stands in this tradition. See Robert Glenn Davis, "The Force of Union: Affect and Ascent in the Theology of Bonaventure," Ph.D. dissertation, Harvard University, 2012. On-line at: <http://nrs.harvard.edu/urn-3:HUL.InstRepos:9385627> (Accessed 12/19/2019)

indivisible living community. In that sense this paradigm is actively tolerant and genuinely democratic by definition, as the awareness of mutual inter-dependency grows and the hierarchies between different cultures dismantle.

Transmodernity is also essentially *postpatriarchal* in a sense that women's visions and intuitions are to be recognized as indispensable in order to invent together innovative urgent solutions. This is radically different from the (preceding and necessary) (post)modern feminist movements that fight for women's rights only. Rather it is about a joint effort of men and women to fight for the better world of tomorrow by rejecting values of control and domination.

It is also essentially *postsecular* in a sense that redefines a new relation between religions and politics in a way that re-enchants the world towards a new openness to spiritual awareness and presence as a basis for private behaviour and public policy, whilst rejecting any religious divisions and dogmas. It is open to the transcendental, while resisting any authoritarian imposition of religious certainty. In doing so it tries to rediscover the *sacred* as a dimension of life and of our societies.

Transmodernity opposes the endless economic progress and obsession with material wealth and instead promotes the concept of *quality of life* as the measure of progress. This is expressed in the form of the knowledge economy which moves the emphasis from material capital to intangible assets and the nourishment of human potential. It challenges the rationalized notions of work in its artificial divorce from life. It combines rationalism with intuitive brainwork.

It moves away from vertical authority toward "flatter," more "horizontal," organizations; away from "recommend-dations-up-orders-down" management and toward more *con-sensual decision-making*. It downsizes the concept of clergy, technocrats and experts in order to raise the self-awareness, self-knowledge and individual accountability of all, yet it simultaneously uses the modernist achievements of science, technology and social innovation. It promotes *Earth citizenship* and draws from the highest potentials of humanity. It redefines the relation between science, ethics and society to reach for real and radical *transdisciplinarity*.

Yet it is not a uniforming view as *global reconciliation* around a sustainable future and a broad range of cultural diversity is maintained at the same time. Within the global vision of connected humanity it claims that each community or region needs to be free to develop in ways that are uniquely suited to its culture, ecology, climate and other characteristics. It wants us to see that the danger of today is less between cultures and religions, than the conflict *between* different paradigms. As such it offers a powerful path to peace and a new platform of dialogue between world cultures.[142]

This is an example of the kind of thinking—the comprehensiveness—that is required in our time by the dire global conditions we are facing in the areas of environment and climate change, political discourse and governance, and relations with non-human creatures. Contemporary Anglican theologian and philosopher, John Milbank, has called attention to the seventeenth century Czech philosopher, John Amos Comenius (d. 1670), who proposed an ecumenical, philosophical, and pedagogic project, "Pansophia," rooted in the long-term Catholic legacy and in medieval and Renaissance thought, especially that of Nicholas of Cusa. At the heart of Pansophy, according to Milbank, lay the attempt to articulate a fully Trinitarian ontology. This was associated, in Comenius's mind, with the endeavor to secure peace in Europe after the Reformation and to restore the unity of Christendom on a common doctrinal basis. Comenius's quest has been referred to as an attempt to lay the foundations for an "Integral Enlightenment."[143] The Marian spirituality that we are discussing in this book is, I believe, a central element of what any new integral and Trinitarian Enlightenment of the future might look like. This is the necessarily on-going project of Sophiology in our time—a project that is concerned both

---

[142] Irena Ateljevic, "Visions of Transmodernity: A New Renaissance of our Human History?," *Integral Review*, Volume 9, Number 2, June 2013. On-line at: <https://integral-review.org/issues/vol_9_no_2_ateljevic_visions_of_transmodernity.pdf> (Accessed 12/3/2019)

[143] See Professor John Milbank's presentation at the New Trinitarian Ontologies Conference in Cambridge, England, in September 2019. Videos of this and other associated presentations can be found on-line at the Conference website at: <https://www.newtrinitarianontologies.com/> (Accessed 12/5/2019)

with individual well-being and also with the common good. Benedictine teacher, Joan Chittister, writes:

> Authority and self-determination are two of the major problems of the spiritual life. Are we our own masters or not?
>
> The Benedictine answer is a simple one. Benedictine communities cannot be pictured correctly by either the pyramid or the circle. Benedictine communities are not meant to be either hierarchical or egalitarian. On the contrary, Benedictine communities are better pictured as a wheel with a hub and spokes. In the Benedictine community, there is a center to which all the members relate while they all relate to one another.
>
> The role of authority in Benedictine community is to unify the community and to direct its attention to God who is the center of life of each and all of them. Benedictine authority is not for its own sake.[144]

This manner of relating is, it seems to me, characteristic of cooperative life and work in the vicinity of the Grail and in service to the Grail.

7. Hierophanies

The term "hierophanies" is used here as an umbrella term for all the various modes of manifestation of the Blessed Virgin Mary in human experience. Included in this general category are what are called apparitions or appearances as well as auditions, locutions, realizations and various paranormal phenomena associated in some way with the Blessed Virgin Mary.[145]

Reference has been made, above in this present text, to the kinship between the Blessed Virgin Mary and the Holy Sophia of God. As such, apparitions of Sophia have been noted as well as apparitions of the Blessed Virgin Mary. In her Introduction to *Pavel Florensky: Beyond Vision: Essays on the Perception of Art*, Nicoletta Misler (Professor of

---

[144] Joan Chittister O.S.B., *Wisdom Distilled From the Daily: Living the Rule of St. Benedict Today* (New York: HarperSanFrancisco, 1990), pp. 134-135.

[145] With regard to locutions or "voices," see Christopher C. H. Cook, *Hearing Voices, Demonic and Divine: Scientic and Theological Perspectives* (New York: Routledge, 2019). On-line at: <http://dro.dur.ac.uk/27003/> (Accessed 12/27/2019)

Russian and Art History of Eastern Europe, University of Naples, L'Orientale, now retired) writes:

> In fact, the very title, "Celestial Signs," [an essay by Florensky] bears an immediate reference to religious apparitions, a mystery that, from the initial use of *znameniia* (heavenly bodies or phenomena) rather than *znaki* (semiotic indicators), pervades the whole text. The Russian *Znamenie Presviatoi Bogoroditsy*, for example, means the "miraculous apparition of the Virgin Mary" and connotes one of the different visages of Sophia—of Sophia, the "true sign of Mary Full of Grace in Her Virginity, the Beauty of Her soul." Consequently, the word "signs" could also encompass the different apparitions of Sophia to which Florensky refers in his footnotes to "Letter No. X" on the concept of Sophia in [his book,] *The Pillar and Ground of the Truth*. The experience of these religious apparitions was long, starting with the Holy Fathers and ending with the Symbolist philosophers and poets such as Vladimir Solov'ev and Viacheslav Ivanov, and the theme of Sophia fascinated Florensky, too, inspiring his recourse to religious meditation in the 1910s and the thesis of his magistral dissertation, a major contribution to Orthodox theology.[146]

For the Orthodox polymath and New Martyr, Fr. Pavel Florensky (d. 1937), "the transparent is apparitional." The full context of this remark is as follows:

> When we examine a transparent body of considerable thickness, such as an aquarium full of water, a solid glass cube (an inkwell), and so on, the consciousness is split with an exceptional sense of unease between the perceptions of both facets of the transparent body, which occupy different positions in the consciousness, but are homogeneous in content (this last circumstance being the cause of the unease). The body fluctuates in the consciousness between a reading of it as *something*, a body, and as *nothing*, visually nothing insofar as it is trans-

---

[146] Nicoletta Misler, editor, *Pavel Florensky: Beyond Vision: Essays on the Perception of Art*, translated by Wendy Salmond (London: Reaktion Books, 2002), p. 115-117.

parent. This *nothing* to vision is *something* to the touch; but this something is transformed by visual memory into something that *seems* visual. The transparent is apparitional.

In his various essays on art, Florensky was particularly concerned with aspects of icons and their production as well as with the art of the iconostasis in Orthodox churches. The iconostasis is similar to what is called the Rood Screen in some medieval churches in the West. For Florensky, the apparitional is a particular characteristic or quality of both our experience of certain icons and the occasional presentations of Sophia and of the Virgin Mary to those blessed to be their witnesses.

According to Michael O'Neill, a Chicago-based Catholic author with particular interest in miracle reports concerning the Virgin Mary, "Some scholars estimate the total number of apparition claims throughout history to be approximately 2,500 (with about five hundred of those coming in the twentieth century alone)."[147] We will share the context for this statement in a more extended excerpt of observations by Michael O'Neill further below, in this same section.

Consider the possibility that the holy icons, in the most literal sense of iconicity, and the variety of other manifestations commonly called apparitions are structurally the same, which is to say they are presentations of the divine energies in a perceptual space that does not fit scientistic grids of subjective/objective, material/immaterial, and other such binaries. These grids do not contain or allow what is required for these manifestations—namely, the ontological presence of intermediary realms that we may name the angelic.

Most of us do not, or have not, witnessed appearings or apparitions of the Virgin Mary. We may, however, read the accounts of apparitions or their messages or we may visit their shrines. The question for us becomes one of discernment and of our edification. In the early Church there were recognized gifts of prophecy. However, according to Jim Marion, at some point in the history of the Church emphasis was placed on what he calls the "mythic" dimensions of the faith to the exclusion or suppression of the "psychic" dimensions.[148] The pro-

---

[147] From the webpage on Marian apparitions at Michael O'Neill's *The Miracle Hunter* website. On-line at: <http://www.miraclehunter.com/marian_apparitions/index.html> (Accessed 10/30/2019)

[148] See Jim Marion, *Putting on the Mind of Christ: The Inner Work of Christian Spirituality* (Charlottesville, Virginia: Hampton Roads Publishing Company,

phetic and cultivation of the psychic (inner seeing) have continued, but not always (or never?) under the control of the Church as a set of institutions.

One of Our Lady's many titles is the ancient title of Queen of Prophets.[149] Her appearances throughout history and her messages are best understood as instances of the prophetic. The seers who witness Our Lady's appearing and hear her messages become, themselves, prophets in otherwise dry lands as they share, in unreceptive environments, what they have seen and heard. Authentic prophets do not enact that role except as the divine world reveals itself to them and lays upon them the mandate of truthful witness. Authentic prophets do not act in self-interest. They are servants of the revelation.[150] There is, however, always an ambiguity surrounding claims of revelation. It is as if we have to do with another Moebius strip, of divine revelation/authorial sub-creation. If the Virgin Mary is understood to have a prophetic role, she also has—it has been argued—a priestly role:

> The Priesthood of the Virgin Mary has, since the late Middle Ages, become a very popular topic in Roman Catholic theology, with influence also on the iconography of the Latin West. In Byzantine theology this theme has never been articulated as doctrine, whether positively or negatively. However, in Eastern Christian homiletics and hymnography the notion and metaphor of the Virgin's priesthood is easily perceived. Some church fathers compared the Virgin with the Priest and at the same time with the Altar Table, on which "she has offered to us Christ as Heavenly Bread for the redemption of sins."[151]

Inc., 2000), especially Chapter 9, "Psychic Consciousness." This text by Jim Marion reflects the maps of consciousness developed by Integral philosopher, Ken Wilber, and others who perceive a progression (or an evolution) through stages of human consciousness.

[149] See Dudley Plunkett (Medjugorje Network, England), *Queen of Prophets: The Gospel Message of Medjugorje* (New York: Doubleday, 1992.

[150] Fr. John Dear has referred to Mary as a "Prophet of Nonviolence." See John Dear, "Mary of Nazareth: Prophet of Nonviolence," an essay at his website, December 2001. On-line at: <http://johndear.org/pdfs/Mary_of_Nazareth.pdf> (Accessed 11/6/2019)

[151] Alexei Lidov (Moscow State University), "The Priesthood of the Virgin Mary as an Image-Paradigm of Christian Visual Culture," *IKON: Journal of*

The phenomena of apparitions of the Blessed Virgin Mary over the centuries are a clear indicator that the reality of the Blessed Virgin Mary has to do with the imaginal realms and how we understand these.[152] The philosopher, Jean-Luc Marion, makes a distinction between "saturated" phenomena (icons) that can be said to be revelatory and "idols."[153] An apparition of the Blessed Virgin Mary could be understood as an instance of the former. Mikkel B. Tin (Department of Folk Culture, Telemark University College, Norway) writes about Marion's understanding of saturated phenomena using Marion's own expressions:

A phenomenon which appears "in full authority, in full glory, as the first morning of a world" may still be a phenomenon, but it is the kind of "phenomenon that gives (itself) according to a maximum of phenomenality," "a phenomenon taking saturation to its maximum." This kind of phenomenon is one "in which givenness not only entirely invests manifestation but,

---

Iconographic Studies, Volume 10, 2017, pp. 9-26, p. 9. Other resources on the priesthood of Mary can be found on-line at: <http://www.womenpriests.org/devotion-mary-priest-overview/> (Accessed 11/20/2019). Some of the materials at the website reproduce arguments from Rene Laurentin's well-documented book on the topic, *Maria-Ecclesia-Sacerdotium* (Paris 1952). See also Christopher Smith, "Virgo Sacerdos: Mary and the Priesthood of the Faithful," License Thesis, 2005, Pontificia Universitas Gregoriana. On-line at: <https://www.academia.edu/7910168/Virgo_Sacerdos_The_Priesthood_of_the_Virgin_Mary> (Accessed 11/20/2019)

[152] Following Carl Jung, Henry Corbin, James Hillman, and Tom Cheetham, alchemy can be understood as the interpretive key, *par excellance*, for engaging with the imaginal. Seyyed Hossein Nasr writes: "Alchemy ... enlarges the dream of the individual soul to cosmic dimensions, breaking the prison of individual existence by the love of the beauty of Nature. The dream of the individual soul becomes that of the World Soul.... In the end ... the alchemist realizes that it is not he but the Divine Principle of the universe that is truly dreaming the cosmos." From Seyyed Hossein Nasr, *Science and Civilization in Islam*, Plume Series (New York: New American Library, 1970), p. 246.

[153] See Amy E. Antoninka, "Without Measure: Marion's Apophatic-Virtue Phenomenology of Iconic Love," Ph.D. dissertation, Baylor University, 2009. On-line at: <https://baylor-ir.tdl.org/bitstream/handle/2104/5519/Amy_Antoninka_phd.pdf> (Accessed 12/19/2019)

surpassing it, modifies its common characteristics." It differs so radically from the "poor phenomena" and "common-law phenomena" of classical phenomenology that it calls for a new phenomenology. In fact, in its extreme form, as we shall see, a "saturated phenomenon" is a revelation. At one point at least, Marion thought that a revelation can be accommodated only in a phenomenology of religion.[154]

The ambiguous character of such phenomena has been recognized. It has been suggested, for example, that Marian apparitions are "boundary objects—polymorphous realities stable and graspable enough, yet belonging to different worlds at once"—"that of modern medicine and mental health on one hand, and that of pastoral care and religious life on the other."[155] Again, from Michael O'Neill, here is an overview of Marian apparitions in history:

> The earliest known claim was from St. James the Greater who saw the Virgin Mary while he was in preaching on the banks of the Ebro River in Saragossa, Spain, in 40 A.D. Today, apparition reports occur more frequently. Some scholars estimate the total number of apparition claims throughout history to be approximately 2,500 (with about five hundred of those coming in the twentieth century alone). According to the *Dictionary of Apparitions of the Virgin Mary*, throughout history 308 apparitions are attributed to Saints or Blesseds. They are generally unofficially recognized by Church authorities (or at least the orders and congregations that they have founded or belonged to). Only seven Popes throughout history have witnessed Marian apparitions.

---

154 Mikkel B. Tin, "Saturated Phenomena: From Picture to Revelation in Jean-Luc Marion's Phenomenology," *Filozofia* 65, 2010, No. 9, p. 861. On-line at: <http://www.klemens.sav.sk/fiusav/doc/filozofia/2010/9/860-876.pdf> (Accessed 10/21/2019)
155 Zdeněk Konopásek and Jan Paleček, "Apparitions and Possessions as Boundary Objects: An Exploration into Some Tensions between Mental Health Care and Pastoral Care," *Journal of Religion and Health*, Vol. 51, No. 3 (September 2012), pp. 970-985. Preview on-line at: <https://www.jstor.org/stable/41653882> (Accessed 9/14/2019)

Although not officially approved by the Roman Catholic Church, visionaries in Medjugorje, Bosnia-Hercegovina and elsewhere currently distribute messages attributed to the Blessed Virgin.

The most famous apparitions have been those reported in Guadalupe, Mexico (1531), Rue du Bac, France (1830), Lourdes, France (1858), Fatima, Portugal (1917), and Medjugorje, Bosnia-Hercegovina (1981).

The most recently Vatican recognized apparitions are those from Le Laus, France (1664) which were approved in 2008. The most recently occurring apparitions with Vatican recogntiion are those from Kibeho, Rwanda which ended in 1989. The apparitions in Itapiranga, Brazil (specifically those from 1994-98) were declared to be supernatural by the local bishop in 2009. The 1859 Robinsonville, WI, USA, apparitions which were declared authentic on December 8, 2010, are the first and only episcopally approved apparitions in the history of the United States. The most recent approval by a local bishop was that of the Bishop of San Nicolas [Argentina], Most Reverend Hector Cardelli, who in May 2016 approved the apparitions received by Gladys Quiroga de Motta as supernatural from the years 1983-1990 (although the messages continue to this day).[156]

Mary in Russia and in Christian religious thought in Russia is pervasive:[157]

Looking back into Russia's history, it's clear that that the Virgin Mary has had a very strong cultural influence in the country—from its religion to its art and architecture. In fact, before the revolutions of 1917 which overthrew the Russian Empire and led to the establishment of the Soviet Union, Russia was colloquially known as the "house of Mary," since there were

---

[156] From Michael O'Neill, *The Miracle Hunter* website, previously cited.

[157] See Walter Nunzio Sisto, "The Soul of the Human Race: The Mother of God in the Theology of Sergius Bulgakov," Ph.D. dissertation (2013), University of St. Michael's College, University of Toronto. On-line at: <https://tspace.library.utoronto.ca/handle/1807/43428> (Accessed 8/24/2019)

more shrines and churches dedicated to Our Lady than in any other country at the time.[158]

Russian expatriate and religious philosopher, Nikolai Berdyaev (d. 1948), discerned an emphasis on motherhood in the Russian national character:

> The religion of soil is very strong in the Russian people; it lies deep down in the very foundation of the Russian soul. The land is the final intercessor. The fundamental category is motherhood. The Mother of God takes precedence of the Trinity and is almost identified with the Trinity.[159]

Marian apparitions signal some pressing need for change. The pressing need for change concerns some situation or situations so dire that direct warning from the divine realms may seem necessary.[160] This need for change may not concern the visionaries specifically, but more likely concerns the wider cultures in which the visionaries may be embedded. The apparition serves to create networks of people that did not exist before. These networks—which may be transnational—serve to effect change.[161] The visionaries themselves are typically persons

---

[158] From Catholic News Agency, "Our Lady of Kazan and Mary's affinity for Russia," *Angelus*, August 13, 2017. On-line at: <https://angelusnews.com/faith/our-lady-of-kazan-and-marys-affinity-for-russia/> (Accessed 11/20/2019)

[159] Nikolai Berdyaev, *The Russian Idea*, translated by R. M. French (Hudson, New York: Lindisfarne Press, 1992), p. 24.

[160] See John Kirby, "The Day of Mary: The Coming of Mary and Our Mutual Transformation of the World," DuVersity website, Library. On-line at: <https://www.duversity.org/PDF/The%20Day%20of%20Mary.pdf> (Accessed 1/11/2020)

[161] Agnieszka Halemba (Associate Professor at the Institute of Ethnology and Cultural Anthropology, University of Warsaw), cited further below, makes a distinction between institutions and organizations, the latter being the structural means by which these kinds of networks spread. For Halemba, according to Konrad Siekierski (in a review, "Negotiating Marian Apparitions: The Politics of Religion in Transcarpathian Ukraine," more completely cited further below), within this dichotomy, "organizations are perceived as agents" and "are unlike [...] institutions because they always involve conscious monitoring and control of the relationship between means and ends on a fairly

embedded in social/cultural circumstances that can be seen as having in some way marginalized them. Such generalizations as this cannot, however, be relied upon because the initiative remains with the divine world. From a global perspective, Marian apparitions (or, more generally, apparitions of the divine feminine) are not limited to visionaries who happen to be Christian in a sociological sense.

Marian apparitions sometimes evolve into new religious movements. As we note further below, the messages of Mary do also have political implications. At the beginning of this section (*For the Healing of Nations*) of this present text, reference was made to advocacy for a Fifth Marian Dogma. Mary, herself, as Lady of All Nations, spoke about this in a message given to the visionary, Ida Peerdeman (d. 1996), in Amsterdam on May 31, 1951:

> I stand here and come to tell you that I wish to be Mary, the Lady of All Nations. Look carefully. I am standing before the Cross of the Redeemer. My head, hands and feet as of a human being, as of the Son of Man; the body as of the Spirit. I have firmly placed my feet upon the globe, for in this time the Father and the Son wants to bring me into this world as Coredemptrix, Mediatrix and Advocate. This will be the new and final Marian dogma. This image will precede. This dogma will be much disputed, yet it will be carried through. I have repeated these things so that you may once more clarify this to your spiritual director and theologians and refute their objections.[162]

The apparition may or may not be immediately intuited as being that of the Blessed Virgin Mary. As mentioned above, this entails dis-

---

regular basis." He quotes Halemba's words, "the processes of interaction between religious institutions and religious organizations generate some of the most important and pregnant questions concerning the ways in which religion is present in human life."

[162] As quoted in Peter Jan Margry, "Marian Interventions in the Wars of Ideology: The Elastic Politics of the Roman Catholic Church on Modern Apparitions," in *History and Anthropology*, Volume 20, September 2009, Issue 3: Ethnographies of "Divine Interventions" in Europe, pp. 243-263, at p. 250. On-line at: <http://www.academia.edu/3633595/Marian_Interventions_in_the_Wars_of_Ideology> (Accessed 10/26/2019)

cernment, not only by those at some distance from the apparition in space and time, but also by witnesses to the apparition. In a sermon given at the shrine at Lourdes, here is what the then-Archbishop of Canterbury, Rowan Williams, said:

> When Mary came to Bernardette, she came at first as an anonymous figure, a beautiful lady, a mysterious 'thing,' not yet identified as the Lord's spotless Mother. And Bernardette—uneducated, uninstructed in doctrine—leapt with joy, recognising that here was life, here was healing. Remember those accounts of her which speak of her graceful, gliding movements at the Lady's bidding; as if she, like John in Elizabeth's womb, begins to dance to the music of the Incarnate Word who is carried by his Mother. Only bit by bit does Bernardette find the words to let the world know; only bit by bit, we might say, does she discover how to listen to the Lady and echo what she has to tell us.[163]

This brings to mind the question of the function of privacy in the modern world. Perhaps it has something to do with safety? How is it related to the realms where Our Lady chooses to appear? We may remember here the admonition in the Gospel to go into one's "inner room" and close the door, praying to the Father "in secret."

The key to justice is distribution and that to miracles is generosity.[164]
— From a Celtic proverb

The above proverb resonates because distribution and generosity are characteristic of the *flowingness* that is the deep reality of both God and the world—the world that both is and is not God. Hoarding and withholding are sins against the common life.

---

[163] Rowan Williams, "Archbishop of Canterbury's sermon for the International Mass at Lourdes," September 24, 2008. On-line at: <http://aoc2013.brix. fatbeehive. com/articles.php/1221/archbishop-of-canterburys-sermon-for-the-international-mass-at-lourdes> (Accessed 9/5/2019)
[164] As quoted in Richard J. Woods O.P., *The Spirituality of the Celtic Saints* (Chicago, Illinois: New Priory Press, 2014), p. 224.

It may be that the way to understand our present crisis, in the Western world in general and in the United States in particular, is to view it as the birth-pangs of a people yet in formation. We are not yet who we shall be. The Americas are a crucible of peoples.[165]

Hierophany manifests not only in what are called apparitions. The umbrella term, hierophany, also includes the phenomena of "far-seeing" vision that manifests in such written texts as *The Life of the Blessed Virgin Mary* from the visions of Anne Catherine Emmerich (d. 1824), *The Poem of the Man God* by Maria Valtorta (d. 1961), and *Mystical City of God* by Mary of Agreda (d. 1665). The term, hierophany, is sufficiently broad to include, as well, the experiences and writings of any number of others such as, for example, Luisa Piccarreta (d. 1947), *The Book of Heaven*; Gitta Mallasz (d. 1992), *Talking with Angels*; and Vassula Rydén (b. 1942), *True Life in God*.

Mary of Agreda (d. 1665) plays an important part in the story of who we shall become. Mary of Jesus of Agreda was a Franciscan abbess in Spain who, remarkably, is credited with helping to evangelize Native American Indians of the American Southwest through stories of her bilocation and appearance to the Indians as a "blue nun" who taught them while never having left Spain.[166] Mary of Agreda is also noted for her profound writing, *Mystical City of God*, as mentioned above, on the life of the Virgin Mary. Marilyn H. Fedewa, author of a book about Mary of Agreda writes:

> … we can easily appreciate Sor Maria's treatment of Mary, through three complimentary approaches. First, Sor Maria's practice and achievement of Quiet Prayer provided the foun-

---

[165] See, for example, the work of Virgilio Elizondo (d. 2016), a Mexican-American Roman Catholic priest and community activist. A leading scholar of Liberation and Hispanic theology, Elizondo is widely regarded as "the father of U.S. Latino religious thought."

[166] The phenomenon of bilocation in the case of Mary of Agreda is similar if not identical to the "exosomatosis" (conscious out-of-the-body experience) of the contemporary Cypriot Christian healer and sage, Stylianos Atteshlis (also known as Daskalos, d. 1995) as described in books by the sociologist, Kyriacos Markides (University of Maine). The phenomenon of bilocation also figures in the stories of the lives of St. Anthony of Padua (d. 1231), Padre Pio (d. 1968), St. Paisios (d. 1994) of Mount Athos, and perhaps other wonder-working saints.

dation from which she chronicled her internal dialogues with God the Father, Christ, and Mary. Second, Sor Maria's reverence for—and personal relationship with—Mary as paragon, teacher, and role model, informed the abbess throughout her lifelong quest to be a worthy bride of Christ. Third, in understanding Sor Maria's writing as a "grand theological poem" replete with devotional metaphors, we may derive inspiration from her portrayal of Mary as the "New Jerusalem."[167]

Mary's message, when she appears, is a political message.[168] She urges not only the individual but society as a whole to change and to repent. Focusing on Medjugorje alone, the concerns of her messages have been classified as: prayer, penance, conversion, faith, and peace.[169] Melanie Barbato (University of Münster, Germany) writes:

> Of course, the status of Marian apparitions is highly contested. Catholics are not obliged to believe in any of the accepted apparitions, and not only rationalists may find it difficult to believe that God sends Mary today to speak on day-to-day politics. Yet one should keep in mind that those who write off Marian apparitions as degenerated forms of religion and hence as imagined have an agenda, too. Religion, politics, modernity and the market do not come in neat boxes, and we should be wary of anyone trying to package these terms according to their needs. Marian apparitions are an underestimated phenomenon of modernity that can shed new light on the contested concep-

---

[167] From Marilyn H. Fedewa, "Beyond Baroque Style: A New Look at Maria of Agreda's Treatment of Mary's Life and Person in the Mystical City of God," *Marian Studies*, Volume 60, Article 10, 2009, pp. 173-188, p. 176. Online at: <https://ecommons.udayton.edu/marian_studies/vol60/iss1/10/> (Accessed 11/27/2019). See also the biography by Marilyn H. Fedewa, *Maria of Agreda: Mystical Lady in Blue* (Albuquerque: University of New Mexico Press, 2009).

[168] A survey of worldviews that tend to associate with various Marian apparitions can be found in Chapter Seven, "The Fundamentals of Modern Apparition Worldviews" in Zimdars-Swartz, *Encountering Mary*, previously cited.

[169] This classification is from Plunkett, *Queen of Prophets*, previously cited, p. 46.

tualisation and construction of religion from the nineteenth century onwards.[170]

The history of the spiritual phenomena that are Medjugorje today reflects both the opposition of political authorities as well as as the discerned intentions of the Blessed Virgin Mary:

After the tenth anniversary of the alleged apparitions in Medjugorje, on August 25, 1991, according to the Medjugorje visionary Marija Pavlović-Lunetti, Our Lady said that what she had begun in Fátima, she would fulfill in Medjugorje:
[On that day she said that Satan is strong and wants to sweep away her plans. She called people to help her, with prayers and fasting, to fulfill everything she wanted through the secrets she began in Fátima].
The Message of Fátima encourages praying the rosary for peace in the world and the end of war, for conversion and penance, for devotion to the Immaculate Heart of Mary and for sinners who have no one to pray for them. Secular interprettations of the message of Fátima involve political events the Lady of Fátima had forseen: the October revolution, the end of World War I and the beginning of World War II. The message also says that if Russia does not devote itself to the Immaculate Heart of Mary, it would turn into a source of evil that wages war and casts out all religion. With Mary's message in Fátima, the Church waged an anti-communist campaign against the Iron Curtain countries from the end of World War I through to its collapse in 1989. In that sense the message of Fátima is an urgent call to conversion and penance.
The alleged apparitions in Medjugorje started on the evening of June 24, 1981. According to the six visionaries, the apparations have been occurring continuously till today.
The apparitions in Medjugorje started several years before the fall of Communism and the Iron Curtain. As the distinguished Croatian theologian Tomislav Pervan states,

---

[170] From Melanie Barbato, "Marian apparitions—a challenge to established categories," *The Critical Religion Association* blog, September 2, 2013. On-line at: <https://criticalreligion.org/2013/09/02/marian-apparitions-a-challenge-to-established-categories/> (Accessed 9/14/2019)

already the election of the uncompromising Polish cardinal Karol Jozef Wojtiła in 1978 caused the then director of the soviet KGB, Jurij Andropov, to sense a catastrophe for communism in the making.

Pervan calls the election of Pope John Paul II, who placed his pontificate under the protection of Mary, and the Medjugorje apparitions, "the trumpets of Jericho playing together to sound the fall of the communist beast."[171]

The writer of the report, from which the above excerpt is taken, goes on to detail the extent to which the local government initially went to oppose and discredit the Medjugorje visionaries and the local Franciscan priests who served the visionaries and the pilgrims to Medjugorje.

It is the character of hierophanies (or theophanies) to sometimes be the occasion of various kinds of disorientation (with respect to "where" the hierophany occurred). St. Paul, for example, wrote: "I know a person in Christ who fourteen years ago was caught up to the third heaven—whether in the body or out of the body I do not know; God knows. And I know that such a person—whether in the body or out of the body I do not know; God knows—was caught up into Paradise and heard things that are not to be told, that no mortal is permitted to repeat." (2 Corinthians 12:2-4, NRSV) The question of the "place" of any particular hierophany is a significant one. However that question may be answered, the necessity of discernment is always present, whether concerning our own experience or reports of the experience of others. In the absence of an overwhelming persuasiveness of an experience, the status and character of the experience can be questioned or doubted. While there is no concensus among scholars in accounting for experiences of hierophany, the language of explanation continues to evolve and diversify in the efforts to bring every expe-

---

[171] Marijana Belaj (University of Zagreb), "'We all laughed at the secret of the collapse of Communism, only Communists believed in that': the first ten years of the Medjugorje apparitions," *SIEF 2015: Utopias, Realities, Heritages: Ethnographies for the 21st Century.* 12th SIEF Congress Zagreb (Croatia), 21–25 June 2015. On-line at: <https://www.academia.edu/15228383/_We_all_laughed_at_the_secret_of_the_collapse_of_Communism_only_Communists_believed_in_that_the_first_ten_years_of_the_Medjugorje_apparitions> (Accessed 11/20/2019)

rience into and within the nets of prevailing conceptual schemes. For example:

> Historians too often study visions as if they are a determinate "thing." While many accounts of visions may give this impression, closer analysis often reveals a variety of perceptions (visual, auditory, tactile, proprioceptive, and the like) that seem very real to subjects but are most likely, like dreams, generated from internal rather than external sources. Such experiences are often associated with mental states such as sleep, trance, hypnosis, dissociation, and psychosis. Theoretical integration across various lines of psychological research is laying the foundation for an increasingly sophisticated understanding of such experiences in terms of cognitive processing and fluctuations in consciousness. Considering visions as arising, like dreams, from internally rather than externally generated percepts and both as grounded in fluctuating states of consciousness, allows us to analyze the range of perceptions that arise without external stimulation of the senses, the extent to which they morph into other unusual states, and, in cases where this happens, the factors that seem to encourage this.[172]

The above excerpt makes reference to dreams, which have traditionally been regarded as a "place" or scene of divine revelation. The contemporary classicist and scholar of Pre-Socratic philosophy, Peter Kingsley, has called attention to the ancient Greek wisdom practice of incubation, by which an *iatromantis* (shamanic healer-prophet) would sleep in a cave or other sacred area with the intention of experiencing a divinely-inspired dream or cure or would guide others in doing so.[173] The practice of entering into incubation allowed one to experience a

---

[172] Ann Taves, "Channeled Apparitions: On Visions that Morph and Categories that Slip," *Visual Resources*, Volume 25, Numbers 1–2, March–June 2009, pp. 137-152, p. 137. On-line at: <https://www.religion.ucsb.edu/wp-content/uploads/2009-Channeled-apparitions-On-visions-that-morph-and-categories-that-slip.-Visual-Resources-251-137-52..pdf> (Accessed 12/10/2019)

[173] In this connection, see also Olga Kharitidi, *Master of Lucid Dreams: In the Heart of Asia a Russian Psychiatrist Learns How to Heal the Spirits of Trauma* (Charlottesville, Virginia: Hampton Roads Publishing Company, 2001).

fourth state of consciousness different from sleeping, ordinary dreaming, or ordinary waking. In the late medieval West, the French Benedictine monk, John of Morigny (d. early fourteenth century), advocated a devotional practice for acquiring knowledge through dreams. This practice associates with what is called the gift of prophecy. The Benedictine theologian, Rupert of Deutz (d. c. 1129) has been seen as representing an association between vision (focused in the liturgy) and knowledge. Prophecy, prayers, and dreams come to be associated in certain streams of medieval monastic culture.[174] The Blessed Virgin Mary presides over this (perennial) wisdom culture, then and now.

The human being has been referred to as a "breathing cathedral." (Bruteau's "Prayer and Identity" paper relates to this.) The human being is created as (literally) the "temple of the Holy Spirit." As such, the Blessed Virgin Mary is emblematic of who we are created to be.

If the Blessed Virgin Mary has seemed to have a preference for remote, wooded or undeveloped geographic areas having springs of water, this is not always the case. The apparition in 1945 to Joseph Vitolo Jr. (d. 2014) in Bronx, New York, occurred in New York City. Among her many titles, Our Lady is referred to as fountain of grace. At La Salette she is associated with a miraculous fountain.[175] In some of her apparitions, such as at Zeitun in Egypt and at Knock in Ireland, Our Lady is silent—she appears but does not speak. Her image alone does the work she intends. In these instances is highlighted a connection with the Primordial Silence, from out of which comes the everlasting Word.

What I say to you in the dark, tell in the light; and what you hear whispered, proclaim from the housetops.
— Matthew 10:27 (NRSV)

---

[174] Claire Fanger (Rice University) has written on matters touching this topic in an essay titled, "Inscription on the Heart: Medieval Christian Knowledge Practices," *The Side View* website, October 4, 2018. On-line at: <https://thesideview.co/articles/inscription-on-the-heart/> (Accessed 12/18/2019)

[175] Fr. John Sheehan, "The Miraculous Fountain of La Salette," at the website of the La Salette Missionaries, as reprinted from the La Salette publication, *Our Lady's Missionary*, September, 1934, pp. 129-130, 132. On-line at: <https://www.lasalette.org/about-la-salette/reconciliation/spirituality-and-charism/1895-the-miraculous-fountain-of-la-salette.html> (Accessed 6/15/2019)

Therefore whatever you have said in the dark will be heard in the light, and what you have whispered behind closed doors will be proclaimed from the housetops.
— Luke 12:3 (NRSV)

Two delightful stories having some relevance to the Blessed Virgin Mary, and which may evoke a sense of wonder in some readers, can be found in Chapter 7, "Signs & Wonders," of *The Mountain of Silence*, a book by Kyriacos Markides.[176] These two stories are summarized here by Fr. Bill Olnhausen:

After the Turkish invasion of Cyprus a Cypriot deacon, despondent about the destruction and loss of lives, especially among his relatives, went to visit the Elder. He said Father Paisios asked him to spend the night at his cell saying, I'll wake you early so we can chant Matins (Orthros). At 2 a.m. Father Paisios woke him and began the service. (Orthros begins very early in monasteries of the Athonite tradition.) At the Fifth Ode of the Canon the chapel was filled with a white-blue light. The flames of the oil lamps became blue as well and began to move in a slow rhythm, and there was a fragrance so lovely he couldn't describe it. The deacon asked: Father what's happening? Paisios whispered Be still and say the Jesus Prayer; the Virgin Mary is visiting us. After a while the lamps stopped moving and the light faded and as it faded the deacon said the sorrow and grief also faded from his heart.

Father Maximos spoke of a night he was there himself, when "a very subtle wind rushed into the chapel even though the door as well as the window were firmly shut. The lamp in front of the icon of the Holy Virgin [but none of the other lamps] began swinging back and forth... I turned with curiosity toward Elder Paisios trying to figure out what was happening. He signaled to remain quiet as he knelt down and touched the floor with his forehead remaining in that posture for some time. I stood perplexed... while the strange phenomena went on around me. After about half an hour while the lamp in front of

---

[176] Kyriacos C. Markides, *The Mountain of Silence: A Search for Orthodox Spirituality* (New York: Image/Doubleday, 2001), pp. 78-93.

the icon of the Holy Virgin continued its back and forth motion, I resumed reading the service. When I reached the Seventh Prayer of the blessing of Saint Symeon the lamp gradually stopped swinging. The luminosity that had inexplicably filled the room…vanished and everything went back to normal. Elder Paisios stood up and signaled me to follow him outside. What was that all about? I asked him. What? he replied, pretending not to have a clue what I was talking about. That phenomenon in the chapel. What happened? I asked. What did you see? he asked me. I told him everything that took place. He asked me whether I saw anything else. I said no. Oh, he said, it was nothing, it was nothing, waving his hand." Another night, another visitor, similar happenings. Paisios explained to him that the Theotokos goes around Athos at night checking things out and this time "all she saw here was two idiots saying their prayers."[177]

Phenomena of hierophanies are commonly referred to and discussed in language using the terms "miracle" and "the miraculous." What is reasonably meant by these terms is all that is experienced as being both wonderful and delightful. This may also include what we often refer to as happy synchronicities. The Brazilian essayist, Olavo de Carvalho, suggests we might attempt to understand the concept of the miraculous in terms of the symbol as conceived by the philosopher, Susanne K. Langer (d. 1985):

Symbol was defined by the philosopher Susanne K. Langer … as the matrix of all intellection. That is to say, a symbol is not something that you understand in itself, but something that helps you to understand a number of other things. Take, for instance, the biblical narratives. Many times you do not understand what is going on there, but later on, as you start to find facts in real life analogous to the facts in the narratives, the observed facts become intelligible, thanks to the unifying power

---

[177] From Fr. Bill Olnhausen, "133. A Late-Twentieth-Century Saint: The Holy Elder Paisios," Father Bill's Blog, *Ancient Faith Blogs*, July 5, 2019. On-line at: <https://blogs.ancientfaith.com/frbill/133-a-late-twentieth-century-saint-the-holy-elder-paisios/> (Accessed 12/21/2019)

of symbols; several facts are joined under a species that is condensed into the symbol.

That is exactly what the miraculous fact does; we do not understand it, but it throws light on innumerable causal connections that are usually not visible to us. This characteristic is proper to the miraculous phenomenon. Any phenomenon, of course, if regarded in a certain manner, can be symbolic, but the fact regarded as miraculous already has a symbolic structure in itself, and it is inseparable from this symbolic structure. It is this inseparability of its presence from its symbolic character that is the distinctive feature of the miraculous phenomenon.

In the first instance, it is not the miracle that has to be understood. Rather it is everything else that has to be understood in the light of the miracle. Each and every fact may be regarded symbolically, but the miracle has to be so. It does not admit of being looked on otherwise. Why? Because it is the nature of the miracle to physically show those connections between several causal orders which usually do not appear to us, and that is precisely what symbols do.

Do you understand this? Seen in this manner, the miraculous fact does not have to be explained, because the miraculous fact is the source of all explanation; it is the miraculous fact that throws light on all the rest. And that is precisely whence its name—*miraculum*—comes: something worthy of being looked at, worthy of being contemplated. So what Aristotle said about rites of mysteries in general also applies to miracles: they teach us nothing, but leave a deep impression upon us (these are not Aristotle's words, but my own way of putting it) that acts like a vitamin, so to speak, upon our intelligence. He thus anticipated Susanne K. Langer's definition of symbol as the matrix of all intellection. A miracle is not to be explained in itself but to be contemplated (distinguished, obviously enough, from other phenomena) and to be used thereafter as a matrix for the understanding of many things that are happening at that same time and that are to happen from that time on.

The miraculous phenomenon has characteristics that no other phenomenon does. One of these characteristics is that it cannot be understood in itself, i.e., it cannot be explanatory comprehended in itself, but it throws some light on other facts. This is the true criterion for the study of miraculous facts.[178]

The miraculous, in this account, is not that which requires explanation, but is rather that which serves to explain other phenomena. The miraculous reveals internal connections between and among events that were not previously seen or recognized. Another account of the miraculous that I have found particularly helpful is based on the recognition of degrees of reality. The miraculous is, in that context, understood as the "breaking in" of one level of reality into another.[179] It may be useful to ask ourselves this general question: Have we chosen to live in a world where revelation (from other levels of reality) is a possibility? Or have we chosen to live in a world of a single (flat) reality where "revelation" is not possible? It seems to me that the Christian faith entails the possibility of revelation (as revealing or unveiling).[180]

Whereas the spiritual culture of Islam seems to engender an ahistorical perspective, mainstream Christian cultures in the West have tended to emphasize the historical dimensions of the faith. The hazard or risk of this historical emphasis is that we come to see events as

---

[178] These are the final paragraphs of a longer essay by Olavo de Carvalho, "What is a Miracle?," *VoegelinView*, January 25, 2009. On-line at: <https://voegelinview.com/what-is-a-miracle/> (Accessed 1/1/2020)

[179] In my book, *The Anthropocosmic Vision: For a New Dialogic Civilization* (2017), I discussed the concept of the miraculous in connection with Alexei Losev's view of myth and in connection with Basarab Nicolescu's view of levels of reality.

[180] For a doorway into this question, I commend the work of Kyriacos C. Markides (University of Maine), previously referenced, on the emerging scholarly field of transpersonal sociology. See Markides, "Eastern Orthodox Mysticism and Transpersonal Theory," *The Journal of Transpersonal Psychology*, 2008, Volume 40, Number 2. On-line at: <https://pdfs.semanticscholar.org/9bcb/f3c9735a53a280e420c4465fc1bc680df0d9.pdf> (Accessed 1/3/2020). See also Markides, "The Healing Spirituality of Eastern Orthodoxy: A Personal Journey of Discovery," *Religions*, June 8, 2017. On-line at: <https://www.mdpi.com/2077-1444/8/6/109/htm> (Accessed 1/3/2020). See also Steven F. Cohn and Kyriacos C. Markides, "Religion and Spiritual Experience: Revisiting Key Assumptions in Sociology," *International Journal of Transpersonal Studies*, Volume 32, Issue 2, 2013, pp. 34-41. See also Dan Wigner, "What is Transpersonal Sociology," Dan Wigner website, August 31, 2018. On-line at: <http://www.dannwigner.com/?p=542> (Accessed 1/3/2020)

connected by causal "chains" that operate at a single level of reality. What is missing, it seems to me, is the recognition of, and an openness to, what is called *metahistory*, or the sense that there are larger and more comprehensive stories that comprehend the particular stories of history.[181] The emanation of the Glory of God that some saints are privileged to behold is not part of any causal chain.

8. Confluence of Spiritual Streams and Imagery

It is as if the Celtic stream is emblematic of an energetic pole whereas the Benedictine stream is emblematic of a container (or crucible) wherein the energies are canalized and directed.[182] We might say that the "container" of Benedictine life enables the alchemical processes of transformation to occur. If we enlarge the perspective, we might shift the metaphor and speak of a garden (the Virgin Mary's garden) that contains many lovely and fragrant flowers and herbs—comprehending not only these ancient Celtic and Benedictine streams but, together with these, the Franciscan and Dominican friars and other spiritual traditions as well. Most recently, there is the appearance of what is called New Monasticism and, within the Anglican world, Fresh Expressions of the church.

---

[181] A good illustration of uses to which metahistory can be put can be found in Daniil Andreev's *The Rose of the World* (Location not specified: Lindisfarne Books, 1997). A synopsis of Andreev's book, including its references to metahistory, can be found in the Appendix to Mikhail Epstein's chapter on "Daniil Andreev and the Russian Mysticism of Femininity" in Bernice Glatzer Rosenthal, Editor, *The Occult in Russian and Soviet Culture* (Ithaca, New York: Cornell University Press, 1997), pp. 346-355. The Appendix can also be found on-line at: <https://www.emory.edu/INTELNET/fi.andreev. synopsis.html%20> (Accessed 1/3/2020)

[182] This perspective in articulated by Esther de Waal in an essay titled, "Where Celtic and Benedictine Traditions Meet," in Linda Burton and Alex Whitehead, editors, *Christ is the Morning Star: When Celtic Spirituality meets the Benedictine Rule* (Dublin, Ireland: Lindisfarne Books, 1999). The essays in this book were originally prepared for the National Conference for Licensed Readers within the Church of England, College of St. Hild & St. Bede, Durham University, Autumn 1998.

Walsingham

The principal Marian shrine in England is at Walsingham. To begin with the environment of Walsingham, here is a recent account of a visitor to Walsingham traveling from London:

> What stands out in my mind was the journey to Walsingham, I was acutely aware of the spatial and physical changes that were occurring around me. There was a stark contrast between the obnoxiousness of London and the calming atmosphere in Walsingham. I felt rather claustrophobic in London as the dense buildings seemed to tower over you and block out the light. The modern architecture is cold and dark that creates an ominous presence. There is a type of nervous energy that radiates out of London that comes from the thousands of people wandering through the streets amongst the thousands of cars and bicycles. There is a never-ending constancy of everything, nothing ever sleeps. While travelling on the coach, I could feel that the urgency that London conveyed began to weaken as the buildings and cars began to spread out. I could feel that I was losing touch with the core or centre and moving further and further away to some peripheral place. Entering Walsingham I felt that we had "arrived" somewhere totally different. The atmosphere was calm, quiet and serene.
>
> There was a subtlety in Walsingham that was missing in London, everything was more peaceful and still. The red bricked houses emphasized the warmth of the area. Everything was much smaller in Walsingham; the houses, roads, shops and the entire village. The village seemed strangely familiar as it has a quaint charm that resembled the villages that I had visited as a child. The Anglican shrine itself was contradictory in its presentation as the architecture of the area infused modern and old architectural designs. The shrine was placed amongst modernist garden landscaping with minimalist designs and carefully manicured gardens. This juxtaposes against the rustic and more authentic feel of the village with its cobble stoned houses and winding streets and alleyways. Nevertheless, I felt that the modern aesthetics did not detract from the potency of the shrine, it seemed to have a power over people that changes the way they acted, becoming more reflective and sombre in their

mood and actions. Both [those who had and those who did not have] a religious affiliation with Walsingham felt at least a calmness that was not present with them in London.[183]

Here is the famous prophecy of Pope Leo XIII in 1897: "When England goes back to Walsingham, Our Lady will come back to England."

Mary's Dowry and National Dedications

While the Greek monastic pennensula, Athos, is known as the Garden of the Mother of God, England has been known as "Mary's Dowry" at least since the Middle Ages. There is a tradition that the title goes as far back as St. Edward the Confessor (d. 1066).[184] Pope Leo XIII in 1983 referred to England's long association with this title. In an essay on "The Blessed Virgin Mary in the Theology and Devotion of the Seventeenth-Century Anglican Divines," the Rev. William L. Lahey S.S.C. wrote:

> England, not only in church but also in nation, has been known in history as "Our Lady's Dowry." There the Blessed Virgin was most frequently spoken of and addressed as "Our Lady Saint Mary." The image of Mary with the Christ was set in the crown of the early monarchs. Many colleges, particularly at Oxford and Cambridge, were placed officially "under her pro-tection." Many flowers found in England have the term "Lady" in their names, for example, Lady's smock, Lady's-mantle, Lady's-slipper and Marigold (Mary's gold). Many places still employ her title such as Lady Grove, Lady Mead, and Mary Well. In quoting from an early source, we find the inscription, "One could not honor Mary and hold women in despite for it is not wisdom to despise that which God loveth." Even the patron saint of England, Saint George, was known as "Our

---

[183] Excerpt from Chloe Evans, "Walsingham Field Notes Write-Up," for a course in the Anthropology of Christianity at the London School of Economics, 3/26/2010. On-line at: <https://studylib.net/doc/15680972> (Accessed 9/17/2019)

[184] According to the *Dowry Tour* web page at <http://dowrytour.org.uk/dowryofmary/> (Accessed 12/19/2019)

sovereign Lady's knight." More, therefore, is the pity that, in the tragic era of the Reformation and following closely thereafter, thought and devotion concerning her suffered as it did in the English Church.[185]

At the initiative of the Roman Catholic Church, England is to be re-dedicated as Dowry of Mary in 2020.

I commend myself to you, true Throne of the Trinity!
Oh Meek Maid, now the Mother of Jesus,
Queen of Heaven, Lady of Earth,
and Empress of Hell be ye!
— From Gabriel's valediction in
   "The Parliament of Heaven,"
   a late Medieval English mystery play[186]

Scotland was dedicated to Our Lady in 2017 by action of Roman Catholic bishops in Scotland,[187] but such dedications should never be interpreted as rationale for any particular political agenda.[188]   The

---

[185] William L. Lahey, "The Blessed Virgin Mary in the Theology and Devotion of the Seventeenth-Century Anglican Divines," *Marian Studies*, Volume 38, 1987, Article 14, pp. 137-170, p. 137. On-line at: <https://ecommons.udayton.edu/marian_studies/vol38/iss1/14/> (Accessed 12/19/2019)

[186] The title "Empress of Hell" was commented above in this present text, in Section 4, *The Marian Reality*, under the sub-heading of *In the Darkest Nights.*

[187] See Philip Kosloski, "Scottish Parliament recognizes consecration to the Immaculate Heart of Mary," *Aleteia*, September 6, 2017. On-line at: <https://aleteia.org/2017/09/06/scottish-parliament-recognizes-consecration-to-the-immaculate-heart-of-mary/amp/> (Accessed 12/30/2019)

[188] As an example of what may happen when attempts are made to move images of the Virgin Mary into places of prominence in the public sphere, consider the recent history of efforts to restore the Marian Column in Prague. In 2017, Chloe Langr, a contributor to the *EpicPew* website, wrote: "City Hall considered two petitions relevant to the issue. The first was petition signed by more than 3,000 people, all in favor of the restoration of the column. The second petition was signed by more than 1,000 people and it was against the restoration. Citizens who signed the petition against the monument argued that the Marian column was still a symbol of the Habsburg reign. The restoration of the Marian column would mean the denial of the Czech history

Blessed Virgin Mary is the solvent of every ideological crystallization that is opaque to the Light.[189] What is called "civil religion," for example, is an ideological crystallization. Civil religion always serves the interests of the governing powers.

Blessing of the Grapes

The reference to "a confluence of streams" in the heading of this section is also a reference to all the received wisdom traditions—teachings and practices—from all times and all places where Our Lady is honored. This traditional array is the manifestation of Marian culture. One delightful instance of this is the annual (Orthodox) ceremony of the Blessing of the Grapes in Armenia and in other places wherever memory of viticulture is kept alive. The Blessing of the Grapes occurs in the month of August following celebration of the liturgy of the Assumption of the Holy Mother of God. As such, it has particular associations with the Blessed Virgin Mary that can be discerned, for example, in the use of seedless grapes, a fruit that came into being without seed as Christ was conceived in the Virgin Mother without human agent. Here is an excerpt from the Order of Blessing used in the Armenian Church. Similar to imagery in Celtic Christian spiritual writing, language in this Order of Blessing reflects an intimacy with the natural world:

> Blessed art Thou, Son and Word of the Father, inexpressible radiant of the first light, form and image of the invisible God ... who didst call thyself the vine; Thy followers in love, the

---

developments,' the petition read. Meanwhile, supporters of the monument argued that the Marian column symbolizes and honors those who defended Prague's Old Town during the Thirty Year's War. They also called the column a 'spiritual artifact'." From Chloe Langr, "Prague Won't Allow Marian Column Restoration," *EpicPew* website, September 19, 2017. On-line at: <https://epicpew.com/marian-column-removed-prague/> (Accessed 10/31/2019)

[189] Cyril Hovorun is an important resource for the ideological temptation within the Orthodox world. See, for example, his *Political Orthodoxies: The Unorthodoxies of the Church Coerced* (Minneapolis, Minnesota: Fortress Press, 2018). His observations may apply, by analogy, to situations of non-Orthodox religious communities in the West.

branches; and Thy Divine Father cultivator, who sanctifies those who are fruitful in righteousness and cuts off the unfruitful and condemns them to the eternal fire. The juice of the grape makes the wine which dispels sadness and creates gladness, as the Holy Bible states: "Wine that maketh glad the heart of man." And Thou, O Lord, on the occasion of Thy last supper, dispensed this same pleasure-giving wine to Thy disciples as Thy expiatory blood and representing the wisdom of the Holy Spirit and thus Thou didst establish the Sacrament of the Holy Eucharist, saying: "This is my blood which is shed for the salvation of mankind."

Therefore, O Lord, bless these bunches of grapes which have been donated to Thine Altar and grant remission of sins and spiritual and physical well-being to all who partake of this blessed offering with faith.

Bless, O Lord, the vineyards and the vinestock from which these grapes came to Thy Holy Church for blessing. Make them fruitful like fertile fields.

O Lord, protect the vineyards and the farms against all kinds of accidents which happen because of our sinful acts. Keep them free of hail, frosts, sunburn and harmful insects, so that through Thy bountiful mercy we may be deserving of sharing the product of Thy vinestock, at Thy Father's heavenly table, and to glorify the Holy Trinity, the Father and the Son and the Holy Spirit, now and forever unto the ages of ages. Amen.[190]

The Pomegranate

Beyond the blessing that is grapes, we might also consider the pomegranate, an ancient fruit that is mentioned in both the Bible and the Qur'an. In Christian tradition, this fruit is regarded as a symbolic of eternal life and of resurrection. In Islamic tradition the pomegranate is

---

[190] From Arman Shokhikyan, "Ceremony of Blessing of Grapes," text utilizing the "Bless, O Lord: Services of Blessing in the Armenian Church" by Fr. Garabed Kochakian with some linguistic revisions. On-line at: <https://ism.yale.edu/sites/default/files/files/2018%20Liturgy%20Conference/Arman%20Shokhikyan%20-%20Blessing%20of%20Grapes.pdf> (Accessed 12/26/2019)

regarded as a fruit of Jannah (Paradise) and is sometimes associated with prosperity, wellness, and wealth. In some religious paintings (by Botticelli and by da Vinci, for example), the pomegranate is seen in the hands of the Virgin Mary or in the hands of the infant Jesus. Sometimes the pomegranate is depicted as bursting open.

The Honeybee and Perennial Wisdom

Yet another association with the Blessed Virgin Mary is the honeybee:

> Bees are symbols of the Virgin Mary throughout the western world and especially in Eastern Europe. In the Slavonic folk tradition the bee is linked with the Immaculate Conception. July 26, the Feast of St. Anna, mother of Mary, whose birth also resulted from an immaculate conception, is the time when beekeepers pray for the conception of new healthy bees. In the Ukraine bees are the *tears of Our Lady* and the Queen Bee of any hive is called *Queen Tsarina*, a name associated with Mary, Queen of Heaven. Throughout Eastern Europe, Mary is protectress of bees and beekeepers and consecrated honey is offered on altars on the Feast of the Assumption of the Virgin Mary on August 15th, the date linked with her ascension into heaven.[191]

Saint John Chrysostom (d. 407) said: "The bee is more honored than other animals, not because she labors, but because she labors for others."[192] A twentieth century saint, Elder Paisios (d. 1994) of Mount Athos, said this about the bee: "When a bee is found in a room full of dirt and there is a small piece of sweet in a corner, it will ignore the dirt and will go to sit on top of the sweet. Now, if we ask the bee to show us where the garbage is, it will answer: 'I don't know. I can only tell you where to find flowers, sweets, honey and sugar;' it only knows the good things in life and is ignorant of all evil."[193] To labor for others

---

[191] From Anavrin, "Animal Symbolism of Honey Bees," *The Daily Spell*, September 19, 2010. On-line at: <http://thedailyspell.com/profiles/blogs/animal-symbolism-of-honey-bees> (Accessed 12/30/2019)
[192] Ibid.
[193] As quoted in Fr. Dn. Charles Joiner, "Flies and Bees - Advice from Elder Paisios," *Orthodox Way of Life: Walking the Path to Theosis*, December 17, 2009.

and to be disposed to see the good in all beings is deeply characteristic of Marian spirituality.

The honeybee is also associated with the accumulation of wisdom.[194] Contemporary Sufi teacher, A. H. Almaas, explains this association:

> There was a secret Work school that existed in Afghanistan for thousands of years called "Sarmoun Darq," which means "The Beehive" or the "Collectors of Honey." The purpose of this beehive was to collect human knowledge during the times when knowledge was dissipating and store it for future times when it could be used again. Most often undertaken in times of difficulty on earth, times of turmoil or war, this activity is so profound that most people cannot even conceive of what is involved and what significance it has.
>
> When we say the Sarmoun Darq stores human knowledge, we do not mean information. Information can be collected in books. There, is no need to form a school or a secret society to store information. Unlike information, this knowledge is material in the way that honey is material. The knowledge is actually collected in the same way that bees collect nectar from flowers and change it into honey. This is why the school is called The Beehive; its function is to collect all kinds of nectars—aspects of essential knowledge. The members have the capacity to concentrate it and change all the aromatic, beautiful nectars into very thick, sweet honey which they can then store in special flasks. When the right time comes, the

---

On-line at: <http://orthodoxwayoflife.blogspot.com/2009/12/flies-and-bees-advice-from-elder.html> (Accessed 12/30/2019)

[194] Essene teachers were sometimes referred to as "bees" because of their integral role, within their communities, as keepers of spiritual wisdom. See Hilda M. Ransome, *The Sacred Bee in Ancient Times and Folklore* (Mineola, New York: Dover Publications, 2004; originally published by George Allen & Unwin, London, 1937), p. 58. In his book, *The Masters of Wisdom: An Esoteric History of the Spiritual Unfolding of Life on This Planet* (Santa Fe, New Mexico: Bennett Books, 1995, p. 53), J. G. Bennett (d. 1974) wrote: "It seems clear that some at least of the Essenes were Masters of Wisdom." In the visions of Anne Catherine Emmerich, previously mentioned, the Virgin Mary is seen to have Essene progenitors.

flasks are opened and the knowledge is given out according to what is needed.

The nectars are the different aspects of knowledge about Essence, and the honey is the distilled pure knowledge of Essence. The image of the bees and the honey and the hive and the nectar is the closest description of the actual reality of the school. It is the closest description of the actual reality because knowledge of Essence is material that can be collected, concentrated, and distilled. This becomes obvious when we understand that Essence actually exists just as honey exists, just as nectars exist. The real knowledge about Essence is Essence itself. Essence is itself the knowledge.

This school, the Sarmoun Darq, collects the human Essence during difficult times on earth and stores it in special flasks. These special flasks are actually carefully prepared human beings. In this way, knowledge is preserved and passed on to other flasks until it is needed. Then these flasks, these human containers, are sent to different places to give out a particular material, material of whatever density or profundity can be absorbed.[195]

In times such as ours, with its array of challenges, it may be that attention to the Blessed Virgin Mary is associated with a particular way of being in the world that is also both wisdom and wisdom school.[196] The sweetness of this honey is manifest in the range of Biblical images

---

[195] From "Gathering Honey," Chapter 17, in A. H. Almaas, *Diamond Heart: Book One: Elements of the Real in Man* (Boulder, Colorado: Shambhala Publications, 1987), p. 243. Essential knowledge, in the second paragraph, can be understood as wisdom or sapiential truth. Essence, in the third paragraph, can be read as essential knowledge or truth, often understood as Perennial Wisdom.

[196] The wisdom of Mary is the wisdom of love. Fr. Slavko Barbarić O.F.M. (d. 2000), spiritual director to the visionaries of Medjugorje, wrote: "To be in a school where love is taught means to be in the most beautiful school. Whoever is with the Mother is in the school of love and whoever wants to be in the school of love, unconditionally has to be with the Mother." –From Fr. Slavko Barbarić, *In the School of Love* (Milford, Ohio: Faith Publishing Company, 2018), p. 1.

in the language of the (Ethiopian) *Harp of Glory,* a text previously noted. This is an extensive text, but here are some additional lines:

My Lady Mary, at night, and at the dawn of day,
    I bow before you,
Offering praises to that womb which contained
    the awesome radiance of God.
My Queen, humble in heart, and merciful of soul,
Raise me up from the sleep of indolence,
    to be a herald of your name.
Make me zealous and skillful in the cause of your praise,
Cast down upon me the great radiance of the light
    of your loveliness,
Let me never be cut off or exiled from your peaceful court.
My Lady Mary,
Gate of Peace from which the perfume
    of the spirit of life issues forth,
Which no wintry wind or rust can ever mar,
You are the House of Shem, which fell to him by lot,
    before his other brothers.
You are that in which his father Noah's blessing
    was made effective.
You are the Oak of Mamre where Abraham dwelt
    as an old man
And whose shade contained the threefold God,
When he made covenant with him, and all his seed thereafter.
You are that Fragrant Mountain of Isaac
Which produced the ram caught by its horns in the thorn bush.
You are the Golden Ladder, on which the angels of the Most
High ascended and descended,
Which Jacob saw when he was in flight from his brother.
O Virgin, holy shrine of the heavenly God,
You are the Mount of Horeb in which his splendor appeared,
And on which His very feet were placed,
When He made his law known to Jacob
    and his judgment to Israel.
You are the Field of Araunah in which David
    offered a sacrifice of salvation to his Maker,
When all his people were laid low under devastating plague.
You are the Temple of Solomon whose inner chambers

were filled with the glory of God,
On that occasion when the priests were unable
    to perform their service.
You are that Cluster of Figs that became a healing poultice
    for Hezekiah
When his days had come to an end,
    yet God added years to his life.
O beautiful lady, see how I have compared you
    to all manner of good and lovely things,
For the roots of the tree of your love
    are entwined within my heart.[197]

The sensuousness of the language brings to mind the Song of Solomon or Song of Songs from the Old Testament. The wisdom of the Blessed Virgin Mary is an embodied wisdom in deep connection with the Earth and all that Heaven has made manifest in it. This wisdom is comprehensive and trans-religious, although it is embodied in particular religious traditions. Hieromonk Silouan writes:

> In Jewish mysticism, known as Kabbalah, and in Islamic mysticism or Sufism, harmony is a divine name that transmits uncreated deifying energy that heals what division destroys and cures what confusion dissipates. In Orthodox Christian Hesychasm, harmony is a deifying divine energy accessed through the remembrance of God. Harmony is seen when harmony sees who sees, God in the midst, God seeing seer and seen. Holy Trinity is triune opening, triune revelation awakening the eye and ear of the heart so that separation turns back into union. In Buddhism, the practice of harmony is grounded in the practice of compassionate mindfulness. In Advaita Vedanta, harmony is rooted in realisation of the uncreated Self, *Atman*, and entails discernment as well as knowledge, *jnana*. It is not a mere change of opinion, but accesses the transcendent depths of pure awareness ever present beneath the phenomena of the conditioned self or *jiva*. Each wisdom tradition bears witness in its own language to the transcendent source of harmony,

---

[197] From John Anthony McGuckin, *The Path of Christianity: The First Thousand Years* (Downers Grove, Illinois: InterVarsity Press, 2017). Page number(s) not identified.

expressing wisdom in a different way. Wisdom, however, remains wisdom and in Christian tradition, Christ is wisdom revealed in the wisdom of the Holy Spirit, unveiling the wisdom of the Father. Just as there is no revealed meta-religion transcending the religions, so there is no metaphysical way of accessing harmony outside the sacred wisdoms that open to it. We are given these wisdoms so that harmony may restore us, and harmony heals us when wisdom is awake in the heart. We turn and see so that wisdom, the state of seeing, cures all that destroys harmony within us, between us, and among us wherever we turn, for divine harmony is always already present awaiting us, calling us to turn and see.[198]

An Ethiopian Story

On this topic of the confluence of spiritual streams, we may recall a beautiful story of the welcoming of some Armenian children into Ethiopia following the Armenian Genocide. This was a group of forty orphans who had escaped from the atrocities in Turkey and were afterwards adopted by Haile Selassie I of Ethiopia, then Crown Prince Ras Tafari. The children performed as a marching band in Jerusalem. The Crown Prince met the children while visiting the Armenian Quarter in Jerusalem. They impressed him so much that he obtained permission from the Armenian Patriarchate of Jerusalem to adopt and bring them to Ethiopia, where he then arranged for them to receive musical instruction. The children arrived in Addis Ababa in 1924 and, along with their bandleader, became the first official orchestra of the nation. It is of note that, in this small and particular instance, music played a role in making possible a blending of these two Christian cultural traditions. Music was the occasion of some movement in the heart of the Crown Prince that had life-changing impact on the children but also, over time, on the Christian people of Ethiopia.[199] So

---

[198] Hieromonk Silouan, "Practice of Harmony in Orthodox Christian Wisdom," The Harmony Project website. On-line at: <https://www.theharmonyproject.org.uk/practice-of-harmony-in-orthodox-christian-wisdom/> (Accessed 1/8/2020)

[199] P.H., "See How Armenian Genocide Orphans Sparked a Revolution in Ethiopian Music," How Africa: The Rise of Africa, website, undated. On-line

far as I can tell, the Virgin Mary does not directly figure in the story that is told, but this is nevertheless how Our Lady works.

Virgin Mary in the Writing of Evelyn Underhill and J. R. R. Tolkien

It is not well known that the Anglican scholar of mysticism, Evelyn Underhill (d. 1941), in her early writing, gave attention to the Virgin Mary who remained central to Underhill's spirituality throughout her life. Carol Poston (professor emerita, St. Xavier University) writes:

> Underhill's early devotion to Marian sacrifice comes to bloom later in her career as pacifism, that mandate for personal and radical self-sacrifice represented not just by Jesus on the cross but also Mary at the manger, Mary at the foot of the cross, Mary of the Pieta, and Mary at the Pentecost. Toward the end of her life, when bombs were landing regularly on Hampstead Heath near where she and Hubert [her husband] had taken refuge, Underhill speaks of true Christian pacifism as being a lonely, though sacred, journey: unable as a Christian may be to "cast out Satan by Satan" by killing the enemy, "the true charter of Christian pacifism" is found "in the declaration of One who has conquered the rebel universe at its heart by letting violence do its worst, triumphing over principalities and powers by the costly application of sacrificial love." In her final letter (Eastertide 1941) to the select few women of a prayer group she had established once the war had begun and she was a virtual shut-in, she warns that Christianity is not an easy journey. "It is a stem business. It is concerned with salvation through sacrifice."[200]

With regard to the English philologist, J. R. R. Tolkien (d. 1973), it has been observed by writer and publisher, Philip Kosloski, that particular qualities or characteristics of Our Lady are embodied in four

---

at: <https://howafrica.com/armenian-genocide-orphans-sparked-revolution-ethiopian-music/> (Accessed 1/7/2020)

[200] From Carol H. Poston, "Evelyn Underhill and the Virgin Mary," article at The Evelyn Underhill Association website, December 1, 2015. On-line at: <http://evelynunderhill.org/evelyn-underhill-and-the-virgin-mary-by-carol-h-poston/> (Accessed 12/27/2019)

women appearing in the writings of Tolkien. In a blog entry, Kosloski writes:

> "I think I know exactly what you mean by the order of Grace; and of course by your references to Our Lady, upon which all my own small perception of beauty both in majesty and simplicity is founded." (*The Letters of J. R. R. Tolkien*, #142)

J. R. R. Tolkien, being a devout Catholic, was well acquainted with the indispensable role of the Blessed Virgin Mary in Christianity and had a deep devotion to her. He saw her importance in being the "Mother of God" and venerated her as the "Queen Mother" who sits enthroned with her Son in Heaven. This devotion to the "Morning Star" would find its way into four women in the realm of Middle-Earth:

> *Lúthien*—While she is a character featured in *The Silmarillion*, her story does find its way into *The Lord of the Rings* and is a constant reference in regards to the relationship of Aragorn and Arwen. In any case, Lúthien is half-elven and half-divine and possessed such pure beauty that she captivated the heart of the man Beren after he saw her dancing in the woods. This beauty earned her the title of "the most beautiful of all the Children of Iluvatar" and it is said that her beauty was "as the dawn in spring." Lúthien reflects that pure beauty of the Blessed Virgin Mary who is the "Tower of Ivory" and "Lady Immaculate." The Blessed Virgin Mary, while completely human, was preserved from sin and conceived Divine Life in her womb. Lúthien then reflects that pure beauty of the "Fairest Daughter of the Father," who is also the "Morning Star."
>
> *Galadriel*—Daughter of Finarfin, Prince of the Noldor, and cousin to Luthien, Galadriel is an excellent reflection of many characteristics of the Blessed Virgin Mary. She is said to be the fairest of all the elves and was granted the ability to see into the mind's of others, seeing their thoughts. She was called the "Lady of Light" or the "White Lady." Her hair was so beautiful that even Gimli desired to have a single strand of her

hair. She also dispensed many gifts to the Fellowship when they stopped in Lothlorien. Galadriel reflects that heavenly beauty of Our Lady and reminds us of the role of the Blessed Virgin Mary as the "Mediatrix of All Graces;" the one who intercedes most powerfully for us and dispenses many gifts to the faithful who call upon her.

Arwen—Daughter of Elrond and granddaughter of Galadriel, Arwen was called the "Evenstar" and was accounted as the most beautiful of the final generation of elves. She was a descendant of Lúthien and often compared to her for her beauty and for her relationship with Aragorn. She was described by Frodo as, "Young she was and yet not so. The braids of her dark hair were touched by no frost, her white arms and clear face were flawless and smooth, and the light of stars was in her bright eyes, grey as a cloudless night; yet queenly she looked, and thought and knowledge were in her glance, as of one who has known many things that the years bring." Thus, Arwen reflects that regal beauty of Our Lady, who is exalted as Queen.

Éowyn—Daughter of Théodwyn and sister to Éomer, Éowyn was a woman who longed for battle and despised being sequestered to the "cage" that was her life. In the end it was her heroism in battle that defeated the Witch-King, where she proclaimed, "Begone, if you be not deathless! For living or dark undead, I will smite you." After her victory, she would eventually devote herself to "be a healer, and love all things that grow and are not barren." Éowyn reflects that power of the Blessed Virgin Mary, who crushed the head of the serpent and is called the "Terror of Demons;" for when called upon, demons fly away from the sound of her name. Éowyn also reflects that healing power of the Blessed Virgin Mary, who is called the "Health of the Sick," "Comfort of the Afflicted" and "Help of Christians."

As you can see, Tolkien infused his most prominent women in Middle-Earth with such great beauty as befits the

Blessed Virgin Mary. He made certain that they each possessed a beauty in "majesty and simplicity," for each had a regal beauty that was simple and pure. Each woman can not be said to fully represent Our Lady, yet they each had a specific attribute of the Blessed Virgin Mary.

In the end, these women reflect the incomparable beauty of the "Fairest Daughter of the Father" and beckon us to call upon her in our need for she is also our Mother.[201]

Varda or Elbereth, the Queen of the Stars, in Tolkien's legendarium has also been identified as having resonance with the Blessed Virgin Mary.[202] More generally, in an essay in *Parabola*, Tracy Cochran wrote:

The late Lex Hixon, Sufi teacher and author, saw the American Marian phenomenon as an interplay of disparate social and spiritual causes. On the one hand, it expresses a conservative apocalyptic movement. On the other, our rationalistic bias against mystical experience, what he called "living water, a kind

---

[201] Philip Kosloski, "4 Women in Tolkien's Middle-Earth who reflect the beauty of the Virgin Mary," *Voyage Comics & Publishing*, March 22, 2019. On-line at: <https://voyagecomics.com/2019/03/22/4-women-in-middle-earth-who-reflect-the-beauty-of-the-virgin-mary/> (Accessed 6/15/2019). See also Mahmoud Shelton, *Alchemy in Middle-earth: The Significance of J. R. R. Tolkien's The Lord of the Rings* (Temple of Justice Books, 2002), p. 78, where the author writes: "Like the Philosopher's Stone and the legendary Grail, the veneration of the Virgin Mary belongs both to Christianity and Islam. Indeed, the Cult of the Virgin only came to dominate Catholicism with the Age of Chivalry, which is the age of encounter with Islam that likewise produced the Grail legends. As Tolkien himself admitted, perhaps the clearest expression of Catholic religiosity in his work is the example of the Elven Lady Galadriel. Although very little explicitly identifies Galadriel with the Virgin Mary, there can be little doubt that both in the love and devotion she inspires as well as in her intercessionary role, the 'White Lady' appears in the image of the Virgin. Concerning the alchemical work, the stage called the 'whitening' is particularly associated in Christendom with the Blessed Virgin."
[202] See Farid Mohammadi, "In search of the Holy Presence of the Blessed Mary in Tolkien's Middle-earth," *International Journal of Applied Linguistics & English Literature*, Vol. 2 No. 4; July 2013, pp. 200-211. On-line at: < http://www.journals.aiac.org.au/index.php/IJALEL/article/view/998> (Accessed 11/3/2019)

of stream of higher intelligence," is beginning to erode. "In the old days," he told me, "in villages like Garabandal and Lourdes, apparitions would arise because there was a kind of spiritual openness or atmosphere of faith that would allow these underground springs to come up. In modern culture, we've laid a kind of parking lot over all of that, even inside our religious congregations. Lately, the parking lot has been dissolving because there's uncertainty all over the world, and these things are rising up again. Of course, we can't discount the role of the mass media in publicizing these events, but something much deeper is happening as well."[203]

It is to this "something much deeper" that readers of this book are encouraged to attune. This concerns the realm of the *imaginal*.[204] What follows is not so much *about* the Blessed Virgin Mary as it is about seeing the presentations of our life as occurring under the *omophorion* or protection of the Blessed Virgin Mary.[205] The Age to come—and whose premonitions are already occurring—is the Age of the Blessed Virgin Mary.[206]

The New Epoch

There are various ways of describing or characterizing the Age to come or the drawing near of the Kingdom of Heaven. We are likely acquainted with expressions having currency in popular culture, such as the "New Age" or the coming "Age of Aquarius." The Age of Bles-

---

[203] Tracy Cochran, "Queen of Angels," *Parabola*, April 30, 2015. On-line at: <https://parabola.org/2015/04/30/queen-of-angels/> (Accessed 6/14/2019)

[204] The realm of the imaginal is not unrelated to what is meant by "waking dream" as used by the kabbalist of light, Colete Aboulker-Muscat (d. 2005), in Jerusalem, and her students.

[205] See the painting of the Blessed Virgin Mary as protector at: <http://www.pravmir.com/the-theotokos-protects-all-equally/> (Accessed 6/15/2019)

[206] Consider the history of the movement, within Roman Catholicism, on behalf of a promulgation by the Vatican magisterium of a "fifth Marian dogma." For this history, see, for example, Gloria Falcão Dodd (University of Dayton), *The Virgin Mary, Mediatrix of All Grace: History and Theology of the Movement for a Dogmatic Definition from 1896 to 1964* (New Bedford, Massachusetts: Academy of the Immaculate, Franciscans of the Immaculate, 2009, 2012).

sedness in Planet Earth does not arrive except following on times of crisis, such as the times in which we are currently living—times in which some choose to head for the (human) exits.[207] The Bulgarian philosopher and spiritual teacher, Beinsa Douno (Peter Deunov) (d. 1944), spoke of a "New Epoch" on this planet. Among his followers and in associated literature he was often referred to as "the Master." As he often did, he spoke in response to questions that were asked. The experiential background of this teaching is Bulgaria in the aftermath of World War II:

> The world was in darkness. Humankind was caught in the madness of destruction. One could not find a way out, nor could a light be seen. Anxiety filled the hearts of all; uncertainty was pervasive. In such moments, the Master possessed the ability to bring peace and to inspire faith. He revealed opportunities for a bright future, describing the image of renewed, reborn, and enlightened humankind. A question about the coming new epoch was asked. The Master said:
>
> Our Solar System will depart from heavier matter and enter into a less dense medium. Because of this, there will exist conditions for the manifestation of a higher consciousness for humankind. The Solar System departs from the so-called "13th sphere." At the same time, the Sun will enter the Age of Aquarius. Now is the end of the dark epoch, the Kali Yuga. Because the Earth is entering a new realm, all the old forms will change. New forms will destroy the old ones. People will not notice how they will grow and become new people. Old forms will fall away as do the leaves in autumn. In the place of the "old" people, new ones will come with new ideas.

---

[207] See discussion of the possibility and the actuality of the human exit in the work of the contemporary Russian philosopher, Sergey S. Horujy, and in my book, *The Anthropocosmic Vision: For a New Dialogic Civilization*, a Perennials Study Group publication, Memphis, Tennessee (CreateSpace / Kindle Direct Publishing, 2017). As an illustration of the human exit, consider the prevalence of zombies as a theme in recent popular films. For the psychoanalytic implications of this phenomenon, see discussion by Professor John Vervaeke (University of Toronto) on-line at: <https://youtu.be/iSwAbQD-gZU> (Accessed 8/31/2019)

The Earth, after making many millions of rotations, makes one exception from its usual rotation. This departure is occurring today.

New organs are forming in the human brain for the human beings of the future. Until they are formed, many things will remain unexplained. When a great artist begins to paint a painting, is it possible for the beauty of it to emerge immediately? No. On the first day, he will only dash colors on the canvas with a brush. Even if we do not like the painting, he would only smile. On the second day, you will see that the painting is in the same state. The artist will tell you, "Do not hurry with your judgment. When I finish the painting, then you can express your opinion." You hurry to express your opinion about Life now, but Life is not yet finished.

A sister asked, "Master, when will the time come when everything will become clear to us?"

We are now in this time. Today, the world comes to a specific stage, a stage of transformations that will become its new principles of organization. Today a new type of human being, a new generation of Love, is being formed.

God leaves to people the free will to arrange the small things, yet the big ones He arranges by Himself. The contemporary epoch is one of the birth of the human being of Love.

Every new epoch begins with a new rhythm. Today a new rhythm to Life comes. The Divine makes its way everywhere. The Wave, which is coming now, will elevate not only us, but all minerals, plants, and animals as well. Those who cannot be uplifted by this Wave will remain for the future. Remember: There will be no other Wave such as this because in Nature there is no repetition of phenomena. If you wait until the future, the conditions will be more difficult then.

A New Knowledge, a New Culture is coming into the world. I call it: the Culture of Divine Love, Wisdom, and Truth. It will teach people how to live.

The old life is suffering, but the new, joy. The roots are the old life, and the branches the new one. Today we are at the end of the deprivation of Love and at the beginning of Divine, unconditional Love.

Who awakens the human being? That one who is taking care of him. The mother awakens the child. This shows that

142

she is taking care of her infant. God is the Watcher for humans, which shows that He is taking care of them.

Those who do not awaken during the modern epoch will be left for other times. We wonder what will happen to those people who are not able to accept the Divine. The issue is clear. I come to a fruit tree and collect the ripe fruit, and for the others, I will wait. When they ripen, I will pick them as well, and the bad fruit I will use as fertilizer. Afterward, they will become beautiful fruits as well. You ask, "Why is it so?" Because it is not possible to be otherwise.

It is said in the Scriptures, "Search for Me until I am close." (See also Jeremiah 29:13, "And you will seek Me and find Me, when you search for Me with all your heart.") This means: use the favorable conditions until I am close to you. If people were to be surprised by what the future is bringing to them, this surprise would deprive them of the opportunity to make use of the Good that is coming. Therefore, in order to make use of the conditions of Life, one needs to possess the knowledge that brings peace into one's soul. Ignorance fills people with worry. Today the New is coming into the world everywhere. What is the New? In what form it will manifest that can be understood only by a few? A new cycle is being formed. Those who can enter into it will find before themselves great opportunities. If you are not ready, then you will miss the favorable conditions. The Divine is coming into the world.

Today is a most dangerous time. You could fall asleep and remain on the outside. The Divine Train is very punctual! You may be late by only a second. Therefore, your consciousness, your heart, and your mind need to be vigilant. The one who has lived for thousands and millions of years on the Earth and has been through so much suffering—does that person want to miss this moment, to miss the Train and not receive the Divine? If God finds you vigilant when He comes to you, you will grow up like the seed; you will develop and will give fruit.

The day has two halves. One is when the Sun is rising, and the second is when the Sun is setting. Until noon, we have ascent; and in the afternoon, descent. The Law is the same with relation to this epoch. The current epoch is in descent and this cannot be stopped. The forces of darkness are leaving. The Good will come exactly at the determined time, just as the spring comes at its time. When Spring comes, everything blossoms. The same will happen with the coming of the Divine.

An illuminated epoch is coming. The idea of brotherhood will come into realization. This Divine Spring will come gradually, not all at once. People will change without noticing. They simply will not notice how they will change. One day they will awaken, and they will find themselves in a new stage similar to the caterpillar, which enfolds into the cocoon, and, once inside, transforms itself into a butterfly that cannot feed on leaves any more. What is coming now can be called "Manifestation of the Divine Origin in the human being." The new generation that is coming will renew the world. This means that we are in the epoch when the caterpillars will transform into butterflies. Those caterpillars that did not become butterflies yet will ask how one can live in the air. When they become butterflies, then they will learn. As caterpillars, they cannot learn.

Today life is more active. Years ago infants could open their eyes not earlier than three weeks after birth. But today, they open their eyes the moment they are born. This exists everywhere, in every nation.

Humble people will put the world in order. Who are the humble? Once two people went to court. The son of one of them came and told his father, "Father, we do not need that for which you are in court. Let's forget and forgive." This son was considered unassertive, but he stopped the trial.[208]

---

[208] From Beinsa Douno, *The Wellspring of Good: The Last Words of the Master* (Sofia, Bulgaria: Bialo Bratstvo Publishers, 2013), pp. 292-296 on "The New Epoch." On-line at: <http://petardanov.info/Knigi/Wellspring_of_Good.pdf> (Accessed 8/31/2019). Harrie Salman, in his Preface to that book, wrote: "Very significantly, Peter Deunov discovered two small wellsprings on the slope in front of the house where he was staying. One of them he named, 'The Wellspring of Good,' and the other, 'The Wellspring of Health.' Together with his disciples he built basins for the water and made paths to them. These sacred acts of making the 'living water' available to human beings had a deep symbolic meaning as well. The Teaching that he brought from the School of the Great Universal Brotherhood is a Wellspring of the new spiritual Life." Note also the synchronicity of the word, "Wellspring," with overall theme of this present book.

The Faith in its fullness entails confidence in the manifestation, in time, on this our planet Earth, of the New Epoch. It is the manifestation, the "drawing near" of the Kingdom and it is experienced most profoundly as a Marian Age. Here is one description of the main elements of contemporary Marian spirituality as seen from the perspective of a Roman Catholic scholar:

- Its strong *iconic* character, i.e. devotion, identification with the Marian image from icons to medals and scapulars as expression of personal and visual contact.

- A strong *narrative* dimension which takes us to Mary as in pilgrimmages to Marian sanctuaries or with her into the commemoration of our salvation history as in the prayers of the rosary and angelus.

- A *mystagogical* development, meaning the growing importance of entrustment to Mary in acts of consecration in order for her to lead us closer to Jesus (Eucharist) or to associate us to her own mission. Not to forget a resurgence of intercessory devotions.[209]

The implications of this are varied. Some perceive it as a "New Pentecost."[210] In this context, at least one contemporary commentator has referred to the Virgin Mary as a "New Gideon."[211] Manifestation, it should be noted, is intimately connected with (and entails) perception. Perception, in turn, depends upon our having "eyes to see" and "ears to hear." Perception of the arriving Kingdom—experience of living in an Age of Mary—depends upon who we are. Perception of Paradise (Paradise-Consciousness) is a matter of whether or not we have allowed ourselves to become People of Paradise! As at the Wedding at Cana, to hear and to follow the instructions of the Blessed

---

[209] Fr. Johann Roten, S.M. (International Marian Research Institute, University of Dayton) in undated Q&A on the Age of Mary. On-line at: <https://udayton.edu/imri/mary/a/age-of-mary.php> (Accessed 1/3/2020)

[210] This descriptive expression was particularly associated by Pope John XXIII with his hopes for the Second Vatican Council and its potential.

[211] This expression was used by Mark Mallett in reference to the Virgin Mary in an essay, "The New Gideon," published at his website on August 22, 2017. On-line at: <https://www.markmallett.com/blog/2017/08/22/the-new-gideon/> (Accessed 10/31/2019)

Virgin is to experience the festival of Paradise.[212] The martyred Fr. Alexander Men (d. 1990) said, "We are moving into an age of Love." These words of Fr. Men are cited by the iconologist, Irina Yazikova, in her 2005 essay on Fr. Men. Here are a few sentences from her essay that suggest what Fr. Men may have meant by his words:

> Fr. Alexander often repeated that the Gospel has not yet been fully read or understood by mankind, since history is full of wars, revolutions, catastrophes. Each person must discover Christ and believe that God is Love. And when the Good News enters his heart, he will look at the world, at people, and his mission in the world with different eyes. And if this happens, then evil, hatred, conflicts will disappear from the world of man. Love teaches us to look on the other as a part of ourselves. Mankind is one, and therefore every enmity against the other is waged against us as well. Christ came in order to put an end to this chain reaction of hatred, in order to teach people to love. "We are moving to an age of Love," said Fr. Alexander Men. His entire life was a powerful striving to it and a witnessing to that fact, that already here on earth man can realize in complete fullness God's plan, and to make near the Kingdom of Heaven.[213]

Among Russian Old Believers there is the legend of Belovodia—sometimes associated with Kitezh and sometimes with Shambhala—an actual physical place on Planet Earth where the New Epoch timelessly manifests.[214]

---

[212] The phrase "festival of Paradise" appears in Canto XIV of Dante's *Paradiso*. A similar phrase, "festival of the Kingdom," appears in Allchin, *The Joy of All Creation*, previously cited, at p. 64.

[213] From Irina Yazikova, "We are Moving into an Age of Love" (2005), an essay uploaded to the Alexander Men website at: <http://www.alexandermen.com/We_are_Moving_into_an_Age_of_Love> (Accessed 11/7/2019). The author/translator might have chosen to use inclusive language with no change to the meaning.

[214] Reference to Belovodia can be found in Stefanie Scherr, "'As Soon As We Got Here We Lost Everything:' The Migration Memories and Religious Lives of the Old Believers in Australia," Ph.D. dissertation, Swinburne University of Technology (Australia), 2013. On-line at: <https://pdfs.semanticscholar.org/

To consider this from a different perspective, we might make reference to the divine-humanity.[215] In other words, a new age or epoch requires a new people—or requires that we be different, in some way, than we currently are. This difference has been articulated in various ways. Rudolf Steiner (d. 1925), for example, referred to a "sixth race" to be identified with its spiritual character rather than its physical characteristics. Similarly, some years later, the Bulgarian teacher, Beinsa Douno, referred to above, also used this expression which his editors have felt required some explanation:

Another sensitive issue which may lead to misunderstandings of the word of Beinsa Douno is related to the word "race" mentioned in different contexts. This word was widely used at the time as a classification system that categorizes humans in large and distinct populations or groups. Although the term is still used today it is often replaced by other words which are less questionable.

According to the Master so far there have been five stages (or races) in human civilization. The Master explained that at any of those stages each distinct group of people was characterized by certain qualities. He believed that the "sixth stage," which he called the "new epoch of Love," was approaching and that it will include advanced people from all nations, races, ethnical, and social groups. He called the people of that new epoch of Love the "sixth race."

We replaced, when possible, the word "race" by another word. However, in some passages this was difficult without

---

f02f/4e47846fab69ca65bfb69d52b6221108ed17.pdf> (Accessed 12/29/2019). Reference to Belovodia also appears in Olga Kharitidi, *Entering the Circle: Ancient Secrets of Siberian Wisdom Discovered by a Russian Psychiatrist* (New York: HarperCollins/HarperSanFrancisco, 1997).

215 Humanity as a single entity permeated with (or transparent to) the divine energies has been a central concern of modern Russian (Orthodox) spiritual writing. This concern is also reflected in my three previous books—*From Glory to Glory: The Sophianic Vision of Fr. Sergius Bulgakov* (2016); *The Anthropo-cosmic Vision: For a New Dialogic Civilization* (2017); and *Taliesin's Harp: A Poetics of the Divine-Humanity* (2019).

changing the meaning of the Master's message which always focuses on uniting all human beings in Love.[216]

Whether one uses the term, "sixth race," or as I prefer, the "divine-humanity," in either case the Blessed Virgin Mary is at the head of this new people in their self-understanding.[217] This is the content of our hope for future generations, however dire empirical present trends may be. Prior to the horrors of the September 11, 2001, attacks and all that followed in their aftermath, Pope John Paul II included the following language in his speech to the United Nations in October 1995:

> We must *overcome our fear of the future. But we will not be able to overcome it completely unless we do so together.* The "answer" to that fear is neither coercion nor repression, nor the imposition of one social "model" on the entire world. The answer to the fear which darkens human existence at the end of the twentieth century is the common effort to build the civilization of love, founded on the universal values of peace, solidarity, justice, and liberty. And the "soul" of the civilization of love is the culture of freedom: the freedom of individuals and the freedom of nations, lived in self-giving solidarity and responsibility.
>
> *We must not be afraid of the future. We must not be afraid of man.* It is no accident that we are here. Each and every human person has been created in the "image and likeness" of the One who is the origin of all that is. We have within us the capacities for wisdom and virtue. With these gifts, and with the help of God's grace, we can build in the next century and the next

---

[216] From the Explanatory Notes to the book, *The Wellspring of Good,* p. 12, previously cited.

[217] Nemanja Radulović writes that, according to the self-understanding (emic history) of one strand of contemporary neo-Bogomilism, "… Bogomilism is of hyperborean origin, five billion years old, representing the Ur-religion of mankind; it is universal spirituality which can unify religions under the guidance of the Virgin Mary." From N. Radulović, "The Question of Neo-Bogomilism" in *Ways of Gnosis. Mystical and Esoteric Traditions and Gnostic Worldview from Antiquity to the Present Time,* edited by Sergey V. Pahomov and Anna A. Tesman, 169–184. St. Petersburg: Russian Christian Academy for Humanities, 2013. On-line at: <https://www.academia.edu/9844763/The_Question_of_ Neobogomilism> (Accessed 9/1/2019)

millennium a civilization worthy of the human person, a true culture of freedom. *We can and must do so!* And in doing so, we shall see that the tears of this century have prepared the ground for a new springtime of the human spirit.[218]

It is this confidence within humankind that enables us to grieve at what is passing away and irretrievably lost while at the same time confident in the power and love God that brings all things to their destined end in the most beautiful ways that we can neither imagine nor comprehend. We are invited to attune to and cooperate with that.[219] As the Psalmist writes: "Put not your trust in rulers, nor in any child of earth, for there is no help in them. When they breathe their last, they return to earth, and in that day their thoughts perish." (Psalm 146:2-3, *Book of Common Prayer*) Instead, the divine-humanity puts its trust in heaven, wherein there is Life-everlasting.

9. A Coherent Life Ethic

To serve Mary and to be her courtier is the greatest honor one can possibly possess, for to serve the Queen of Heaven is already to reign there, and to live under her commands is more than to govern.
— St. John of Damascus[220]

For many persons, the notion of hierarchy is suspect because they imagine a tendency toward government by compulsion. The above apothegem of St. John of Damascus, however, suggests a different

---

[218] Address of His Holiness John Paul II to the Fiftieth General Assembly of the United Nations Organization at the United National Headquarters (New York), Thursday, October 5, 1995. On-line at: <https://w2.vatican.va/content/john-paul-ii/en/speeches/1995/october/documents/hf_jp-ii_spe_05101995_address-to-uno.html> (Accessed 10/15/2019)

[219] For both the poignancy and the potential of the present crisis, see Llewellyn Vaughan-Lee, *Darkening of the Light: Witnessing the End of an Era* (Point Reyes, California: The Golden Sufi Center, 2013) and Mary Evelyn Tucker and John Grim, editors, *Living Cosmology: Christian Responses to Journey of the Universe* (Maryknoll, New York: Orbis Books, 2016).

[220] As quoted in Jill Haak Adels, *The Wisdom of the Saints: An Anthology* (Oxford, UK: Oxford University Press, 1987), p. 21. John of Damascus is understood to have lived and breathed the spirituality of St. Dionysius the Areopagite.

situation, a paradox—to serve is to reign. Hierarchy, in Christian tradition stemming from St. Dionysius the Areopagite (late fifth to early sixth century) in which St. John of Damascus stands, however, exhibits this paradox. According to a contemporary interpreter of St. Dionysius, Georgia J. Williams (Th.M. student, Holy Cross Greek Orthodox School of Theology), hierarchy of this type has a "fractal" character. She writes:

> Now because fractals are mid-points between randomness and predictability, because they incorporate a degree of freedom, and because of the intense and dynamic interrelationships between fractal levels, fractal becomes an appealing word to use to refer to Dionysian hierarchy, which seems to have all these elements and to be "built" of moments of relationship that constitute instances of creative power being released. There is a recurring image used by Dionysius, that of the mirror. Creatures assimilated to the life of God—who are living according the shape of the life of God—are "spotless mirrors." Light reflected in one mirror is immediately magnified in a host of other mirrors throughout the multi-dimensional, vital organism that is reality, and in this way we truly create and are truly co-workers (*synergoi*) with God himself.
>
> By this description it begins to look as if participation in hierarchy is the beginning of empowerment for anything and everything, independent of level. I am struck by the fashion in which such a picture could explain the effectiveness of prayer, or the effect of *mitzvah*—of doing the commandment of God. [Eric D.] Perl says, for instance, that in hierarchy as conceived of by Dionysius "every being has an active role not only in its own production, but in the production of all things."[221]

If reality itself is constituted in this way as hierarchies—"mid-points between randomness and predictability"—then service to the Queen of Heaven puts all things in order. As St. John of Damascus said: "… to live under her commands is more than to govern." As a life ethic, this

---

[221] Georgia J. Williams, "An Exploration of Hierarchy as Fractal in the Theology of Dionysios the Areopagite," in *Power and Authority in the Eastern Christian Experience: Papers of the Sophia Institute Academic Conference, New York, December 2010* (New York: Theotokos Press, 2011), pp. 110-111, pp. 103-118.

is consistent only in that one journeys through life consistently listening for the divine guidance.

Teach me to go to the country beyond words and beyond names.
— Thomas Merton[222]

If we are able to move through life beyond words and beyond names it is because we give priority to relationships that make for community and because we have begun to bring our mind (our ways or styles of thinking) into relationship with our heart. A "consistent life ethic" is possible only to the extent that our heart is attuned to the divine world and its guidance. Hearts attuned in this way may begin to see the broad implications of a commitment to compassion—implications, for example, in our food practices that now become vegetarian, without question. We begin to see that a commitment to compassion includes compassion for our fellow-creatures of the animal kingdom.[223]

In the history of the evolution of human consciousness (as self-awareness), we are moving toward what Owen Barfield termed "Final Participation." What Final Participation may signify, for our purposes, is the manifestation of wisdom, but it is wisdom of a certain kind. It is virtue wisdom as opposed to law-based or rule-based wisdom. This is wisdom as practical intelligence. It is sometimes called "practical wisdom." There is a fearless playfulness and freedom about it.[224]

In considering the topic of a "coherent life ethic" we may be led to reflect on the larger contexts in which we may find ourselves. One of

---

[222] For a good summary of Fr. Thomas Merton's appreciation of the Blessed Virgin Mary, see Kenneth M. Voiles, "The Mother of All the Living: The Role of the Virgin Mary in the Spirituality of Thomas Merton," *The Merton Annual*, Volume 5, 1992, pp. 297-310. On-line at:
<http://merton.org/ITMS/Annual/5/Voiles297-310.pdf> (Accessed 9/15/2019)

[223] For resources on the rationale for a Christian vegetarian practice, see the work of Charles Camosy, Ph.D., Associate Professor, Christian Ethics, Fordham University, Bronx, New York. His books include *For Love of Animals: Christian Ethics, Consistent Action* (Cincinnati, Ohio: Franciscan Media, 2013). See, also, relevant videos at: <https://www.charlescamosy.com/ask-charlie-anything> (Accessed 11/27/2019)

[224] See psychotherapist, Mark Vernon, video, "John Vervaeke, Romanticism & Owen Barfield," where he discusses Owen Barfield and Final Participation. On-line at: <https://youtu.be/GQQ7Qb30TS4> (Accessed 8/23/2019)

these contexts may reveal itself as the unholy and heretical trinity of Capital-Nation-State.[225] We may come to understand that borders are meant to be permeable. Consider the significance of the obstacles to travel along the Central and Eastern European pilgrim routes caused by impermeable state borders. We will have more to say about pilgrimage further below.

A coherent life ethic, in this context, is nothing other than harmonizing, in all that we are and in all that we do, with the appealing beauty of the intra-divine life of the Trinitarian Council—the Holy Trinity. This is Sophianic life. Orthodox lay theologian, Paul Evdokimov (d. 1970), wrote: "King Midas turned everything he touched into gold. A Christian by his inner attitude can made all things transparent, can transform them into icons, images of their truth. Style, once it has become an authentic spiritual category, will become more naturally efficacious than sermons."[226] As we are drawn into the all-pervasive life of the Holy Trinity we may come to a realization that God's Mercy does not negate God's Justice with respect to ourselves. In this realization, our fear of suffering may be overcome. The Christian faith becomes more a way of living, a way of journeying through the world, than a set of rituals or beliefs or even a way of envisioning the world.

Finding One's Own Personal Rhythm (Rule)

Learning to blend or harmonize with the rhythms of the days, months, years of our life and with the rhythms of our various relationships and communities is the intention embedded in any vaiable Rule of life. Here is how the previously mentioned Italian mystic, Luisa Piccarreta, commends that we seek to begin each day in conformity with the Divine Will for us:

How to Begin the Day in the Divine Will

Thus let us make all our being rise in the light of the Will of God and let us begin our rounds.

---

[225] For some discussion of this shadow trinity, see Gil Anidjar, *Blood: A Critique of Christianity* (New York: Columbia University Press, 2014), where he cites the work of Kojin Karatani.
[226] Paul Evdokimov, "Message aux Eglises" (1950), *L'Amour fou de Dieu* (Paris: Seuil, 1973), p. 172.

The first act must be an act of love in The Divine Will. Let us make this act diffuse into all the intelligences of creatures, in all glances, in the words, in the movements, in the steps, in the heartbeats and in each breath. Let us then tie all our acts to the last one done by Adam in the Holy Will of God. Let us also tie all our acts to the acts which the creatures who will live in the Will of God will do unto that last one that will be completed upon the earth.

Let us then elevate ourselves a little higher in the creation. For the love of the creature, God has created the sun, the stars, the sea, the earth, the birds, the flowers; and we take all this love spread in the Creation. Let us make it ours and offer it to our Creator as so many other acts of homage, of love, of blessings and of praise. And now let us go higher, up there in Paradise; let us make our rounds for all the Angels and for the Saints; let us unite ourselves to all the heavenly Court and for each and every one let us give an act of love to Jesus.

Let us then draw near to the Blessed Virgin, to our dear mother. She is ready to make a gift to us of all her merits; and we, with the confidence of children, let us take that which She has done from the first instant of her Conception to the last breath; and, as if all were ours, let us offer it to our God as the most beautiful act.

And then, let us go to the Word, and let us ask Him to make us partakers of all His acts: His Conception, His Birth, His escape into Egypt, the thirty years of His hidden life, the years of His public life, His Passion, His Death and His Ascension to Heaven; He did all this for us. Let us make it ours and offer it to the Sacrosanct Trinity. Only thus, as miserable creatures that we are, can we offer Him an act, the most complete and most holy, because in such a way the creature does not give anything of his own, but returns to God all the Glory that is his due from that which He Himself has done.[227]

---

[227] From "A Prayerlife in The Divine Mercy and Will of God," Divine Mercy Apostolate for Cardiff and South Wales, 2006, p. 30. On-line at: <https://irp-cdn.multiscreensite.com/7827db40/files/uploaded/

In the British Isles, the Benedictine and the Celtic are blended traditions. In Benedictine life, particularly, there are rhythms of prayer and work—both together and alone. If and when in the course of one's life there forms a desire to develop some kind of personal "Rule," in this context it is simply a matter of finding ways to become aware (and to remain aware) of the seasonal and daily rhythms of nature and of monastic life and to harmonize with these rhythms.

Consider the image of the Virgin Mary as engaged in the art and craft of spinning.[228] Allow this and other sacred images, from scripture and from nature, to do their work. The Celtic Christian tradition is particularly rich in verbal and craft images. Faith and reason in this tradition relate playfully to one another.[229] John O'Donohue is a valuable teacher about the reality and the spiritual significance of beauty. Beauty's reality and spiritual significance, which connects us with these rhythms, may be revealed, over time, in silence, in our practice of meditation. For O'Donohue, dedication to the threshold where silence becomes language is the mark of the poet. Orthodox lay theologian and historian, Olivier Clément (d. 2009), for example, was both a poet and a friend of poets (Pierre Emmanuel). John Butler, English poet and organic farmer, writes:

> This blessed practice of meditation, which I owe so much to really, gradually, gradually, gradually—it's, you know, meditation works because it's sometimes described like following a trail of grains of sugar, you know. It works because it leads you to something that we recognize as preferable. It's like this trail

Divine%2BMercy%2BPrayer%2BBook-2.pdf> (Accessed 1/1/2020). A slightly different translation from the Italian can be found in John Kirby, "Will and Reconciling Our Evolution," *DuVersity 45*, Spring 2018, p. 9. On-line at: <https://www.duversity.org/sites/default/files/files/DuVersity%2045%20%20%20%20%20%20%20%20%20%20%20%20%20%20Spring%202018.pdf> (Accessed 1/1/2020)

[228] See Florentina Badalanova Geller, "The Spinning Mary: Towards the Iconology of the Annunciation," *Cosmos: The Journal of the Traditional Cosmology Society*, Volume 20, 2004, pp. 211-260. On-line at: <https://thisisthetcson.files.wordpress.com/2016/07/cosmos-20.pdf> (Accessed 8/12/2019)

[229] As argued by John Milbank in his *Theology and Social Theory: Beyond Secular Reason*, second edition (Malden, Massachusetts: Blackwell Publishing, 2006, 1990), modern violence can be understood as having its source in the non-recognition of the interplay between faith and reason.

of sweetness which leads you grain by grain over this long trail, like an ant following this trail of grains of sugar. So you don't need anyone to tell you, really, because once you get this first taste of sugar in your mouth you follow that and, eventually, one day, you come to the sugar mountain. You draw nearer it. And then, Oh, ... the idea of a world without it just evaporates; it no longer exists, because, you know, you found out something better.[230]

Commitment to this practice of meditation helps us to discern the divine rhythms to which we seek to attune our lives in our personal rhythm or rule. This is, implicitly if not explicitly, a Marian spirituality. It can be noted, however, that "[a] characteristic mark of the Saints, who are the real members of the Body of Christ, is that they love the Virgin Mary. It is impossible for there to be a Saint who does not love her."[231] The divine Beauty draws persons toward their own particular type of sanctity. It has been suggested that there are types of Christian piety that vary according to one's understanding of the Church: "Ark of Salvation" for zealots/ascetics, "Body of Christ" for the proselytes/ missionaries, "Temple of the Holy Spirit" for the spirituals, "Father's house," for the protestors.[232] Successful and healthy communities find

---

[230] John Butler, *Lanzarote Tapes #4*, at 22:40 in and following. On-line at: <https://youtu.be/UYnj70LWzxA> (Accessed 11/21/2019)

[231] Metropolitan Hierotheos (Vlachos) of Nafpaktos, "The Annunciation of the Virgin Mary," Orthodox Research Institute website. On-line at: <http://www.orthodoxresearchinstitute.org/articles/fasts_feasts/hierotheos_vlachos_annunciation.htm> (Accessed 11/23/2019)

[232] This schema, in its general outline, is from Antoine Arjakovsky, "The Limits of Ecclesiology of Faith and Order: Rethinking in a Postdenominational Way the Foundations Given by K. Barth and G. Florovsky," Chapter 2 in Ashley John Moyse, Scott A. Kirkland, and John C. McDowell, editors, *Correlating Sobornost: Conversations Between Karl Barth and Russian Orthodox Tradition* (Minneapolis, Minnesota: Fortress Press, 2016), p. 52. Arjakovsky, at this same place, also states that it is his view that "... boundaries between Christians are of an anthropological, more than dogmatic, order." This schema receives more extensive discussion in the section on "Three forms of anthropological consciousness" in Chapter 3 of Antoine Arjakovsky, *What is Orthodoxy: A Genealogy of Christian Understanding* (Brooklyn, New York: Angelico Press, 2018), p. 61 ff., and most succinctly at p. 75. Similar schemas can be

ways, over the long term, to accommodate all these various types of Christian piety.[233]

> In the last days it will be, God declares, that I will pour out my Spirit upon all flesh, and your sons and your daughters shall prophesy, and your young men shall see visions, and your old men shall dream dreams. Even upon my slaves, both men and women, in those days I will pour out my Spirit; and they shall prophesy. And I will show portents in the heaven above and signs on the earth below, blood, and fire, and smoky mist. The sun shall be turned to darkness and the moon to blood, before the coming of the Lord's great and glorious day. Then everyone who calls on the name of the Lord shall be saved.
> — *The Acts of the Apostles*, 2:17-21

St. Mechtilde of Hackeborn (d. 1299), a Benedictine nun of the convent of Helfta, experienced three visions of the Virgin Mary. The Virgin asked Mechtilde to "recite three Hail Marys every day, remembering in the first the Power received from the Eternal Father, in the second the Wisdom received from the Son, with the third one the Love that has filled the Holy Spirit." St. Mechtilde was famous for her musical abilities. The Hail Mary prayers simply and unobtrusively fit with the rhythms of the day.

---

found in, for example, Rufus M. Jones, *Studies in Mysitical Religion* (London: Macmillan & Co., Ltd., 1909), on-line at: <http://www.iapsop.com/ ssoc/1909__jones___studies_in_mystical_religion.pdf> (Accessed 11/23/2019); and in Jim Forest's article, "Christian Types, Christian Virtues, Christian Unity: The Evangelical Path to Christian Unity" *Touchstone Magazine*, May/June 1999, on-line at: <https://www.touchstonemag. com/archives/ article.php?id=12-03-031-f> (Accessed 11/23/2019)

[233] The Villages of God initiative of Ray Simpson, Founding Guardian of the Community of Aidan and Hilda in Britain, could be an example of this. See Ray Simpson's discussion of this in several of his publications: in Chapters 7 and 8 of *Church of the Isles: a prophetic strategy for the emerging church in Britain and Ireland*; in Chapter 5 of *High Street Monasteries*; in Chapter 5 of *St. Aidan's Way of Mission: celtic insights for a post-Christian world*, in *Emerging Down Under: creating new monastic villages of God* with Brent Lyons Lee (ATF Press).

Rosary - Garland of Roses

In Marian spirituality, especially in the West, the rosary has played a significant role. According to the *New Advent Catholic Encyclopedia*:

> As regards the origin of the name, the word *rosarius* means a garland or bouquet of roses, and it was not infrequently used in a figurative sense—e.g. as the title of a book, to denote an anthology or collection of extracts. An early legend which after travelling all over Europe penetrated even to Abyssinia connected this name with a story of Our Lady, who was seen to take rosebuds from the lips of a young monk when he was reciting Hail Marys and to weave them into a garland which she placed upon her head. A German metrical version of this story is still extant dating from the thirteenth century. The name "Our Lady's Psalter" can also be traced back to the same period. *Corona* or *chaplet* suggests the same idea as *rosarium*. The old English name found in Chaucer and elsewhere was a "pair of beads," in which the word *bead* originally meant *prayers*.[234]

Here is a fuller telling of the legend referred to above. It is a late thirteenth century legend about the origin of the rosary, in Latin, Catalan and German versions:

> A young boy had the daily practice of making a chaplet [or wreath] of roses, or whatever flower he could find according to the season, and placing it on the head of a statue of Our Lady. He did this with great joy and pious devotion. The Virgin saw the good intention of his heart, and wanting to help him further it, gave him the desire to take up the religious life. And so he became a lay brother in a cloister. But in the cloister he was given so many tasks to perform that he no longer had time to make Mary her chaplet as he was accustomed to do. For this reason, he became dissatisfied. He was about to leave the order and return to the world, when an older priest became aware of

---

[234] Herbert Thurston and Andrew Shipman, "The Rosary," *New Advent Catholic Encyclopedia*, Volume 13. (New York: Robert Appleton Company, 1912). Online at: <http://www.newadvent.org/cathen/13184b.htm> (Accessed 11/26/2019)

his distress. The priest wisely advised him that he should recite each day fifty Ave Marias in place of the chaplet and convinced him that the Virgin Mary would prefer that to all the rose chaplets that were ever made. The boy followed the advice and continued in it for some time.

Then one day he was sent on an errand that required him to ride through a forest that harbored thieves. In the forest he tied his horse to a tree, knelt down and was reciting his fifty Ave Marias when thieves saw him and decided to rob him and steal his horse. But as they approached him, they saw from a distance a wonderfully beautiful maiden standing by him who, every little while, took from his mouth a beautiful rose and added it to a garland that she was making. When the rose chaplet was complete, she placed it on her head and flew off to Heaven. The robbers were thoroughly amazed and ran to the boy asking him who the beautiful maiden was that they had seen beside him. The boy replied: "I did not have any maiden with me. I have only been reciting fifty Ave Marias as a chaplet for Queen Mary, as I was instructed. That is all I know." When the robbers told him what they had seen, the boy and the robbers too realized that it was the Holy Mother of God who, in person, had accepted the rose chaplet that he was accustomed to send to her daily through our angel.

Then the boy rejoiced from the depths of his heart, and from that day forward, made a spiritual rose chaplet of fifty Ave Marias for Queen Mary daily and instructed other good people in the practice. In this manner the rosary was created and made known to us. And one may believe that the robbers bettered their lives as a result, because God's grace had permitted them to behold the Mother of Mercy.[235]

---

[235] From "Rosary: History of the Term" at the *All About Mary* website of the University of Dayton. On-line at: <https://udayton.edu/imri/mary/r/rosary-history-of-the-term.php> (Accessed 12/21/2019). The language of this version of the legend has been edited to replace "good, simple secular man" and "lay brother" with "boy" or "young boy" to conform with the telling of the legend in Clark Strand and Perdita Finn, *The Way of the Rose: The Radical Path of the Divine Feminine Hidden in the Rosary* (New York: Spiegel & Grau / Penguin Random House, 2019) at pp. 55-56.

Very simply, a rosary is a set of beads on a string. Most typically, a rosary (a five-decade rosary) consists of five groups of ten beads (a decade), with an additional large bead before each decade. The *Hail Mary* is said on each of the ten beads within a decade, while the *Lord's Prayer* is said on the large bead before each decade. Meditation on episodes in the life and death of Jesus from the Annunciation to the Ascension and beyond are sometimes added to the basic rosary practice. These meditations are traditionally grouped by fives into themed sets known as the Joyful (or Joyous) Mysteries, the Luminous Mysteries, the Sorrowful Mysteries, and the Glorious Mysteries:

Joyful Mysteries—The Annunciation, The Visitation, The Nativity of the Lord, The Presentation of the Infant Jesus in the Temple, The Finding of Child Jesus in Temple

Luminous Mysteries—The Baptism of Jesus, The Wedding at Cana, The Proclamation of the Kingdom of God, The Transfiguration, The Institution of the Eucharist[236]

Sorrowful Mysteries—The Agony in the Garden, The Scourging at the Pillar, The Crowning with Thorns, The Carrying of the Cross, The Crucifixion

Glorious Mysteries—The Resurrection, The Ascension, The Descent of the Holy Spirit at Pentecost, The Assumption of Mary, The Coronation of Mary as Queen of Heaven and Earth

Use of the rosary as a Christian spiritual practice dates at least from the time of Saint Dominic (d. 1221). According to the Rosary Center, founded by the Dominican friars, use of the rosary has evolved:

We have to keep in mind that over the centuries there has been a considerable evolution in the form that this devotion called the Rosary has taken. We have to remember that in the time of St. Dominic:

---

236 The Luminous Mysteries or Mysteries of Light, as commended by Pope John Paul II, were initially formulated by Saint George Preca (d. 1962) in 1957 and are therefore a late addition to the traditional sets of mysteries.

The *Hail Mary* did not exist as we pray it today. Only the first half of it was then used. The word *Jesus* was not added until the fourteenth century, and the second half of the prayer came later still.

The *Our Father* and the *Glory be to the Father* were not then part of the Rosary.

The *Mysteries of the Rosary* were not fixed as they are now. Even in the fifteenth century in the time of Alan De Rupe, O.P., who was responsible for the revival of the Rosary devotion 250 years after the time of St. Dominic, the Rosary he preached was the *Marian Psalter* of 150 *Hail Marys* and 150 mysteries. These were divided into three groups of fifties dedicated to the Joyful, Sorrowful and Glorious mysteries. The fifteen mysteries in use today [excluding the Luminous mysteries] were officially established by Pope Pius V in 1569.

There was no pendant (the cross and five extra beads) as we have now.[237]

Fr. Paul A. Duffner O.P , author of the article from which the above is excerpted, goes on to write: "The custom of counting repeated prayers by the use of a string of beads or knots, or pebbles in a bowl was prevalent long before the time of St. Dominic. This was common among the Muslims, the Buddhists, and other non-Christian religions as well as among Christians."

Use of the rosary in this way can be understood as being in functional continuity with mantra meditation. Whereas mantras are typically single words or short phrases, the prayed rosary is verbally more extensive. The effect, however, is similar in that both serve as means of ascension or, in other terms, of achieving distance from the turbulence and mimetic power of mental contents. As the alchemical process requires heat be applied to the flask, so the human heart requires

---

[237] Fr. Paul A. Duffner O.P., "The Rosary & St. Dominic: In Defense of a Tradition," Rosary Center & Confraternity website. This article originally appeared in *The Rosary Light & Life*, Volume 49, Number 5, September-October 1996. On-line at: <https://www.rosarycenter.org/homepage-2/rosary/the-rosary-st-dominic/> (Accessed 11/26/2019)

continuous warmth to effect transformation.[238] Use of the rosary in prayer or meditation generates this warmth of heart.[239]

It can also be said that there is no single way to "say" or use a rosary.[240] However, or through whatever channels, it may be taught, the rosary and its uses belong to the people of faith. Its uses are never fully controlled by the teaching authority of the Church. The reason for this is because the rosary "travels"—it goes with a person into his or her "inner room" where the doors of perception are shut. If we

---

[238] For insight into the association of alchemy and the Virgin Mary, see Urszula Szulakowska (University of Leeds), *The Alchemical Virgin Mary in the Religious and Political Context of the Renaissance* (Newcastle upon Tyne, U.K.: Cambridge Scholars Publishing, 2017), a study having to do with the use of Marian theology and iconography in alchemical works composed by Lutheran and Anglican esoteric philosophers. She writes: "From the 14th to the 15th centuries the extreme branch of the Franciscan Order played a decisive role in the production and dispersion of apocalyptic prophecies and eschatological writings. These radical members of the Order were known variously as 'Poverelli,' 'Fraticelli,' 'Joachimites,' or in modern parlance, 'Spirituals.' The radical Franciscans were also responsible for significant developments in alchemical theory and visual illustration. ... [T]he introduction of specifically Marian discourse into alchemy by the Franciscans has not been remarked by scholars. The first time this occurred was when the anonymous Franciscan who composed the *Buch der Heiligen Dreifaltigkeit* employed Marian iconography as an allegory of the alchemical 'mercury.' From this mystical substance the quintessence (fifth essence) was distilled in the production of the Philosopher's Stone. In later sixteenth century alchemy the emblem of Mary represented the white alchemical tincture, or elixir, made from the Philosopher's Stone." (pp. 4-5) Introduction and first chapter on-line at: <https://www.academia.edu/32581197/The_Alchemical_Virgin_Mary_in_the_Religious_and_Political_Context_of_the_Renaissance> (Accessed 12/27/2019)

[239] A phenomenology of rosary usage, with its Hail Mary and Our Father prayer repetitions, can be usefully compared with, for example, the *Ars Notoria* practices of the French Benedictine monk, John of Morigny (b. late thirteenth century) who understood visions as being subject to cultivation. See, as relevant to this topic, Barbara Newman, "What Did It Mean to Say 'I Saw'? The Clash between Theory and Practice in Medieval Visionary Culture," *Speculum*, Volume 80, Number 1 (January 2005), pp. 1-43. On-line at: <https://english.duke.edu/sites/english.duke.edu/files/file-attachments/Newman_Speculum2005.pdf> (Accessed 12/3/2019)

[240] For contemporary uses of the rosary beyond the Christian context, see Clark Strand and Perdita Finn, *The Way of the Rose*, previously cited.

understand the divergence of Church and monastic life since the time of Constantine, the rosary and its uses identify more closely with the spirituality of monastic and especially eremitic life. Part of the joy of bringing the rosary into one's life is making the rosary. Instructions can readily be found on the Internet.[241] Michael Carden (University of Queensland) writes, "As the final two mysteries of the Rosary graphically represent, she is the model and forerunner of the glorification and divinisation that are the goal of Christian hope for all humanity and for the entire cosmos."[242] Some have discerned the presence of the rosary, in a different form, in the mythos of J. R. R. Tolkien. Br. Joseph Bernard Marie Graziano O.P. (Dominicans of the Province of St. Joseph) writes:

> In *The Lord of the Rings*, the Lady Galadriel gives Frodo a gift upon his departure from Lothlórien: a phial, somehow filled with the light of Eärendil, the star that serves as a sort of Polaris or Morning Star to guide the Eldar (elves) to the Undying Lands. When Galadriel gives Frodo the phial, she expresses her purpose for the gift: "May it be a light to you in dark places, when all other lights go out." Frodo first uses the phial as a light in Shelob's lair, a cave which bore a "sense of malice so intense that Frodo reeled" (*Lord of the Rings*, IV.9). As he raises the phial aloft, he exclaims *"Aiya Eärendil Elenion Ancalima!"* which translates to "Hail Eärendil, brightest of stars!" At his words, the light shines forth brighter. Later, when Sam uses the phial, he cries out:

---

[241] A particularly good handout of instructions for making a rosary is available on-line from Loyola Press, a Jesuit ministry, at: <https://www.loyolapress.com/our-catholic-faith/parish-ministry/intergenerational-catechesis/mary/rosary-activity-center> (Accessed 12/4/2019)

[242] Michael Carden, "The Gendered Dynamics of Kenosis and Theosis in the Traditional Rosary of the Blessed Virgin Mary and the Surprising Theological Possibilities for Inclusive Theologies of Gender and Sexuality," p. 19. Article originally published in *Australian eJournal of Theology*, Issue 1, 2009. Article on-line at: <https://staff.acu.edu.au/__data/assets/pdf_file/0010/158545/Carden_ROSARY_Essay_Final_01.pdf> (Accessed 12/10/2019)

O Elbereth Gilthoniel
o menel palan-diriel,
le nallon sí di'nguruthos!
A tiro nin, Fanuilos!

Oh Elbereth Starkindler,
from the high firmament gazing afar,
to thee do I cry amid this horror!
Look kindly upon me, Ever-pure Lady!"

... Elbereth (or Varda) is the Queen of the Stars in Tolkien's mythology. At Sam's words, the light "flamed like a star that leaping from the firmament sears the dark air with intolerable light."

Given by Lady Galadriel and a source of light through prayer, the phial is for us an image of the Rosary. The Blessed Virgin Mary, fairest of all women, gave us the Rosary as a light in dark places. In praying the Rosary, we cry out to Mary the Morning Star that she may guide us to Heaven in her Son. In whispering our Aves, we ask the Queen of Heaven, the Woman robed in stars, for Her aid in the darkest times of life. Even Sam's prayer to Elbereth is suspiciously similar to the Hail Holy Queen, which we pray to end the Rosary: "Hail Holy Queen...to thee do we cry...in this valley of tears! Turn then, most gracious advocate, thine eyes of mercy towards us."

We can identify three effects of the phial which also apply to the Rosary. First, the phial provides light to illuminate the hobbits' path, lest they stumble: By praying the Rosary, we grow in grace and can thus understand better the way we should turn. We have faith that, by praying to God through the powerful intercession of the Mother of God, He will draw us closer to Himself, in Whom is all our joy. Second, the phial gives the hobbits hope. Despite the trials they are facing, the light of Eärendil reminds them of the great stories about how others have triumphed over evil and how, above all the gloom of Mordor, there is yet beauty and goodness and truth. The Rosary of Mary is a source of hope for us, for by meditating on the life of Christ and walking with Him, we come to understand all the more that death is not the end of life, that Christ has conquered death, and that He has promised His kingdom to those who follow Him. The Rosary is Mary's humble way of leading us through this world while keeping us from despairing of the fullness of life to come. Third, the phial is a terror to evil ones. Shelob, an ancient evil in spider form, took to flight at the flame of the shining phial. Similarly, the Holy Rosary is a terror to demons, a sure weapon in our fight against our own vice and against the world's evils. For proof, just take a close look at the lives of the saints. [...][243]

The adventures of the hobbits, seen in a certain light, have the form or shape of pilgrimage.

Pilgrimage

Happy are the people whose strength is in you!
whose hearts are set on the pilgrims' way.
Those who go through the desolate valley will find it a place of springs,
for the early rains have covered it with pools of water.
— Psalm 84:4-5 (*The Book of Common Prayer*, 1979)

This psalm is reassuring because to take up the pilgrim's way is to leave places of relative safety and enter into worlds of hazard, albeit with trust and humility.[244] To begin the pilgrim's way is to enter into the flowingness that may bring to mind other waters—the dark and treacherous waters of sailors at risk of drowning—sailors who, in crisis, appeal to Our Lady, Star of the Sea (*Stella Maris*).

Anna-Karina Hermkens, Willy Jansen, and Catrien Notermans (all of Radboud University Nijmegan, Netherlands) offer the following

---

[243] From Br. Joseph Bernard Marie Graziano, "Where the Rosary Appears in 'The Lord of the Rings'," *Word on Fire Blog*, March 23, 2017. On-line at: <https://www.wordonfire.org/resources/blog/where-the-rosary-appears-in-the-lord-of-the-rings/18699/> (Accessed 12/22/2019). It has been noted above, in Section 8, that some women appearing in the writings of Tolkien seem to embody particular qualities or characteristics of Our Lady.
[244] See, for example, Hans Lyngsgaard, *Teachings of the Virgin Mary* (Alresford, Hampshire, U.K.: Axis Mundi Books / John Hunt Publishing Ltd., 2012), wherein is recounted a story that begins with the Virgin Mary posing this question to author: "Will you rediscover my pilgrimage route?"

description in the Introduction to their book, *Moved by Mary: The Power of Marian Pilgrimage*:

> At the beginning of the twenty-first century, disregarding trends of secularization, Mary, the mother of Jesus, has become a megastar. Both old and new sacred sites dedicated to the Virgin Mary are attracting growing numbers of pilgrims, both in Europe and the United States. Old shrines seem to attract new groups—devout elderly women and patients seeking spiritual or physical healing now mingle with tourists, hikers, migrants, anti-abortion activists, and soldiers—and become sites of new traditions that often eclectically borrow from the past in creating new sources of spiritual engagement. Old pilgrimage sites also use modern approaches and apply the technological innovations of the World Wide Web to reach pilgrims at home with webcam images, online religious stores, and interactive prayer sites. Sanctuaries globally distribute and receive religious messages, prayers, artifacts, and replicas of statues. These sacred words and objects spread across the world on an unprecedented scale to activate Marian devotion in different cultural contexts. New sanctuaries arise in urban spaces or unexpected places. In Clearwater, Florida in the United States, a modern commercial building was transformed into a pilgrim site after an image of Mary was seen on its windows. In these new sanctuaries, replicas, for example, of Lourdes or Guadalupe, effect new devotions. In addition, people keep meeting Mary in visions or dreams as she moves over the entire globe with the times and the needs of her devotees. The question is, what is happening here? Why are so many people around the world 'moved by Mary'?
>
> Considering the popularity of Mary, one would expect a considerable academic interest in Marian pilgrimages. However, although many books have been published about Mary from a theological or devotional perspective and the interest in pilgrimage studies is increasing ..., relatively little academic attention has been paid to Marian pilgrimages .... This is surprising, considering that Marian pilgrimages and Marian sites are among the largest and most well-known events and places around the world. Moreover, they are intrinsically linked with topics that are of interest to contemporary scholars.

It seems that the general preoccupation of contemporary scholars with modernity and charting processes of globalization and secularization has actually led to a neglect of Marian pilgrimmages in contemporary scholarship. At first instance, Marian pilgrimages seem antimodern or resisting modernity. ... [I]t is not associated with processes of modernity and consequently considered to be "an 'obvious' or 'known' phenomenon that does not require fresh and constantly renewed examination." However, increased opportunities for travel, improvements in mass transport systems and in health and medical care, along with economic improvements and the search for national and cultural identity, contribute to the modern expansion of pilgrimage opportunities.

... [W]e particularly want to emphasize that modernity produces power inequalities that may direct people to Mary and religion in general, in order to seek help and empowerment. The global spread of modernity has given rise to growing numbers of people who are deprived of adequate means of survival. In fact, modernization seems to sharpen the inequalities of gender, ethnicity, class, religion, and age that are played out in the religious fields of Marian pilgrimages. For many Catholics, Mary provides the answer to such globally produced problems, and they bond with Mary to gain empowerment and improve their lives. In this process, old and new Marian symbols, places and movements are put to work.

At the same time that the practice of Marian devotion is modernized and goes on with the times, it is also one of the most fundamental, conservative, and militant forces in the Catholic Church, acting against secularism, individualization, and such gender issues as women's emancipation and sexual liberation. These religious forces have often been considered antimodern but actually belong to modernity: they exemplify how in modern times cultural means are employed to oppress others or resist oppression. Religion continues to be a way in which people deal with constraining and violating power inequalities caused by processes of globalization, secularization, gender discrimination, colonialism, violence, economic exploittation, insecurity, changing and disintegrating family structures, and biomedical dominance in health systems. Marian devotion simultaneously uses modernity and acts against certain outcomes of modernity. It helps people—both powerful and powerless—to position themselves in changing modern power relations.

Along with the general idea that Marian pilgrimages have no bearing on the contemporary world and its dynamics, is the erroneous preconception that modernity and religion are oppositional and incompatible. According to [Indian-American anthropologist and globalization theorist], Arjun Appadurai, the modern world has been considered by theorists as "a space of shrinking religiosity," leading to a focus on processes of secularization. While modernity may not … directly result in rising levels of faith, it does shape the conditions in which people can easily intensify and increase their religious activity. Growing evidence indicates that religiosity and religious movements, such as Marian devotions, [as suggested by Appadurai] "may be more consequential than ever in today's highly mobile and interconnected global politics."[245]

With regard to pilgrimage in England[246] as well as elsewhere, the sites or destinations of pilgrimage were and are often sites of apparitions. Chris Maunder (York St John University, England) writes:

At a time around the beginning of the eighth century, a swineherd named Eoves or Eof experienced a vision of three women at a place that we now know as Evesham in Worcestershire, named after him. The woman in the centre was identified as the Virgin Mary, although anyone familiar with the ancient triple goddess in works by Robert Graves and others would probably suggest that this was a christianization of a pagan story. A Benedictine monk Ecgwin, bishop of Worcester, visiting the site, also had a vision of Mary there, and established the abbey which remained until the Reformation; it is now a much-visited ruin with several surviving medieval buildings.

---

[245] Anna-Karina Hermkens, Willy Jansen, and Catrien Notermans, *Moved by Mary: The Power of Marian Pilgrimage* (New York: Routledge, 2016; first published by Ashgate Publishing, 2009).
[246] See Bob Trubshaw, *Pilgrimage in England: A Concise Introduction* (Avebury, UK: Heart of Albion, 2015). On-line at: <https://www.hoap.co.uk/pilgrimage_in_england.pdf> (Accessed 8/13/2019)

The full story of Eoves and Ecgwin is peculiar to Evesham, but the underlying structure is a familiar one in Catholicism. The typical apparition is rooted in local traditions, traditions which stand at the interface between doctrinal Christianity and common religion with its folklore and belief in the spirit world. The visionary is often someone located in the liminal (marginal) region between society and nature, usually a herder of animals at the edge of the village. If the apparition is to take its place in history, however, it has to receive the approval of the church hierarchy. This process of legitimization is also one in which the story sheds much of its common religion element, and becomes instead associated with the establishment of an official religious centre. As the Italian Marxist Antonio Gramsci noted, the Roman Catholic Church is very effective at integrating the popular and official in religious devotion.

Other important medieval apparition shrines in England were also linked to abbeys or priories: Thetford, in Norfolk, where visions were associated with healings and the building of a lady chapel at the already existing priory; Walsingham, also in Norfolk, where the dream vision led to the building of a "holy house," said to duplicate that in Nazareth; Aylesford, in Kent, where the founder of the Carmelite priory, Simon Stock, was also credited with a vision of Mary. The twentieth century saw a strong resurgence of interest in pre-Reformation marian shrines in England; Walsingham and Aylesford receive many visitors, while devotion at former abbey towns like Glastonbury, Guisborough, Doncaster and Evesham is now based in the local Roman Catholic parish churches.

The revival of marian pilgrimage in England in the twentieth century followed in the wake of marian revival in France in the nineteenth. The older French marian shrines, some of which, like Le Puy in Auvergne, had founding apparitions, were overshadowed by a new series of famous visions. Four were approved by the church hierarchy: Rue du Bac, Paris, 1830, with its famous "miraculous medal;" La Salette in the Alps, 1846; Lourdes and its healing spring, 1858; the village of Pontmain in Normandy, 1871. There were, of course, many more, but the bishops promoted these four into the apparition "canon."

The growth of the canonical series of modern apparitions continued into the twentieth century in Europe, and four more were added: Knock, Ireland, 1879, but not authenticated until the 1930s; Fatima, Portugal, 1917; Beauraing and Banneux, Belgium, 1932-3. These have been the last of the series in Europe, although elsewhere in the world there has been some episcopal approval at shrines such as Akita, Japan; Betania, Venezuela; Kibeho, Rwanda. The attitude of the European hierarchy has not been conducive to the authentication of visions since World War II, and several pretenders to a place in the series—notably Garabandal, Spain, 1961-5; San Damiano, Italy, 1964-81; Medjugorje, Bosnia-Hercegovina, 1981—have been ignored or condemned by bishops, although there has been a relaxing of restrictions on pilgrimage and church liturgy at such places since the 1980s. These recent apparitions are in the La Salette-Fatima tradition of apocalyptic prophecy and secrets which inspire curiosity and anxiety.

The increase in pilgrimage to shrines old and new is no surprise in a tourism-loving society; while Guadalupe in Mexico remains the most visited Catholic shrine in the world, Lourdes and now Medjugorje receive their millions. However, this heightened excitement over the internationally known shrines contrasts with the decline in interest in traditional marian devotions at the local level. Vatican II is often regarded as the cause of this trend: the tract on Mary was placed in the Constitution on the Church (*Lumen gentium*), rather than having a chapter to itself, excesses of the marian cult were condemned, and, to generalize, the new post-conciliar clergy are often indifferent to marian devotion. This local minimalism causes marian devotees to look away from home to find the spiritual energy and focus that they seek; traditional marian devotions are central at the apparition shrines, and remain so today: the rosary, the Immaculate Heart, hymns like the Salve Regina, processions, and the feasts of the Assumption and Immaculate Conception. Like Lourdes and Fatima beforehand, Medjugorje has gained an international influence, spawning many "Medjugorje centres," publications and groups in several countries. Many recent apparition messages, such as those in Ireland and the USA, clearly draw upon Medjugorje for the substance, emphasis and style. Apparition messages are quite varied depending on their origin, but there are four basic ingredients:

- The identification of the vision with Mary under a particular title;
- The request for a chapel, processions, traditional devotions like the rosary, prayer and liturgical observance;
- The promise of favours such as peace and healing conditional upon a return to right spirituality;
- The promise of miracles where the visionaries ask for proof of the reality of the apparition, which is unseen by others.[247]

The Catholic anthropologists, Victor and Edith Turner, have argued that "a tourist is half a pilgrim, if a pilgrim is half a tourist."[248] This is even the impression one gets reading Chaucer's *Canterbury Tales*. The landscape begins to work in us—natural landscape as primal revelation. The pilgrim way has significance, even for those destined never to walk it. Consider this poignant language from Hannah Green's book, *Little Saint*, about a village (Conques) in southern France whose ethos is permeated with the spiritual fragrance of its patron saint:

> The people of Conques do not think very often about Le Puy. Le Puy is not on their minds. As the people of Lunel think about Conques, so the people of Conques think of Saint Jacques de Compostelle.
>
> Saint Jacques is there, his image; Compostelle is there, far off to the west, as a kind of dream, a conscious dream, which is in their blood—a destination at the end of the Milky Way, the Chemin de Saint Jacques, where it dips down into the west at that Finis-terre, that end of earth where their Celtic ancestors went, both literally and symbolically to die. The feel for that farthest western place beyond which the earth blends into the

[247] Chris Maunder, "Transforming visions? Apparitions of Mary," *The Way* Supplement, 100, pp. 30-41, pp. 30-32. On-line at: <https://www.theway.org.uk/back/s100Maunder.pdf> (Accessed 11/27/2019)

[248] As quoted in Carole M. Cusack (University of Sydney), "Medieval Pilgrims and Modern Tourists: Walsingham (England) and Meryem Ana (Turkey)," *Fieldwork in Religion*, 11(2), April 2017, pp. 217-234.

sea and the sky when the sun goes down into night has come to them through the wild centuries; and Conques is on the way to there, to Saint Jacques de Compostelle.

So living out one's life here in this bowl, this *conque* in the mountains, one is living out one's life on the way to Compostelle, Starry-field. The words, "Saint Jacques de Compostelle," spoken escape into the air of Conques continually like so many golden birds or bees, like so many glimmering moments of thought or prayer heading out into the heavens to join the stars.

"Again and again," says Madame Fau, "my husband and I were planning to make a trip to Saint Jacques de Compostelle. But always, for one reason or another, we put it off.... Now I will probably never see it," she says sadly. But brightening, for it is her way, she says, "Jean-Claude tells me that althrough the cathedral at Saint Jacques has a baroque façade, inside it is *tout à fait* Conques; it is exactly like Conques! Only much bigger!"

There is a fine, straight, blue-eyed old woman, Madame Dissac, who passes by Rosalie's house going up the Rue du Château and back several times a day at least; she is going to visit her daughter and her family on the far side of the Place du Château, but Rosalie and Charlou refer to her as Saint Jacques de Compostelle—because she is always walking, walking, walking, like a pilgrim, they explain. (She is Monsieur Fabre's older sister, but neither they nor their families have spoken for many years.)

"Life is an envelope," said Madame Benoit. "We come from the unknown and we are going toward we know not where in this envelope we call our life." She was sitting in the evening, knitting, on a little wall by a cousin's house above a garden terrace on the narrow Rue du Château. "Perhaps living in a place of pilgrimage, people in Conques understand this more easily than others," she said. (I think of the Venerable Bede's bird flying in from the winter night to the light and the warmth of the banquet hall and out again into the darkness.) "This was once the principal street of Conques," said Madame Benoit, tapping her cane on its stones. "People came in here by the Porte du Barry to go on down the Rue Charlemagne and over the Pont Romain and so on toward Saint Jacques de Compostelle. Or else they went up there and left by the Porte de Vinzelles to go on to Sainte Anne and Grand Vabre and to take the ferry over the Lot, going on from there, perhaps, to Our Lady of Rocamadour. Some people think this explains the mark like an upside-down Y below the scallop shell on Conques's escutcheon."[249]

The Anglican priest, Fr. Robert Llewelyn (d. 2008), longtime chaplain (until 1990) at the shrine of Julian of Norwich in St. Julian's Church, Norwich, made several pilgrimages to Medjugorje over the years. The following is from an interview with Fr. Llewelyn in Medjugorje in 1992. He is responding to a question about the need for renewal in the churches:

This is the third time I've come to Medjugorje, even though I'm eighty-three years old. For me, Medjugorje is simply a place of prayer. For example, I can pray much better here than in London. Experience tells me that we Anglicans have to bring Mary back to our spiritual area and give Her the place She is worthy of. She is our Mother, and we are truly poor if we do not permit Her to be with us. I think this is where the beginning of our spiritual renewal lies, and with this in mind I started up a prayer community. We pray the Rosary together. There certainly aren't many of these groups. Perhaps it's the only one in our Church, it is very close to Catholic heritage and prayer. I talk to my faithful about Mary and I suggest they pray to Her. What Our Lady says here in Medjugorje is what Jesus says, it's what Jesus says is the will of God. Here, in your land, Mary is inspiration. There is a real Christian atmosphere in church, and in many of your families true devotion to Mary shines out and in the visionaries, joy, peace and simplicity. This change came about because of my new filial relationship with Mary our Mother, and it started in Medjugorje. I live in the hope that if this happened to me, it can also happen to others. The renewal is needed by all.

The Rosary is a prayer of meditation, it brings us closer to Jesus. Since Mary is in the beginning and the end of this prayer, what else could happen to me if not learn to love Mary and be convinced that we Anglicans have to find place in our

---

[249] Hannah Green, *Little Saint* (New York: The Modern Library / Random House, 2001, 2000), pp. 177-178.

prayer for Her too? She is our Mother. Without Her we are nothing but poor orphans. Because of my love of the Rosary, I have been able to urge Catholics at meetings to pray it. I know many of your faithful have forgotten it or recite it superficially.

Let Mary instruct you. The world looks at you, do not tire! Through Mary you can renew the world and you will be helping us Anglicans to accept Her too, and we will be brothers! Since I met you I pray for you all, for the monks, the visionaries and the entire parish. Remain one in spirit, like Mary wants. That is the only way you will be able to present His luminous face to the world, and show the way to God. You pray for us too so we will know how to jump over the obstacles and see each other as brothers and sisters as soon as possible. May God, through the intercession of Mary, protect you and watch over you in these difficult times. And may He grant you peace through the intercession of the Queen of Peace.[250]

Via Maria

Mary's Way or Via Maria (Austria, Hungary, Romania, Slovakia, Poland, Croatia, and Bosnia) inscribes a large cross upon the map of Central and Eastern Europe. The Way of Mary pilgrimage network has an East-West arm running from Mariazell (Austria) in the west, through Budapest (Hungary) and Máriapócs (Hungary) to Csíksomlyó (Romania) in the east. It has a North-South arm running from Czestochowa (Poland) in the north through Esztergom (Hungary) and Budapest (Hungary) to Medjugorje (Bosnia and Herzegovina) in the south.

King Saint Stephen I of Hungary, according to one account, dedicated both himself and his people to the Blessed Virgin Mary. Almost as if this action of King Saint Stephen were a seed, the contemporary Flame of Love movement (associated with the seer, Elizabeth Kindelmann, d. 1985) that began in Hungary has blossomed

---

[250] From an interview with Fr. Robert Llewelyn, conducted by Nasa Ognjista in Medjugorje, Bosnia-Herzegovina, December 1992. On-line at: <http://medjugorje.altervista.org/doc_en/testimonies/conv_anglicano.html> (Accessed 1/2/2020). Information about Fr. Llewelyn can be found on-line at: <http://www.lightforthejourney.org.uk/robert-llewellyn.html> (Accessed 1/2/2020)

into associated prayer groups around the world. The quintessential pilgrim people, the Roma (commonly referred to as gypsies), in Hungary keep an annual pilgrimage to the Marian shrine at Csatka, about seventy-five miles west of Budapest.[251] Further east, in Transcarpathian Ukraine, apparition sites draw significant crowds.[252] With respect to Hungary, the Way of Mary (Via Maria) pilgrimage network serves to maintain the coherence of the Hungarian people as a nation. The meaning of Nagy Magyarország, referred to in the excerpt below, has historical roots but is now taken to mean something like the Hungarian nation under divine guidance, or the Hungarian people as divinized, the condition to which its people, in their hearts, aspire:

> The avid search for the re-unification of the Hungarian peoples has become a persistent and prevalent theme within contemporary nationalistic circles, especially following the Treaty of Trianon which was signed in June 1920 when the Austro-Hungarian Empire was broken off into several entities, and 75% of Hungary's territory was sectioned off and redistributed to Romania, Czechoslovakia, and what was to become Yugoslavia. In an effort to link back to the idealized identity of the past and in order to develop a stronger relationship to the historical memory of the Nagy Magyarország, the new location for religion has shifted. The "initial euphoria" that epitomized the attitudes of select members of post-communist Hungarian society eventually subsided, and was replaced by "malaise, widespread exasperation, fatigue and a general sense of ex-

---

[251] Krisztina Than, "Roma seek luck and love at Catholic shrine in Hungary," *Reuters*, September 11, 2017. On-line at: <https://www.reuters.com/article/us-hungary-religion-roma/roma-seek-luck-and-love-at-catholic-shrine-in-hungary-idUSKCN1BM1GR> (Accessed 10/31/2019)

[252] An important anthropological study of these phenomena was done by Agnieszka Halemba in her book, *Negotiating Marian Apparitions: The Politics of Religion in Transcarpathian Ukraine* (Budapest & New York: Central European University Press, 2015). For an insightful review of Professor Halemba's book, see Konrad Siekierski, "Negotiating Marian Apparitions: The Politics of Religion in Transcarpathian Ukraine," *Religion, State and Society*, Volume 45, 2017, Issue 2. On-line at: <http://dx.doi.org/ 10.1080/09637494.2017. 1314081> (Accessed 11/15/2019). Various articles related to Marian studies by Agnieszka Halemba can be found at her Academia.edu page at: <https://pan-pl.academia.edu/AgnieszkaHalemba> (Accessed 12/19/2019).

haustion." Returning to the idealistic "fatherland" of the Nagy Magyarország, a sacred space that does not exist in the tangible, physical world is an effort to re-create a community where Hungarians from all over the world can unite in equality and solidarity through heightened emotional catharsis.

The idea of the collective, shared Hungarian nation stands as a new realm of the sacred, which remains guarded and guided by Christian symbols and saints, regardless of the push away from religion during the Communist era. Subsequently, those who identify as Hungarian have been led to reignite latent symbols of the Nagy Magyarország in order to collectively re-define and re-characterize the nation. Figurative images, such as a coloured geographic map of the historic Nagy Magya-rország with an iron Cross of Lorraine placed at the center of the country, have become prevalent signs and signals of post-communist fervor. This double cross symbol was most likely introduced to Hungary during the reign of King Béla III, who was raised in the Byzantine court in the twelfth century. Nine of the twelve heraldic coats of arms that have been used as national symbols of Hungary since that time bear the motif of the double cross in some shape or form. The official Hungarian coat of arms is composed of three distinct parts. A red and white shield that contains the double cross symbol on top of a crown on a three curved hill, is situated underneath a highly decorative presentation of the royal crown of St. Stephen, the first Christian king of the Kingdom of Hungary. This coat of arms, which has been in use again since 1990, was initially instigated [sic] around the reign of King Matthias Corvinus (1458-1490), who is often revered as the greatest humanist Hungarian King of the Renaissance. Corvinus was born in 1443, in Cluj-Napoca (Kolozsvár), Transylvania which is located half-way between the eastern Hungarian borderline and the city of Csíkszereda. Csíkszereda is the capital of the Hargita County and is located near the city of Ghimeş-Făget (Gyímesbükk), where the thousand-year old eastern border of Hungary used to be prior to the Treaty of Trianon. A large double cross lies on top of a triple curved altar approximately three kilometers from the center of Csíkszereda; this altar is reminiscent of the right side of the Hungarian coat of arms, which is also decorated with a double cross on top of three

175

"mountains" (the Tátra, Mátra and Fátra mountain ranges). These nationalistic symbols are prevalent in this geographic area and often appear as emblems of the physical border between Hungary and Romania. These symbols also represent the ideological border between the historical Nagy Magyarország and the "martyred" post-communist Hungary as well as the spiritual border between the sacred land of the Catholic *Magyars* in comparison to the profane landscape of the Romanians.[253]

10. The Way of Mary – *Festina lente!*

Blessed is that person of love who has caused God, who is love, to dwell in his heart. Blessed are you, O heart so small and confined, yet you have caused Him whom heaven and earth cannot contain to dwell spiritually in your womb, as in a restful abode. Blessed is that illumined eye of the heart which, in its purity, clearly beholds Him before whose sight the Seraphs veil their faces.
— Sahdona (early seventh century), *Book of Perfection*, II.4.8[254]

An emblematic image of one who inhabits the rhythms of nature under the mantle of the Blessed Virgin Mary is the gardener, the one who cares for or tends the garden. The gardener is generally an obscure figure, one who does not call attention to oneself. Mary Magdalene saw the resurrected Jesus at the tomb (John 20:15) but, "supposing him to be the gardener," she failed to recognize him. The same obscurity typically veils Our Lady who, in the eyes of Thomas Merton, is characterized by poverty and hiddenness.[255] The Blessed Virgin Mary moves

---

[253] From Zsofia Lovei (University of Toronto, M.A., Art History), "The Vehicle of Pilgrimage: Spanning the Geographical and Ideological Horizons of the Way of Mary through Mariazell to Csíksomlyó," 2015. On-line at: <https://www.academia.edu/22108005/The_Vehicle_of_Pilgrimage_Spanning_the_Geographical_and_Ideological_Horizons_of_the_Way_of_Mary_through_Mariazell_to_Cs%C3%ADksomly%C3%B3> (Accessed 11/19/2019)
[254] As quoted at Sebastian Brock's webpage of resources in Syriac spirituality. On-line at: <http://syri.ac/brock/spirituality> (Accessed 11/26/2019)
[255] See Chapter 23, "The Woman Clothed with the Sun," in Thomas Merton, *New Seeds of Contemplation* (New York: New Directions, 1972, 1962), pp. 167-

under the radar, to use a familiar expression, also inviting small-scale remembrances of her.

There is perhaps no better way of connecting with Our Lady, especially in the season of Spring, than by creating a Mary garden, which can be done outdoors or indoors at relatively little expense. It has been suggested that St. Fiacre of Ireland planted the first Mary garden in the seventh century. Whether this is true or not, people have been creating quiet spaces full of fragrant and colorful flowers and other plants, in honor of Our Lady, for a very long time. Mary gardens are essentially meditation gardens serving a therapeutic purpose, allowing contemplative re-connection with reality and the divine Presence. Know that the Blessed Virgin Mary presides over even the least gestures manifesting goodness, truth, and beauty. Life in the vicinity of the Blessed Virgin engenders chivalrous and noble relations among all beings.

There is a famous line, "The world shall come to Walsingham," in a poem ("The Quaker Graveyard in Nantucket") by Robert Lowell. Section VI of that poem is reproduced here:

Our Lady of Walsingham

There once the penitents took off their shoes
And then walked barefoot the remaining mile;
And the small trees, a stream and hedgerows file
Slowly along the munching English lane,
Like cows to the old shrine, until you lose
Track of your dragging pain.
The stream flows down under the druid tree,
Shiloah's whirlpools gurgle and make glad
The castle of God. Sailor, you were glad
And whistled Sion by that stream. But see:

Our Lady, too small for her canopy,
Sits near the altar. There's no comeliness
At all or charm in that expressionless
Face with its heavy eyelids. As before,
This face, for centuries a memory,

---

175. See also Voiles, "The Mother of All the Living: The Role of the Virgin Mary in the Spirituality of Thomas Merton," previously cited.

Non est species, neque decor,
Expressionless, expresses God: it goes
Past castled Sion. She knows what God knows,
Not Calvary's Cross nor crib at Bethlehem
Now, and the world shall come to Walsingham.[256]

The Litany of Our Lady of Walsingham

Our Lady of Walsingham,	pray to the Lord for us
Mary conceived without sin,	pray to the Lord for us
Mary the Virgin,	pray to the Lord for us
Mary, the Mother of God,	pray to the Lord for us
Mary taken up into heaven,	pray to the Lord for us
Mary at Bethlehem,	pray for all mothers
Mary at Nazareth,	pray for all families
Mary at Cana,	pray for all married couples
Mary who stood by the Cross,	pray for all who suffer
Mary in the Upper Room,	pray for all who wait
Mary model of womanhood,	pray for all women
Woman of Faith,	keep us in mind
Woman of Hope,	keep us in mind
Woman of Charity,	keep us in mind
Woman of Suffering,	keep us in mind
Woman of Anxiety,	keep us in mind
Woman of Humility,	keep us in mind
Woman of Poverty,	keep us in mind
Woman of Purity,	keep us in mind
Woman of Obedience,	keep us in mind
Woman who wondered,	remember us to God
Woman who listened,	remember us to God
Woman who followed Him,	remember us to God
Woman who longed for Him,	remember us to God
Woman who loves Him,	remember us to God
Mother of God,	be our Mother always
Mother of Men,	be our Mother always

---

[256] As reproduced at the Poetry Foundation website, on-line at: <https://www.poetryfoundation.org/poems/48984/the-quaker-graveyard-in-nantucket> (Accessed 1/13/2020)

Mother of the Church,	be our Mother always
Mother of the World,	be our Mother always
Mother we need,	be our Mother always
Mother who went on believing,	we thank God for you
Mother who never lost hope,	we thank God for you

All holy and ever-living God, in giving us Jesus Christ to be our Saviour and Brother, you gave us Mary, his Mother, to be our Mother also; grant us, we pray you, that we may be worthy of so great a Brother and so dear a Mother. May we come at last to you the Father of us all through Jesus Christ Your Son, who lives and reigns with you and the Holy Spirit for ever and ever.

Amen.

Appendix

The following sets (heptads) of traids originally appeared as inscriptions on a wooden "talking stick" created by this author some years ago and given away. The present whereabouts of the inscribed talking stick is unknown and it is presumed now lost.

> *I must work the works of him that sent me, while it is day: the night cometh, when no man can work. As long as I am in the world, I am the light of the world.*
> — John 9:4-5 (KJV)

Is not the light of day the Light of Consciousness? Perhaps the following can be regarded as notes or keys on the musical instrument of our lives. May the Divine Breath, as on an Aeolian Harp, sound beautiful melodies in you, as it carries you gently Home!

Sanctus - Sanctus - Sanctus

Heptad One

Wine - Love - Wisdom
Priest - Prophet - King
Bread - Wine - Presence
Wheat - Mill - Grain
Roots - Trunk - Branches
Reality - Awareness - Joy
Father - Son - Holy Spirit

Heptad Two

Truth - Goodness - Beauty
Time - Eternity - Vision
Intelligence - Heart - Instinct
Justice - Compassion - Wisdom
Faith - Hope - Love
Body - Soul - Spirit
Theosis - Theophany - Kingdom

Heptad Three

Master - Disciple - Apprenticeship
Incarnation - Metanoia - Theosis
Renunciation - Enlightenment - Theosis
Mandala - Temple - Liturgy
Virtue - Truthfulness - Humility
Willingness - Wilfulness - Will-lessness
Rest - Prayer - Work

Heptad Four

Metaphysics - Therapeutics - Paedogogics
Macrocosm - Microcosm - Mesocosm
Mythos - Logos - Cosmos
Unity - Duality - Harmony
Speech - Silence - Manifestation
Meditation - Medicine - Moderation
Word - Image - Melody

Heptad Five

Oracle - Synchronicity - Blessing
Fate - Freedom - Providence
Initiation - Illumination - Transformation
The Question - Sage - Word of Life
Tradition - Scripture - Insight
Wisdom of Heaven - Written Tradition - Oral Tradition
Gold - Frankincense - Myrrh

Heptad Six

Outer - Inner - The Tempter
Hero - Chaos - Order
Affirming - Denying - Reconciling
Fascination - Attention - Balance
Air - Food - Impressions
Moving Center - Emotional Center - Intellectual Center
Greek - Hebraic - Egyptian

Festina lente!

Resources

Here are some suggested readings on the Marian reality:

Geoffrey Ashe, *The Virgin: Mary's Cult and the Re-Emergence of the Goddess* (History Press, 1976, 2008). Useful historical background.

Sarah Jane Boss, editor, *Mary: The Complete Resource* (New York: Continuum, 2007).

Madonna Sophia Compton, *The Mother of God: Symbolic Theology of the Virgin Mary* (Independently published, 2010). Informed by Eastern Orthodox perspective.

Catherine de Hueck Doherty, *Bogoroditza: She Who Gave Birth to God* (Madonna House, 1998). Orthodox and Catholic perspective.

Mary Ford-Grabowsky and Andrew Harvey, *Spiritual Writings on Mary: Annotated & Explained* (SkyLight Illuminations, 2005).

Mary Ford-Grabowsky, *The Way of Mary: Following Her Footsteps Toward God* (Paraclete Press, 2007).

Andrew Harvey, *Mary's Vineyard: Daily Meditations, Readings, and Revelations* (Quest Books, 1996).

Andrew Harvey, *The Return of the Mother* (Tarcher Perigree, 2000). Not limited to the Virgin Mary.

William Hart McNichols and Mirabai Starr, *Mother of God Similar to Fire* (Orbis Books, 2016).

Chris Maunder, *Our Lady of the Nations: Apparitions of Mary in 20th-Century Catholic Europe* (Oxford University Press, 2016).

Jaroslav Pelikan, *Mary Through the Centuries: Her Place in the History of Culture* (New Haven: Yale University Press, 1998, 1996).

Charlene Spretnak, *Missing Mary: The Queen of Heaven and Her Re-Emergence in the Modern Church* (Palgrave Macmillan, 2004).

Mirabai Starr, *Our Lady of Guadalupe: Devotions, Prayers & Living Wis-dom* (ReadHowYouWant, 2012).

Sandra L. Zimdars-Swartz, *Encountering Mary: Visions of Mary from La Salette to Medjugorje* (Harper Perennial, 1992).

Other resources:

Marian Library, University of Dayton (Ohio):
    <udayton.edu/marianlibrary/index.php>
International Marian Research Institute, University of Dayton (Ohio):
    <udayton.edu/imri/index.php>
Marian Research Institute Blog:
    <udayton.edu/blogs/imri/>

Some religious communities that have chosen to honor the Blessed Virgin Mary in their name:

Community of Saint Mary (Founded in 1865, Episcopal)
    and
Community of the Mother of Jesus (Founded in 2011, Episcopal)
Companions of Our Lady of Walsingham (Founded in 2014, Episcopal)
    <www.facebook.com/Companions.OLW/>

Marian Feast Days in the Anglican Communion:[257]

February 2 – Purification of the Blessed Virgin
February 11 – Our Lady of Lourdes
March 25 – Annunciation to the Virgin Mary (Lady Day)
May 1 – Queen of Heaven
May 31 – Visitation of the Blessed Virgin Mary
August 15 – Falling Asleep of the Blessed Virgin Mary
September 8 – Nativity of the Blessed Virgin Mary
October 15 – Our Lady of Walsingham
December 8 – Conception of the Blessed Virgin Mary

---

[257] From <https://en.wikipedia.org/wiki/Marian_feast_days> (Accessed 9/13/2019)

11. Works Cited

A.K. John Sanidopoulos, translator. "The Panagia, the Life-Giving Spring," *Mystagogy Resource Center*, April 25, 2014. On-line at: <https://www.johnsanidopoulos.com/2014/04/the-panagia-life-giving-spring.html> (Accessed 8/9/2019)

"A Prayerlife in The Divine Mercy and Will of God," Divine Mercy Apostolate for Cardiff and South Wales, 2006, p. 30. On-line at: <https://irp-cdn.multiscreensite.com/7827db40/files/ uploaded/Divine%2BMercy%2BPrayer%2BBook-2.pdf> (Accessed 1/1/2020)

Adels, Jill Haak. *The Wisdom of the Saints: An Anthology*. Oxford, UK: Oxford University Press, 1987.

Agreed Statement on the Blessed Virgin Mary between Anglicans and Roman Catholics on-line at: <https://www.anglicancommunion. org/media/105263/mary-grace-and-hope-in-christ_english.pdf> (Accessed 11/13/2019).

Allchin, A. M. *The Joy of All Creation: An Anglican Meditation on the Place of Mary*. London: New City, 1993.

Almaas, A. H. *Diamond Heart: Book One: Elements of the Real in Man*. Boulder, Colorado: Shambhala Publications, 1987.

Anavrin, "Animal Symbolism of Honey Bees," *The Daily Spell*, September 19, 2010. On-line at: <http://thedailyspell.com/profiles/ blogs/animal-symbolism-of-honey-bees> (Accessed 12/30/2019)

Andreev, Daniil. *The Rose of the World*. Location not specified: Lindisfarne Books, 1997.

Anidjar, Gil. *Blood: A Critique of Christianity*. New York: Columbia University Press, 2014.

Anonymous. *Meditations on the Tarot: A Journey into Christian Hermeticism*. New York: Jeremy P. Tarcher / Putnam, 1985, 2002.

Antoninka, Amy E. "Without Measure: Marion's Apophatic-Virtue Phenomenology of Iconic Love," Ph.D. dissertation, Baylor University, 2009. On-line at: <https://baylor-ir.tdl.org/bitstream/ handle/2104/5519/Amy_Antoninka_phd.pdf> (Accessed 12/19/2019)

Arentzen, Thomas. *The Virgin in Song: Mary and the Poetry of Romanos the Melodist*. Philadelphia, Pennsylvania: University of Pennsylvania Press, 2017.

Arjakovsky, Antoine. *What is Orthodoxy?: A Genealogy of Christian Understanding*. Brooklyn, New York: Angelico Press, 2018.

Ateljevic, Irena. "Visions of Transmodernity: A New Renaissance of our Human History?," *Integral Review*, Volume 9, Number 2, June 2013. On-line at: <https://integral-review.org/issues/vol_9_no_2_ateljevic_visions_of_transmodernity.pdf> (Accessed 12/3/2019)

Averintsev, Sergey S. "The Image of the Virgin Mary in Russian Piety," *Gregorianum* 75, 4 (1994), pp. 611-622. On-line at: <https://www.jstor.org/stable/pdf/23579744.pdf> (Accessed 11/20/2019)

Baker, Andrew. *Dancing Before God: A Franciscan Composer's Theology of Creation*. September 12, 2018. On-line at: <https://andrewbakercomposer.files.wordpress.com/2018/10/dancing-revised-september-20th-with-new-ending-2018-complete.pdf> (Accessed 12/27/2019)

Barbarić, Fr. Slavko. *In the School of Love*. Milford, Ohio: Faith Publishing Company, 2018.

Barbato, Melanie. "Marian apparitions—a challenge to established categories," *The Critical Religion Association* blog, September 2, 2013. On-line at: <https://criticalreligion.org/2013/09/02/marian-apparitions-a-challenge-to-established-categories/> (Accessed 9/14/2019)

Barker, Margaret. "The Images of Mary in the Litany of Loreto," *Usus Antiquior*, Vol. 1 No. 2, July, 2010, pp. 110–31, p. 110. On-line at: <http://www.margaretbarker.com/Papers/USU_Barker.pdf> (Accessed 11/2/2019)

Barker, Margaret. *The Mother of the Lord: Volume 1: The Lady in the Temple*. New York: Bloomsbury/T & T Clark, 2012.

Barnhart, Bruno. *The Future of Wisdom: Toward a Rebirth of Sapiential Christianity*. New York: Continuum, 2007.

Belaj, Marijana. "'We all laughed at the secret of the collapse of Communism, only Communists believed in that': the first ten years of the Medjugorje apparitions," *SIEF 2015: Utopias, Realities, Heritages: Ethnographies for the 21st Century*. 12th SIEF Congress Zagreb (Croatia), 21–25 June 2015. On-line at: <https://www.academia.edu/15228383/_We_all_laughed_at_the_secret_of_the_collapse_of_Communism_only_Communists_believed_in_that_the_first_ten_years_of_the_Medjugorje_apparitions> (Accessed 11/20/2019)

Bennett, J. G. *The Masters of Wisdom: An Esoteric History of the Spiritual Unfolding of Life on This Planet*. Santa Fe, New Mexico: Bennett Books, 1995.

Berdyaev, Nikolai. *The Russian Idea.* R. M. French, translator. Hudson, New York: Lindisfarne Press, 1992.

Bolendas, Joa. *So That You May Be One.* Hudson, New York: Lindisfarne Books, 1997.

Bonis, Wim. "The Hidden Wealth of the Virgin Mary," 2018, p. 9. On-line at: <http://eng.wimbonis.nl/wp-content/uploads/2018/09/The-Hidden-Wealth-of-The-Virgin-Mary-Wim-Bonis.pdf> (Accessed 11/19/2019)

Bowman, Marion; and Susan Sutcliffe, editors. *Beyond New Age: Exploring Alternative Spirituality.* Edinburgh: Edinburgh University Press, 2000.

Bowman, Marion. "Vernacular religion and nature: The 'Bible of the Folk' tradition in Newfoundland," *Folklore*, Volume 114, Issue 3, 2003, pp. 285-295. On-line at: <https://www.tandfonline.com/doi/abs/10.1080/0015587032000145333> (Accessed 11/30/2019)

Brenneman, Walter L., and Mary G. Brenneman. *Crossing the Circle at the Holy Wells of Ireland.* Charlottesville, Virginia: University Press of Virginia, 1995.

Brock, Sebastian. Webpage of resources in Syriac spirituality. On-line at: <http://syri.ac/brock/spirituality> (Accessed 11/26/2019)

Bruteau, Beatrice. *God's Ecstasy: The Creation of a Self-Creating World.* New York: The Crossroad Publishing Company, 1997.

Bruteau, Beatrice. *What We Can Learn From the East.* New York: The Crossroad Publishing Company, 1995.

Bulgakov, Sergei. Catherine Evtuhov, translator. *Philosophy of Economy: The World as Household.* Catherine Evtuhov, translator. New Haven, Connecticut: Yale University Press, 2000.

Bulgakov, Sergius. Boris Jakim, translator. *Icons and the Name of God.* Grand Rapids, Michigan: Wm. B. Eerdmans Publishing Co., 2012.

Bulgakov, Sergius. Thomas Allan Smith, translator. *Jacob's Ladder: On Angels.* Grand Rapids, Michigan: Wm. B. Eerdmans Publishing Co., 2010.

Bunge, Gabriel. Andrew Louth, translator. *The Rublev Trinity: The Icon of the Trinity by the Monk-Painter Andrei Rublev.* Crestwood, New York: St. Vladimir's Seminary Press, 2007.

Butler, John. *Concerning Prayer.* Video. On-line at: <https://youtu.be/p-bnP4g9nuU> (Accessed 12/2/2019)

Butler, John. *Lanzarote Tapes #4.* Video. On-line at: <https://youtu.be/UYnj70LWzxA> (Accessed 11/21/2019)

Byron S.J., William J. *The Word Proclaimed: A Homily for Every Sunday of the Year; Year A*. Mahwah, New Jersey: Paulist Press, 2013.

Caldecott, Stratford. "The Deep Horizon," an essay reproduced at The Matheson Trust website by permission of Second Spring (secondspring.co.uk). On-line at: <https://www.themathesontrust. org/library/the-deep-horizon> (Accessed 12/27/2019)

Camosy, Charles. *For Love of Animals: Christian Ethics, Consistent Action*. Cincinnati, Ohio: Franciscan Media, 2013. See, also, relevant videos at: <https://www.charlescamosy.com/ask-charlie-anything> (Accessed 11/27/2019)

Carden, Michael. "The Gendered Dynamics of Kenosis and Theosis in the Traditional Rosary of the Blessed Virgin Mary and the Surprising Theological Possibilities for Inclusive Theologies of Gender and Sexuality," *Australian eJournal of Theology*, Issue 1, 2009. Article on-line at: <https://staff.acu.edu.au/__data/assets/pdf_ file/0010/158545/Carden_ROSARY_Essay_Final_01.pdf> (Accessed 12/10/2019)

Carey, John. "Henry Corbin and the Secret of the Grail," *Temenos Academy Review* 14 (2011), pp. 159-178. On-line at: <https://www. temenosacademy.org/JOHN%20CAREY%20Henry%20Corbin% 20and%20the%20Secre%20of%20the%20Grail.pdf> (Accessed 10/16/2019)

Carley, James P. *Glastonbury Abbey: The Holy House at the head of the Moors Adventurous*. Glastonbury, England: Gothic Image Publications, 1996.

Catholic News Agency. "Our Lady of Kazan and Mary's affinity for Russia." *Angelus*, August 13, 2017. On-line at: <https://angelusnews.com/faith/our-lady-of-kazan-and-marys-affinity-for-russia/> (Accessed 11/20/2019)

Cheetham, Tom. *Imaginal Love: The Meanings of Imagination in Henry Corbin and James Hillman*. Thompson, Connecticut: Spring Publications, 2015.

Chittister O.S.B., Joan. *Wisdom Distilled From the Daily: Living the Rule of St. Benedict Today*. New York: HarperSanFrancisco, 1990.

Cochran, Tracy. "Queen of Angels," *Parabola*, April 30, 2015. On-line at: <https://parabola.org/2015/04/30/queen-of-angels/> (Accessed 6/14/2019)

Cohn, Steven F., and Kyriacos C. Markides. "Religion and Spiritual Experience: Revisiting Key Assumptions in Sociology," *International Journal of Transpersonal Studies*, Volume 32, Issue 2, 2013, pp. 34-41.

Compton, Madonna Sophia. *The Mother of God: Symbolic Theology of the Virgin Mary*. Berkeley, California, and Kansas City: The Raphael Group, 2010, 2018.

Conge, Michel. *Inner Octaves*. Toronto: Dolmen Meadows Editions, 2013.

Conge, Michel. "Presence and Prayer," *Parabola*, October 17, 2018. On-line at: <https://parabola.org/2018/10/17/presence-and-prayer-by-michel-conge/> (Accessed 11/20/2019)

Connell, Janice T. *Queen of Angels: Mary's Answers to Universal Questions*. Brewster, Massachusetts: Paraclete Press, 2008.

Consortium of Country Churches. "Our Lady of Glastonbury and Saint Joseph of Arimathaea," 2005, essay at the Full Homely Divinity website. On-line at: <http://fullhomelydivinity.org/Glastonburytraditionsfullpage.htm> (Accessed 10/10/2019)

Cook, Christopher C. H. *Hearing Voices, Demonic and Divine: Scientific and Theological Perspectives*. New York: Routledge, 2019. On-line at: <http://dro.dur.ac.uk/27003/> (Accessed 12/27/2019)

Coolman, Boyd Taylor. *Knowledge, Love, and Ecstasy in the Theology of Thomas Gallus*. Oxford, U.K.: Oxford University Press, 2017.

Cooper, Patrick Ryan. "The Virginal Middle: Towards a Marian Metaxology," *Medieval Mystical Theology*, Volume 25, 2016, Issue 1. Abstract on-line at: <https://www.tandfonline.com/doi/full/10.1080/20465726.2016.1163972>.

Corbin, Henry. *Creative Imagination in the Sufism of Ibn Arabi*. Princeton, New Jersey: Princeton University Press, 1969.

Corbin, Henry. Michel Cazenave, editor. *Jung, Buddhism, and the Incarnation of Sophia: Unpublished Writings from the Philosopher of the Soul*. Rochester, Vermont: Inner Traditions, 2019.

Cosma, Ioana. "Angels In-Between: The Poetics of Excess and the Crisis of Representation," Ph.D. dissertation, Centre for Comparative Literature, University of Toronto, 2009, p. 89. On-line at: <https://tspace.library.utoronto.ca/bitstream/1807/26454/7/Cosma_Ioana_I_200911_PhD_thesis.pdf.pdf> (Accessed 11/3/2019)

Critchley, Peter. "Dante's Enamoured Mind: Knowing and Being in the Life and Thought of Dante Alighieri," 2013. On-line at: <https://www.academia.edu/4771579/Dantes_Enamoured_Mind> (Accessed 11/29/2019)

Cselenyi, Istvan. *The Maternal Face of God?: Explorations in Catholic Sophiology*. Kettering, Ohio: Angelico Press, 2017.

Cutsinger, James S. "Colorless Light and Pure Air: The Virgin in the Thought of Frithjof Schuon," 2007. Previously published in *Sophia: The Journal of Traditional Studies*, 6:2 (Winter 2000); reprinted in *Maria: A Journal of Marian Studies*, 3:1 (August 2002) and in *Ye Shall Know the Truth: Christianity and the Perennial Philosophy*, ed. Mateus Soares de Azevedo (Bloomington, Indiana: World Wisdom, 2005). On-line at: <https://www.cutsinger.net/pdf/colorless_light_and_pure_air.pdf> (Accessed 8/30/2019)

Davis, Robert Glenn. "The Force of Union: Affect and Ascent in the Theology of Bonaventure," Ph.D. dissertation, Harvard University, 2012. On-line at: <http://nrs.harvard.edu/urn-3:HUL.InstRepos:9385627> (Accessed 12/19/2019)

de Carvalho, Olavo. "What is a Miracle?," *VoegelinView*, January 25, 2009. On-line at: <https://voegelinview.com/what-is-a-miracle/> (Accessed 1/1/2020)

de Nicolás, Antonio T., translator. *St. John of the Cross (San Juan de la Cruz), Alchemist of the Soul: His Life, His Poetry (Bilingual), His Prose*. York Beach, Maine: Samuel Weiser, Inc., 1989.

de Souzenelle, Annick. *The Body and Its Symbolism: A Kabbalistic Approach*. Wheaton, Illinois: Quest Books / Theosophical Publishing House, 2015.

de Waal, Esther. "Where Celtic and Benedictine Traditions Meet," in Linda Burton and Alex Whitehead, editors, *Christ is the Morning Star: When Celtic Spirituality meets the Benedictine Rule*. Dublin, Ireland: Lindisfarne Books, 1999.

Dear, John. "Mary of Nazareth: Prophet of Nonviolence," an essay at his website, December 2001. On-line at: <http://johndear.org/pdfs/Mary_of_Nazareth.pdf> (Accessed 11/6/2019)

Del Nevo, Matthew. "Imaginal Psychology's Disability," *Spring: A Journal of Archetype and Culture*, Issue 53, 1992, pp. 113-120. Article available on-line at: <https://www.pantheatre.com/archives/pages/forum_2006_metaphysics.pdf> (Accessed 12/2/2019)

Del Nevo, Matthew. *The Metaphysics of Night: Recovering Soul, Renewing Humanism*. New York: Routledge, 2014.

Delio O.S.F., Ilia. "Bonaventure's Metaphysics of the Good," *Theological Studies* 60 (1999). On-line at: <http://cdn.theologicalstudies.net/60/60.2/60.2.2.pdf> (Accessed 9/5/2019)

Delio O.S.F., Ilia. *The Unbearable Wholeness of Being: God, Evolution, and the Power of Love*. Maryknoll, New York: Orbis Books, 2013.

de Lubac S.J., Henri. *Eternal Feminine: A Study on the Text of Teilhard de Chardin* (London: Collins, 1971).

Dodd, Gloria Falcão. *The Virgin Mary, Mediatrix of All Grace: History and Theology of the Movement for a Dogmatic Definition from 1896 to 1964.* New Bedford, Massachusetts: Academy of the Immaculate, Franciscans of the Immaculate, 2009, 2012.

Doherty, Catherine. *Bogoroditza: She Who Gave Birth to God.* Expanded Second Edition. Combermere, Ontario: Madonna House Publications, 2001.

Douno, Beinsa. *The Wellspring of Good: The Last Words of the Master.* Sofia, Bulgaria: Bialo Bratstvo Publishers, 2013. On-line at: <http://petardanov.info/Knigi/Wellspring_of_Good.pdf> (Accessed 8/31/2019)

Duffner O.P., Fr. Paul A. "The Rosary & St. Dominic: In Defense of a Tradition," Rosary Center & Confraternity website. This article originally appeared in *The Rosary Light & Life,* Volume 49, Number 5, September-October 1996. On-line at: <https://www.rosarycenter.org/homepage-2/rosary/the-rosary-st-dominic/> (Accessed 11/26/2019)

Dupuche, John. *Jesus: The Mantra of God: An Exploration of Mantra Meditation.* Melbourne, Australia: David Lovell Publishing, 2005.

Dupuis, Bishop Paul. "Black Virgin: The French Mother Kali" (video). Presentation at the Vedanta Society of Providence (Rhode Island), October 8, 2017. On-line at: <https://youtu.be/vRahjadv9Kw> (Accessed 12/11/2019)

Ermolaev, Natalia. "The Marian Dimension of Mother Maria's Orthodox Social Christianity," *Philanthropy and Social Compassion in Eastern Orthodox Tradition: Papers of the Sophia Institute Academic Conference.* New York: Theotokos Press, December 2009. On-line at: <https://academiccommons.columbia.edu/doi/10.7916/D8XS64SK> (Accessed 10/26/2019)

Evans, Chloe. "Walsingham Field Notes Write-Up," for a course in the Anthropology of Christianity at the London School of Economics, 3/26/2010. On-line at: <https://studylib.net/doc/15680972> (Accessed 9/17/2019)

Evola, Julius. *The Mystery of the Grail: Initiation and Magic in the Quest of the Spirit.* Rochester, Vermont: Inner Traditions International, 1997, 1994. On-line at: <http://www.cakravartin.com/wordpress/wp-content/uploads/2006/08/Julius-Evola-The-Mystery-of-the-Grail.pdf> (Accessed 10/19/2019)

Fabbri, Renaud. "The Milk of the Virgin: The Prophet, the Saint and the Sage," in M. Ali Lakhani, Editor, *Sacred Web* 20, 2007, p. 11. On-line at: <http://www.worldwisdom.com/public/viewpdf/default.aspx?article-title=The_Milk_of_the_Virgin_the_Prophet_the_Saint_and_the_Sage.pdf> (Accessed 7/24/2019)

Fakhoury, Hadi. "Henry Corbin and Russian Religious Thought." Master of Arts thesis, 2013. Institute of Islamic Studies, McGill University, Montreal, Quebec, Canada.

Fanger, Claire. "Inscription on the Heart: Medieval Christian Knowledge Practices," *The Side View* website, October 4, 2018. On-line at: <https://thesideview.co/articles/inscription-on-the-heart/> (Accessed 12/18/2019)

Fedorov, Nikolai Fedorovich. *What Was Man Created For: The Philosophy of the Common Task: Selected Works.* Lausanne, Switzerland: Honeyglen Publishing/L'Age d'Homme, 1999.

Fedewa, Marilyn H. "Beyond Baroque Style: A New Look at Maria of Agreda's Treatment of Mary's Life and Person in the *Mystical City of God*," *Marian Studies*, Volume 60, Article 10, 2009, pp. 173-188. On-line at: <https://ecommons.udayton.edu/marian_studies/vol60/iss1/10/> (Accessed 11/27/2019)

Fedewa, Marilyn H. *Maria of Agreda: Mystical Lady in Blue.* Albuquerque, New Mexico: University of New Mexico Press, 2009.

Ford-Grabowsky, Mary. Editor. *Spiritual Writings on Mary.* Woodstock, Vermont: Skylight Paths Publishing, 2005.

Forest, Jim. "Christian Types, Christian Virtues, Christian Unity: The Evangelical Path to Christian Unity," *Touchstone Magazine*, May/June 1999. On-line at: <https://www.touchstonemag.com/archives/article.php?id=12-03-031-f> (Accessed 11/23/2019)

Frost, Brian. *Glastonbury Journey: Marjorie Milne's Search for Reconciliation.* Oxford, UK: Becket, 1986.

Geller, Florentina Badalanova. "The Spinning Mary: Towards the Iconology of the Annunciation," *Cosmos: The Journal of the Traditional Cosmology Society*, Volume 20, 2004, pp. 211-260. On-line at: <https://thisisthetcson.files.wordpress.com/2016/07/cosmos-20.pdf> (Accessed 8/12/2019)

Gibran, Khalil. *The Prophet.* As quoted in Bahar Davary, "Forgiveness in Islam: Is it an Ultimate Reality?," *Ultimate Reality and Meaning*, Volume 27 Issue 2, June 2004, pp. 127-141, p. 127. On-line at: <https://www.utpjournals.press/doi/pdf/10.3138/uram.27.2.127> (Accessed 12/30/2019)

Girard, René. "Generative Scapegoating," in Robert G. Hammerton-Kelly, editor, *Violent Origins: Walter Burkert, René Girard, and Jonathan Z. Smith on Ritual Killing and Cultural Formation*. Stanford, California: Stanford University Press, 1987.

Goering, Joseph. *The Virgin and the Grail: Origins of a Legend*. New Haven: Yale University Press, 2005.

Graziano, Br. Joseph Bernard Marie O.P. "Where the Rosary Appears in 'The Lord of the Rings'," *Word on Fire Blog*, March 23, 2017. On-line at: <https://www.wordonfire.org/resources/blog/where-the-rosary-appears-in-the-lord-of-the-rings/18699/> (Accessed 12/22/2019)

Green, Hannah. *Little Saint*. New York: The Modern Library / Random House, 2001, 2000.

Guite, Malcolm. "As If." Video based on his 2019 Laing Lectures at Regent College in Vancouver, British Columbia, on the role of the imagination as a truth-bearing faculty. On-line at: <https://youtu.be/-aQD_W1rSw0> (Accessed 12/5/2019)

Håland, Evy Johanne. "The Life-giving Spring: Water in Greek Religion, Ancient and Modern, a Comparison," *Proteus: A Journal of Ideas*, Spring 2009, Volume 26, Number 1, pp. 45-54. On-line at: <https://www.ship.edu/globalassets/proteus/volume26-45-haland.pdf> (Accessed 8/10/2019)

Halemba, Agnieszka. *Negotiating Marian Apparitions: The Politics of Religion in Transcarpathian Ukraine*. Budapest & New York: Central European University Press, 2015.

Hart, Aidan. "Mary and the Temple in Icons," a talk given at the Temple Studies Group at the Temple Church, London, June 15th, 2013. On-line at: <http://www.templestudiesgroup.com/Papers/Hart_Maryandthetemple.pdf> (Accessed 9/16/2019)

Hayes O.F.M., Zachary. "The Cosmos, A Symbol of the Divine." Synthesis of a paper originally prepared for the United States Catholic Conference U.S.C.C. meeting in Washington, D.C., June 1997. On-line at: <https://www.franciscantradition.org/images/stories/custodians/09_Cosmos_Symbol_of_the_Divine.pdf> (Accessed 9/1/2019)

Hermkens, Anna-Karina; Willy Jansen, and Catrien Notermans. *Moved by Mary: The Power of Marian Pilgrimage*. New York: Routledge, 2016; first published by Ashgate Publishing, 2009.

Hickey, Penny. Editor. *Drink of the Stream: Prayers of the Carmelites*. San Francisco, California: Ignatius Press, 2002.

Hieromonk Silouan. "Practice of Harmony in Orthodox Christian Wisdom," The Harmony Project website. On-line at: <https://www.theharmonyproject.org.uk/practice-of-harmony-in-orthodox-christian-wisdom/> (Accessed 1/8/2020)

Hieromonk Silouan. "Virgin of the Flame," blog entry at *Wisdom Hermitage*, April 13, 2018. On-line at: <http://www.wisdomhermitage.org.uk/2018/04/13/virgin-of-the-flame/> (Accessed 9/13/2019)

Hillman, James. *Re-visioning Psychology*. New York, NY: Harper & Row, 1975.

"Holy Snakes." Essay at Orthodox Wikipedia. On-line at: <https://orthodoxwiki.org/Holy_Snakes> (Accessed 1/6/2020)

Homick, Abbot Joseph. *A Place Prepared by God: Through the Virgin Mary, the New Eve, Paradise Will Not Fail Twice*. Sunnyvale, California: Patsons Press, 2010.

Hovorun, Cyril. *Political Orthodoxies: The Unorthodoxies of the Church Coerced*. Minneapolis, Minnesota: Fortress Press, 2018.

Ibn Gabirol, Solomon Ben Judah. *The Fountain of Life (Fons Vitae)*. Originally translated by Alfred B. Jacob. Revised by Leonard Levin. New York: The Jewish Theological Seminary, 2005.

Iwachiw (Ivakhiv), Adrian. "Places of Power: Sacred Sites, Gaia's Pilgrims, and the Politics of Landscape (An interpretive study of the geographics of New Age and conternporary earth spirituality, with reference to Glastonbury, England, and Sedona, Arizona)," Ph.D. dissertation, York University, Ontario, Canada, June 1997. On-line at: <https://oatd.org/oatd/record?record=oai%5C%3Acollectionscanada.gc.ca%5C%3AOOAMICUS.18222596> (Accessed 8/15/2019)

Johnston, Francis. *The Wonder of Guadalupe: The Origin and Cult of the Miraculous Image of the Blessed Virgin in Mexico*. Charlotte, North Carolina: TAN Books, 1993.

Joiner, Fr. Dn. Charles. "Flies and Bees - Advice from Elder Paisios," *Orthodox Way of Life: Walking the Path to Theosis*, December 17, 2009. On-line at: <http://orthodoxwayoflife.blogspot.com/2009/12/flies-and-bees-advice-from-elder.html> (Accessed 12/30/2019)

Jones, Rufus M. *Studies in Mystical Religion*. London: Macmillan & Co., Ltd., 1909. On-line at: <http://www.iapsop.com/ssoc/1909__jones___studies_in_mystical_religion.pdf> (Accessed 11/23/2019)

Karpodini-Dimitriadi, Effie. "The Descent of the Virgin Mary into Hell: A short presentation and free translation of a handwritten text from the island of Kythira." On-line at: <http://ekarpodini.com/

en/files/2013/03/The-descent-of-Virgin-Mary-into-the-Hell1. pdf> (Accessed 8/24/2019)

Kaspersen, Søren, and Ulla Haastrup, editors. *Images of Cult and Devotion: Function and Reception of Christian Images in Medieval and Post-Medieval Europe.* Copenhagen, Denmark: Museum Tusculanum Press and University of Copenhagen, 2004.

Kharitidi, Olga. *Entering the Circle: Ancient Secrets of Siberian Wisdom Discovered by a Russian Psychiatrist.* New York: HarperCollins/HarperSanFrancisco, 1997.

Kharitidi, Olga. *Master of Lucid Dreams: In the Heart of Asia a Russian Psychiatrist Learns How to Heal the Spirits of Trauma.* Charlottesville, Virginia: Hampton Roads Publishing Company, 2001.

Kilcourse, George. "'The Paradise Ear': Thomas Merton, Poet," *The Kentucky Review*, Summer 1987, Volume 7, Number 2.

Kirby, John. "The Day of Mary: The Coming of Mary and Our Mutual Transformation of the World," DuVersity website, Library. On-line at: <https://www.duversity.org/PDF/The%20Day%20of%20Mary.pdf> (Accessed 1/11/2020)

Kirby, John. "Will and Reconciling Our Evolution," *DuVersity 45*, Spring 2018, p. 9. On-line at: <https://www.duversity.org/sites/default/files/files/DuVersity%2045%20%20%20%20%20%20%20%20%20%2020%20%20%20%20%20%20%20%20%20%20Spring%202018.pdf> (Accessed 1/1/2020)

Konopásek, Zdeněk, and Jan Paleček. "Apparitions and Possessions as Boundary Objects: An Exploration into Some Tensions between Mental Health Care and Pastoral Care," *Journal of Religion and Health*, Vol. 51, No. 3 (September 2012), pp. 970-985. Preview on-line at: <https://www.jstor.org/stable/41653882> (Accessed 9/14/2019)

Kosloski, Philip. "4 Women in Tolkien's Middle-Earth who reflect the beauty of the Virgin Mary," *Voyage Comics & Publishing*, March 22, 2019. On-line at: <https://voyagecomics.com/2019/03/ 22/4-women-in-middle-earth-who-reflect-the-beauty-of-the-virgin-mary/> (Accessed 6/15/2019)

Kosloski, Philip. "Scottish Parliament recognizes consecration to the Immaculate Heart of Mary," *Aleteia*, September 6, 2017. On-line at: <https://aleteia.org/2017/09/06/scottish-parliament-recognizes-consecration-to-the-immaculate-heart-of-mary/amp/> (Accessed 12/30/2019)

Kushner, Laurence. *The River of Light: Jewish Mystical Awareness.* Special Anniversary Edition. Woodstock, Vermont: Jewish Lights Publishing, 2000.

Kvamme, Janet C. "The *Fontalis Plenitudo* in Bonaventure as a Symbol for his Metaphysics," Ph.D. dissertation, Theology Department, Fordham University, 1999. Preview on-line at: <https://fordham.bepress.com/dissertations/AAI9955966/> (Accessed 9/13/2019)

Lahey, William L. "The Blessed Virgin Mary in the Theology and Devotion of the Seventeenth-Century Anglican Divines," *Marian Studies*, Volume 38, 1987, Article 14, pp. 137-170. On-line at: <https://ecommons.udayton.edu/marian_studies/vol38/iss1/14/> (Accessed 12/19/2019)

Langr, Chloe. "Prague Won't Allow Marian Column Restoration," EpicPew website, September 19, 2017. On-line at: <https://epicpew.com/marian-column-removed-prague/> (Accessed 10/31/2019)

Lao Tzu. *Tao Teh Ching.* John C. H. Wu, translator. Paul K. T. Sih, editor. New York: St. John's University Press, 1961.

Laurentin, Rene. *Maria-Ecclesia-Sacerdotium.* Paris 1952.

Lavriotes, Maximos. "Giving Birth to God: Meister Eckhart and Symeon the New Theologian on Spiritual Maternity," *Eckhart Review*, Volume 4, Issue 1, 1995, pp. 36-56. Limied access on-line at: <https://www.tandfonline.com/doi/abs/10.1179/eck_1995_4_1_005> (Accessed 12/2/2019)

Lidov, Alexei. "The Priesthood of the Virgin Mary as an Image-Paradigm of Christian Visual Culture," *IKON: Journal of Iconographic Studies*, Volume 10, 2017.

Lindblom, John. "John C.H.Wu and the Evangelization of China," *Logos: A Journal of Catholic Thought and Culture*, May 2005, pp. 130-164. On-line at: <https://www.academia.edu/7509286/John_C._H._Wu_and_the_Evangelization_of_China> (Accessed 11/29/2019)

Llewelyn, Fr. Robert. An interview conducted by Nasa Ognjista in Medjugorje, Bosnia-Herzegovina, December 1992. On-line at: <http://medjugorje.altervista.org/doc_en/testimonies/conv_anglicano.html> (Accessed 1/2/2020). Information about Fr. Llewelyn can be found on-line at: <http://www.lightforthejourney.org.uk/robert-llewellyn.html> (Accessed 1/2/2020)

Lovei, Zsofia. "The Vehicle of Pilgrimage: Spanning the Geographical and Ideological Horizons of the Way of Mary through Mariazell to Csíksomlyó," 2015. On-line at: <https://www.academia.edu/ 22108005/The_Vehicle_of_Pilgrimage_Spanning_the_Geographic al_and_Ideological_Horizons_of_the_Way_of_Mary_through_Mar iazell_to_Cs%C3%ADksomly%C3%B3> (Accessed 11/19/2019)

Lowell, Robert. "The Quaker Graveyard in Nantucket," a poem, as reproduced at the Poetry Foundation website. On-line at: <https://www.poetryfoundation.org/poems/48984/the-quaker-graveyard-in-nantucket> (Accessed 1/13/2020)

Lubanska, Magdalena. "Life-Giving Springs and The Mother of God / Zhivonosen Istochnik / Zoodochos Pege / Balŭkliyska: Byzan-tine-Greek-Ottoman Intercultural Influence and Its Aftereffects in Iconography, Religious Writings and Ritual Practices in the Region of Plovdiv," *Slavia Meridionalis* 17, 2017, Article No.: 1252. On-line at: <https://www.researchgate.net/publication/320408780_ Life-giving_springs_and_The_Mother_of_God_Zhivonosen_ Istochnik_Zoodochos_Pege_Balikliyska_Byzantine-Greek-Ottoman_intercultural_influence_and_its_aftereffects_in_ iconography_religious_writings_and_rit> (Accessed 1/23/2020)

Lyngsgaard, Hans. *Teachings of the Virgin Mary.* Alresford, Hampshire, U.K.: Axis Mundi Books / John Hunt Publishing Ltd., 2012.

McGregor, Peter John. "Heart to Heart: The Spiritual Christology of Joseph Ratziner." Ph.D. dissertation, 2013. School of Theology, Australian Catholic University. Subsequently published in book form (2016) by Wipf and Stock and its imprint, Pickwick Publi-cations, Eugene, Oregon. Dissertation on-line at: <https://researchbank.acu.edu.au/theses/477/> (Accessed 10/9/2019)

McGuckin, John Anthony, translator. *The Harp of Glory: Enzira Sebhat: An Alphabetical Hymn of Praise for the Ever-Blessed Virgin Mary from the Ethiopian Orthodox Church*, Popular Patristics Series. Yonkers, New York: St. Vladimir's Seminary Press, 2010.

McGuckin, John Anthony. *The Path of Christianity: The First Thousand Years.* Downers Grove, Illinois: InterVarsity Press, 2017.

Mallett, Mark. "The New Gideon," essay published at his website blog on August 22, 2017. On-line at: <https://www.markmallett.com/ blog/2017/08/22/the-new-gideon/> (Accessed 10/31/2019)

Margry, Peter Jan. "Marian Interventions in the Wars of Ideology: The Elastic Politics of the Roman Catholic Church on Modern Apparitions," in *History and Anthropology*, Volume 20, September 2009, Issue 3: Ethnographies of "Divine Interventions" in Europe, pp. 243-263. On-line at: <http://www.academia.edu/3633595/Marian_Interventions_ in_the_Wars_of_Ideology> (Accessed 10/26/2019)

Marion, Jim. *Putting on the Mind of Christ: The Inner Work of Christian Spirituality*. Charlottesville, Virginia: Hampton Roads Publishing Company, Inc., 2000.

Markides, Kyriacos C. "Eastern Orthodox Mysticism and Transpersonal Theory," *The Journal of Transpersonal Psychology*, 2008, Volume 40, Number 2. On-line at: <https://pdfs.semanticscholar.org/9bcb/f3c9735a53a280e420c4465fc1bc680df0d9.pdf> (Accessed 1/3/2020).

Markides, Kyriacos C. "The Healing Spirituality of Eastern Orthodoxy: A Personal Journey of Discovery," *Religions*, June 8, 2017. On-line at: <https://www.mdpi.com/2077-1444/8/6/109/htm> (Accessed 1/3/2020).

Markides, Kyriacos C. *The Mountain of Silence: A Search for Orthodox Spirituality*. New York: Image/Doubleday, 2001.

Martin, Michael. "Catholicism isn't a Religion, it's a Field," Angelico Press, blog, undated. On-line at: <https://angelicopress.org/catholicism-isnt-a-religion-its-a-field/> (Accessed 1/6/2020)

Martin, Michael. *The Incarnation of the Poetic Word: Theological Essays on Poetry & Philosophy • Philosophical Essays on Poetry & Theology*. Kettering, Ohio: Angelico Press, 2017.

Maspero, Giulio. "Life as Relation: Classical Metaphysics and Trinitarian Ontology," *Theological Research*, Volume 2 (2014), Number 1, pp. 31-52. On-line at: <http://dx.doi.org/10.15633/thr.677> (Accessed 12/7/2019)

Maunder, Chris. "Transforming visions? Apparitions of Mary," *The Way* Supplement, 100, pp. 30-41. On-line at: <https://www.theway.org.uk/back/s100Maunder.pdf> (Accessed 11/27/2019)

Meinardus, Otto E. A. "The Virgin Mary as Mediatrix Between Christians and Muslims in the Middle East," *Marian Studies*, Vol. 47, Article 10, 1996, pp. 88-101, pp. 93-94. On-line at: <https://ecommons.udayton.edu/marian_studies/vol47/iss1/10> (Accessed 11/3/2019)

Merchant, Carolyn. *Reinventing Eden: The Fate of Nature in Western Culture*. New York: Routledge, 2003.

Merton, Thomas. *New Seeds of Contemplation.* New York: New Directions, 1972, 1962.

Metallinos, Fr. George. "Paradise and Hell According to Orthodox Tradition," *OrthodoxyToday.org*, 2009. On-line at: <http://www.orthodoxytoday.org/articles-2009/Mettalinos-Paradise-And-Hell-According-To-Orthodox-Tradition.php> (Accessed 9/14/2019)

Milbank, John. *Theology and Social Theory: Beyond Secular Reason.* Second Edition. Malden, Massachusetts: Blackwell Publishing, 2006, 1990.

Misler, Nicoletta, editor. Wendy Salmond, translator. *Pavel Florensky: Beyond Vision: Essays on the Perception of Art.* London: Reaktion Books, 2002.

Mohammadi, Farid. "In search of the Holy Presence of the Blessed Mary in Tolkien's Middle-earth," *International Journal of Applied Linguistics & English Literature,* Vol. 2 No. 4; July 2013, pp. 200-211. On-line at: < http://www.journals.aiac.org.au/index.php/IJALEL/article/view/998> (Accessed 11/3/2019)

Montagu, Jemima. "Earthly Delights: The Art of the Garden," *Tate Etc.,* magazine of the Tate galleries, Issue 1, May 1, 2004. On-line at: <https://www.tate.org.uk/tate-etc/issue-1-summer-2004/earthly-delights> (Accessed 9/10/2019)

Moyse, Ashley John; Scott A. Kirkland; and John C. McDowell. Editors. *Correlating Sobornost: Conversations Between Karl Barth and Russian Orthodox Tradition.* Minneapolis, Minnesota: Fortress Press, 2016.

Nasr, Seyyed Hossein. *Science and Civilization in Islam.* Plume Series. New York: New American Library, 1970.

Naydler, Jeremy. "The Perennial Philosophy and the Recovery of a Theophanic View of Nature." Published on-line at *The Harmony Project,* March 14, 2019, and re-published at *The Matheson Trust* website. PDF version accessible on-line at: <https://www.themathesontrust.org/library/naydler-perennial-philosophy-recovery> (Accessed 12/15/2019)

Newman, Barbara. "What Did It Mean to Say 'I Saw'? The Clash between Theory and Practice in Medieval Visionary Culture," *Speculum,* Volume 80, Number 1 (January 2005), pp. 1-43. On-line at: <https://english.duke.edu/sites/english.duke.edu/files/file-attachments/Newman_Speculum2005.pdf> (Accessed 12/3/2019)

O'Donohue, John. *Anam Cara: A Book of Celtic Wisdom.* New York: HarperCollins, 1998.

O'Donohue, John. "Spirituality as the Art of Real Presence," *The Way* Supplement. London: Burns & Oates, 1998, pp. 85 ff. On-line at: <https://www.theway.org.uk/back/s092ODonohue.pdf> (Accessed 11/25/2019)

O'Neill, Michael. *The Miracle Hunter* website. On-line at: <http://miraclehunter.com/marian_apparitions/index.html> (Accessed 9/13/2019)

Olnhausen, Fr. Bill. "133. A Late-Twentieth-Century Saint: The Holy Elder Paisios," Father Bill's Blog, Ancient Faith Blogs, July 5, 2019. On-line at: <https://blogs.ancientfaith.com/frbill/133-a-late-twentieth-century-saint-the-holy-elder-paisios/> (Accessed 12/21/2019)

Páleš, Emil. *Seven Archangels: Rhythms of Inspiration in the History of Culture and Nature.* Bratislava, Slovakia: Sophia, 200).

Pelikan, Jaroslav. *Mary Through the Centuries: Her Place in the History of Culture.* New Haven: Yale University Press, 1998, 1996.

Petrović, Sonja. "Legends of the Virgin Mary: Miracles of Abundance out of Scarcity," in *Belief Narrative Genres*, International Society for Folk Narrative Research, 2012, pp. 139-146. On-line at: <https://www.academia.edu/5978905/Legends_of_the_Virgin_Mary_Miracles_of_abundance_out_of_scarcity> (Accessed 9/9/2019)

P.H., "See How Armenian Genocide Orphans Sparked a Revolution in Ethiopian Music," How Africa: The Rise of Africa, website, un-dated. On-line at: <https://howafrica.com/armenian-genocide-orphans-sparked-revolution-ethiopian-music/> (Accessed 1/7/2020)

Plunkett, Dudley. *Queen of Prophets: The Gospel Message of Medjugorje.* New York: Doubleday, 1992.

Poston, Carol H. "Evelyn Underhill and the Virgin Mary," article at The Evelyn Underhill Association website, December 1, 2015. On-line at: <http://evelynunderhill.org/evelyn-underhill-and-the-virgin-mary-by-carol-h-poston/> (Accessed 12/27/2019)

Pope John Paul II. Address to the Fiftieth General Assembly of the United Nations Organization at the United National Headquarters (New York), Thursday, October 5, 1995. On-line at: <https://w2.vatican.va/content/john-paul-ii/en/speeches/1995/october/documents/hf_jp-ii_spe_05101995_address-to-uno.html> (Accessed 10/15/2019)

Qadir, Ali, and Tatiana Tiaynen-Qadir. "Deep Culture and the Mystical Agency of Mary in Eastern Christianity," *Religions* 2018, 9, 383; doi:10.3390/rel9120383. On-line at: <https://www.researchgate. net/publication/329155659_Deep_Culture_and_the_Mystical_Age ncy_of_Mary_in_Eastern_Christianity> (Accessed 9/2/2019).

Radulović, Nemanja. "The Question of Neo-Bogomilism" in *Ways of Gnosis. Mystical and Esoteric Traditions and Gnostic Worldview from Antiquity to the Present Time*, edited by Sergey V. Pahomov and Anna A. Tesman, 169–184. St. Petersburg, Russia: Russian Christian Academy for Humanities, 2013. On-line at: <https:// www.academia.edu/9844763/The_Question_of_ Neobogomilism> (Accessed 9/1/2019)

Ransome, Hilda M. *The Sacred Bee in Ancient Times and Folklore.* Mineola, New York: Dover Publications, 2004; originally published by George Allen & Unwin, London, 1937.

Reznik, Larisa. "'We Are All Pussy Riot' But Who Are 'We?'," September 20, 2012. An article in the *Sightings* series at the University of Chicago Divinity School website. On-line at: <https:// divinity.uchicago.edu/sightings/articles/we-are-all-pussy-riot-who- are-we> (Accessed 10/28/2019)

Riain, Nóirín Ní. "The Specificity of Christian Theosony: Towards a Theology of Listening." Ph.D. dissertation (2003). Mary Immaculate College, University of Limerick (Ireland). On-line at: <https://dspace.mic.ul.ie/handle/10395/2039> (Accessed 8/26/2019)

"Rosary: History of the Term," *All About Mary* website, University of Dayton. On-line at: <https://udayton.edu/imri/mary/r/rosary- history-of-the-term.php> (Accessed 12/21/2019)

Rosenthal, Bernice Glatzer. Editor. *The Occult in Russian and Soviet Culture.* Ithaca, New York: Cornell University Press, 1997.

Roten S.M., Fr. Johann. Q&A on the Age of Mary. Undated. On-line at: <https://udayton.edu/imri/mary/a/age-of-mary.php> (Accessed 1/3/2020)

Rozett, Ella. "The Mysterious Black Faces of the Madonna," at Interfaith Mary Page. On-line at: <http://interfaithmary.net/ black-madonna-introduction> (Accessed 12/10/2019)

St. Victor, Owen. *The Masked Madonna: Studies in the Mystical Symbolism of The Secret Sovereign: The Queen of Heaven.* Leuven, Belgium: Sancta Sophia, 1988.

Sanidopoulos, John. "How Did the 'Life-Giving Spring' Get Its Name?'," *Mystagogy Resource Center*, May 10, 2013. On-line at: <https://www.johnsanidopoulos.com/2013/05/how-did-life-giving-spring-get-its-name.html> (Accessed 8/9/2019)

Sanidopoulos, John. "Zoodochos Pege (Life-Giving Spring) Resource Page," *Mystagogy Resource Center*, May 5, 2016. On-line at: <https://www.johnsanidopoulos.com/2016/05/zoodochos-pege-life-giving-spring.html> (Accessed 8/9/2019)

Scherr, Stefanie. "'As Soon As We Got Here We Lost Everything:' The Migration Memories and Religious Lives of the Old Believers in Australia," Ph.D. dissertation, Swinburne University of Technology (Australia), 2013. On-line at: <https://pdfs.semanticscholar.org/f02f/4e47846fab69ca65bfb69d52b6221108ed17.pdf> (Accessed 12/29/2019).

Sheehan, Fr. John. "The Miraculous Fountain of La Salette," at the website of the La Salette Missionaries, as reprinted from the La Salette publication, *Our Lady's Missionary*, September, 1934, pp. 129-130, 132. On-line at: <https://www.lasalette.org/about-la-salette/reconciliation/spirituality-and-charism/1895-the-miraculous-fountain-of-la-salette.html> (Accessed 6/15/2019)

Shelton, Mahmoud. *Alchemy in Middle-earth: The Significance of J. R. R. Tolkien's The Lord of the Rings.* Temple of Justice Books, 2002.

Shoemaker, Stephen J. *The Ancient Traditions of the Virgin Mary's Dormition and Assumption*, Oxford Early Christian Studies (Oxford, UK: Oxford University Press, 2003).

Shokhikyan, Arman. "Ceremony of Blessing of Grapes," text utilizing the "Bless, O Lord: Services of Blessing in the Armenian Church" by Fr. Garabed Kochakian with some linguistic revisions. On-line at: <https://ism.yale.edu/sites/default/files/files/2018%20Liturgy%20Conference/Arman%20Shokhikyan%20-%20Blessing%20of%20Grapes.pdf> (Accessed 12/26/2019)

Siekierski, Konrad. "Charismatic Renewal and Miracular Sensitivity at a Catholic Marian Apparition Site in Poland," *Journal of Global Catholicism*, Volume 2, Issue 2, 2018, Article 6. On-line at: <https://crossworks.holycross.edu/jgc/vol2/iss2/6> (Accessed 11/15/2019)

Siekierski, Konrad. "Negotiating Marian Apparitions: The Politics of Religion in Transcarpathian Ukraine," *Religion, State and Society*, Volume 45, 2017, Issue 2. On-line at: <http://dx.doi.org/10.1080/09637494.2017.1314081> (Accessed 11/15/2019)

Simsky, Andrew. "The Image Paradigm of the Fire of God in the Bible and in the Christian Tradition," in Alexei Lidov, editor, *Hierotopy of Light and Fire in the Culture of the Byzantine World*. Moscow: Theoria, 2013), pp. 73-81.

Sisto, Walter Nunzio. "The Soul of the Human Race: The Mother of God in the Theology of Sergius Bulgakov," Ph.D. dissertation (2013), University of St. Michael's College, University of Toronto. On-line at: <https://tspace.library.utoronto.ca/handle/1807/43428> (Accessed 8/24/2019)

Smith, Christopher. "Virgo Sacerdos: Mary and the Priesthood of the Faithful." License Thesis, 2005, Pontificia Universitas Gregoriana. On-line at: <https://www.academia.edu/7910168/Virgo_Sacerdos_The_Priesthood_of_the_Virgin_Mary> (Accessed 11/20/2019)

Sparks, Robert Logan. "Ambiguous Spaces: A Contextualisation of Shared Pilgrimage in Ephesus," Ph.D. dissertation (2011), Tilburg University (Netherlands). On-line at: <https://research.tilburguniversity.edu/en/publications/ambiguous-spaces-a-contextualisation-of-shared-pilgrimage-in-ephe> (Accessed 8/24/2019)

Steiner, Rudolf. *Christianity as Mystical Fact and the Mysteries of Antiquity*. Fourth edition. Hudson, New York: SteinerBooks/Anthroposophic Press in 1997.

Strachan, Gordan. *Jesus the Master Builder: Druid Mysteries and the Dawn of Christianity*. Edinburgh, Scotland: Floris Books, 2010.

Strand, Clark; and Perdita Finn. *The Way of the Rose: The Radical Path of the Divine Feminine Hidden in the Rosary*. New York: Spiegel & Grau / Penguin Random House, 2019.

Szulakowska, Urszula. *The Alchemical Virgin Mary in the Religious and Political Context of the Renaissance*. Newcastle upon Tyne, U.K.: Cambridge Scholars Publishing, 2017. Introduction and first chapter on-line at: <https://www.academia.edu/32581197/The_Alchemical_Virgin_Mary_in_the_Religious_and_Political_Context_of_the_Renaissance> (Accessed 12/27/2019)

Taves, Ann. "Channeled Apparitions: On Visions that Morph and Categories that Slip," *Visual Resources*, Volume 25, Numbers 1–2, March–June 2009, pp. 137-152. On-line at: <https://www.religion.ucsb.edu/wp-content/uploads/2009-Channeled-apparitions-On-visions-that-morph-and-categories-that-slip.-Visual-Resources-251-137-52..pdf> (Accessed 12/10/2019)

Than, Krisztina. "Roma seek luck and love at Catholic shrine in Hungary," *Reuters*, September 11, 2017. On-line at: <https://www.reuters.com/article/us-hungary-religion-roma/roma-seek-luck-and-love-at-catholic-shrine-in-hungary-idUSKCN1BM1GR> (Accessed 10/31/2019)

Thompson, Robert F. *From Glory to Glory: The Sophianic Vision of Fr. Sergius Bulgakov*. A Perennials Study Group publication, Memphis, Tennessee. CreateSpace, 2016.

Thompson, Robert F. *Taliesin's Harp: A Poetics of the Divine-Humanity*. A Perennials Study Group publication, Memphis, Tennessee. Kindle Direct Publishing, 2019.

Thompson, Robert F. *The Anthropocosmic Vision: For a New Dialogic Civilization*. A Perennials Study Group publication, Memphis, Tennessee. CreateSpace / Kindle Direct Publishing, 2017.

Thurston, Herbert, and Andrew Shipman. "The Rosary," *New Advent Catholic Encyclopedia*, Volume 13. New York: Robert Appleton Company, 1912. On-line at: <http://www.newadvent.org/cathen/13184b.htm> (Accessed 11/26/2019)

Tin, Mikkel B. "Saturated Phenomena: From Picture to Revelation in Jean-Luc Marion's Phenomenology," *Filozofia* 65, 2010, No. 9, p. 860-876. On-line at: <http://www.klemens.sav.sk/fiusav/doc/filozofia/2010/9/860-876.pdf> (Accessed 10/21/2019)

Trubshaw, Bob. *Pilgrimage in England: A Concise Introduction*. Avebury, UK: Heart of Albion, 2015. On-line at: <https://www.hoap.co.uk/pilgrimage_in_england.pdf> (Accessed 8/13/2019)

Tucker, Mary Evelyn, and John Grim, editors. *Living Cosmology: Christian Responses to Journey of the Universe*. Maryknoll, New York: Orbis Books, 2016.

Turnbull, James. *The Prophetic Role of Glastonbury: To be a blessing for the world*. Glastonbury, England: Abbey Press, 2001.

"University" in *Johnson's Universal Cyclopedia: A New Edition*, Volume 8. New York: D. Appleton and Company, 1895.

Varner, Gary R. *Sacred Wells: A Study in the History, Meaning, and Mythology of Holy Wells & Waters*. 2nd Edition. New York: Algora Publishing, 2009.

Vasilyev, Tikhon. "Christian Angelology in Pseudo-Dionysius and Sergius Bulgakov." D.Phil. thesis, Wolfson College, Oxford University, 2019. On-line at: <https://ora.ox.ac.uk/objects/uuid:667ef5e8-a005-4bb4-8e2d-cc7b0424d4a7> (Accessed 10/22/2019)

Vaughan-Lee, Llewellyn. *Darkening of the Light: Witnessing the End of an Era.* Point Reyes, California: The Golden Sufi Center, 2013.

Vernon, Mark. *A Secret History of Christianity: Jesus, the Last Inkling, and the Evolution of Consciousness.* Alresford, Hampshire, United Kingdom: Christian Alternative, an imprint of John Hunt Publishing, 2019.

Vernon, Mark. "John Vervaeke, Romanticism & Owen Barfield," June 23, 2019 (Video). On-line at: <https://youtu.be/GQQ7Qb30TS4> (Accessed 8/23/2019)

Vlachos, Metropolitan Hierotheos of Nafpaktos. *Saint Gregory Palamas as a Hagiorite.* Levadia, Greece: Birth of Theotokos Monastery, 2000.

Vlachos, Metropolitan Hierotheos of Nafpaktos. "The Annunciation of the Virgin Mary," Orthodox Research Institute website. On-line at: <http://www.orthodoxresearchinstitute.org/articles/fasts_feasts/hierotheos_vlachos_annunciation.htm> (Accessed 11/23/2019)

Voiles, Kenneth M. "The Mother of All the Living: The Role of the Virgin Mary in the Spirituality of Thomas Merton," *The Merton Annual,* Volume 5, 1992. On-line at: <http://merton.org/ITMS/Annual/5/Voiles297-310.pdf> (Accessed 9/15/2019)

Voss, Angela. "The Secret Life of Statues." On-line at: <https://www.academia.edu/472457/The_Secret_Life_of_Statues> (Accessed 10/17/2019)

Vox Populi. "The Fifth Marian Dogma." Library at Eternal Word Television Network (EWTN). On-line at: <https://www.ewtn.com/catholicism/library/fifth-marian-dogma-5671> (Accessed 10/26/2019)

Warner, Martin Clive. "Virginity Matters: Power and Ambiguity in the Attraction of the Virgin Mary." Ph.D. dissertation, 2003, University of Durham. On-line at: <http://etheses.dur.ac.uk/3140/> (Accessed 11/19/2019)

Wigner, Dan. "What is Transpersonal Sociology," Dan Wigner website, August 31, 2018. On-line at: <http://www.dannwigner.com/?p=542> (Accessed 1/3/2020)

Williams, Georgia J. "An Exploration of Hierarchy as Fractal in the Theology of Dionysios the Areopagite," in *Power and Authority in the Eastern Christian Experience: Papers of the Sophia Institute Academic Conference, New York, December 2010.* New York: Theotokos Press, 2011, pp. 103-118.

Williams, Rowan. "Archbishop of Canterbury's sermon for the International Mass at Lourdes," September 24, 2008. On-line at: <http://aoc2013.brix.fatbeehive.com/articles.php/1221/archbishop-of-canterburys-sermon-for-the-international-mass-at-lourdes> (Accessed 9/5/2019)

Woods O.P., Richard J. *The Spirituality of the Celtic Saints.* Chicago, Illinois: New Priory Press, 2014.

Yazikova, Irina. "We are Moving into an Age of Love" (2005). An essay uploaded to the Alexander Men website at: <http://www.alexandermen.com/We_are_Moving_into_an_Age_of_Love> (Accessed 11/7/2019)

Zimdars-Swartz, Sandra L. *Encountering Mary: Visions of Mary from La Salette to Medjugorje.* New York: Avon Books, 1991.

12. Index

About the Author

Robert F. Thompson O.S.B. has wide-ranging and long-standing interest in comparative spirituality, especially transformational teachings from Eastern Christian tradition and other spiritual cultures of both East and West, as well as in Anglican poetic tradition, modern Russian religious thought, and literature of encounters with the Blessed Virgin Mary. Robert is a member of the *New Benedictine Community*, a dispersed Benedictine community (Anglican) with members in North America and Europe.

Blog: http://brightmetaphor.wordpress.com/
Books: https://perennialsstudygroup.wordpress.com/

At Amazon:
https://www.amazon.com/Robert-F.-Thompson/e/B01B50WU74
https://www.amazon.com/dp/1548897965
https://www.amazon.com/dp/1519310722

E-Mail: RThomp2272@yahoo.com

Made in the USA
Columbia, SC
24 July 2023

20838531R00115